CW00400307

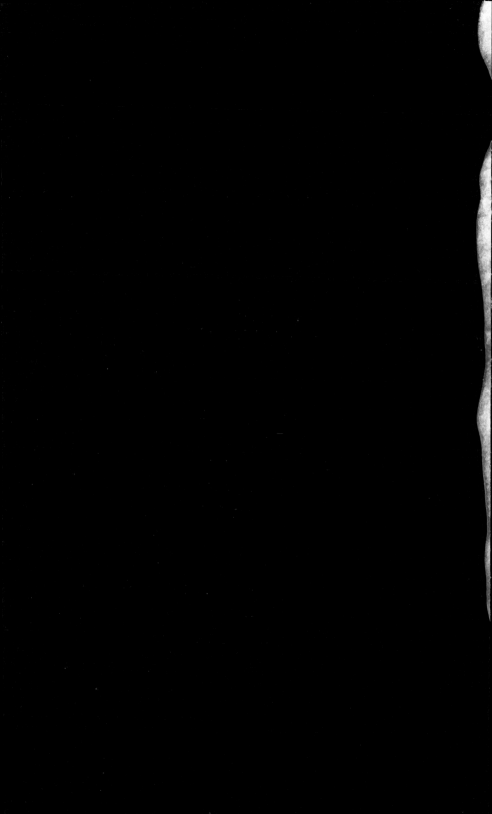

'This liberal author's knowledge of contemporary society is amazingly broad. He exposits the mythic depths (and appearances) of everything from "the myth of science" to superhero attitudes of contemporary American nationalism.

'Along the way he challenges many superficial trivialities about myths functioning in culture. He regards the mythic as a primary, highly effective agent of social ideology, and is never hesitant about demanding that the garments of our truly mythological capitalism are ill-fitting and socially harmful.

'This is the best book I know in terms of disclosing the pragmatic functioning of myth in society.'

William Doty
Professor Emeritus, University of Alabama and author of
*Mythography: The study of myths and rituals*

# the MYTHS of
# REALITY

*Simon*
## DANSER

*the* MYTHS *of* REALITY

*Simon* DANSER

Cover design by Bob Trubshaw

ISBN 1 872883 79 6

Published by
**Alternative Albion**
an imprint of
**Heart of Albion Press**

113 High Street, Avebury
Marlborough, Wiltshire, SN8 1RF

albion@indigogroup.co.uk

Visit our Web site: www.hoap.co.uk

Printed in England by Booksprint

# Contents

# Acknowledgements

The ideas presented in this book have been building up over the last three decades, although at an ever-faster rate during the last ten years. Many have been gleaned from books and articles but some have come from a great many friends. I simply cannot remember everyone who may have challenged and helped to develop my ideas over the years. However since I started writing this book several people have been especially helpful, including Terri Eynon, Munir Hamilton and Anthony Weir. In addition a number of other people read and commented on an earlier draft, including Bhogini, Angela Denham, William Doty, Jeanne Douglas, Dave Everitt, David Lazell, Mariya Limerick, Deborah Sambor, Alby Stone, Steve Taylor, Helen Ward. and Andy Worthington. Discussions with Nigel Pennick also provided helpful suggestions. However none of these people necessarily agree with my opinions or the way in which I have approached the topics.

Much has been compressed in this overview of a vast range of ideas. In my quest for concise and comparatively easily-digested summaries I owe much to other authors. However I did not want to clog up the text with extensive bibliographical references so have simply provided a list of sources at the end of each chapter. Sincere apologies to any persons who are unhappy with their work only being indirectly cited in this way.

Among the many books listed in the bibliography at the end of the book, a small number have been especially influential or helpful, notably those by Alain Badiou, Susan Blackmore, Peter J. Carroll, Dani Cavallaro, William Doty, Christopher Flood, N.J. Girardot, David L. Hall, John Storey, Bob Trubshaw and Mark Turner. To these authors, and all those whose work has helped me with specific sections of this book, my grateful thanks.

I was only made aware of Nikolas Rose's *Governing the Soul* shortly before this book was about to be published. Had I read this work prior to drafting *The Myths of Reality* it would have helped me to clarify a number of arguments and also provided examples for a number of my topics. Those readers who can cope with Rose's dense writing style will find a number of rewarding parallels between his approach and mine.

# acknowledgements

When I first encountered the writings of Alan Watts (1915–65) in the late 1970s they introduced me to nascent versions of some of the ideas in this book. Watts' ability to write about complex philosophical issues in the clearest and most polished of prose remains exemplary. The brilliance of his writing has illuminated my thoughts many times during the writing of this book, and he still casts a clear shadow over many of the topics discussed. Were he still alive I am sure that there is much in this book he would challenge; however I hope he would recognise a fellow traveller, driven by a similar compulsion to disseminate ideas and challenge the consensus. This book is dedicated to his memory.

# Preface

These, in essence, make up the field of activities and
its interactions: the five physical elements, ego,
intellect, the total material substance, the ten senses
and the mind, the five sensory objects, desire and
hatred, pleasure and pain, the combination of all
these, consciousness and one's convictions.
Bhagavad Gita 13.5-6

The voyage of discovery is not in seeking new
landscapes but in having new eyes.
Marcel Proust

By myth man has lived, died and – all too often –
killed.
Jaan Puhvel

What is basic in any social order is how control is
maintained within it.  No society can maintain
control long term through physical coercion alone,
but must promulgate values that are internalized and
transmitted to the next generation.
Joel Kramer and Diana Alstad

Societies, cultures, sub-cultures and all other social groups exist because they share ideas, beliefs, stories, customs, jokes, nicknames and such like. Such ideas and lore both define the group – if you don't understand an 'in joke' you are not part of the group – and help bond the group together.

Most of the time, especially with larger social groups, we are simply unaware of the shared ideas and beliefs – they are simply 'the way things are', the 'deep structures' on which other ideas are constructed. Trying to step outside the belief system is alien. Anyone who appears to have beliefs different to 'the way things are' is ignored, trivialised or demonised.

Becoming more aware of the shared but usually unrecognised belief systems and lore that sustain the implicit 'deep structures' is one of the key themes of this book. In modern western society the pervasive influence of the mass media provides continual reinforcement of specific ideas, beliefs, emotions, desires and aspirations. However we are not simply mindless zombies whose every whim is a response to TV advertising and Hollywood cultural values. In our face-to-face discussions (and, increasingly, their counterparts on the Internet such as emails and personal Web sites) we simultaneously reinforce some aspects of the mass media's 'messages' and contest other aspects. There is a two-way process by which culture is both consumed and produced – and the distinction between 'consumers' and 'producers' is not necessarily clear.

The 'deep structures' of any society include such aspects as religion, politics, economics, technology, and the sense of self and individuality. Just as there is truism that other cultures have mythology while we have religion, so too there is a sense that we have politics while other cultures have ideologies. Clearly this is pure relativism. All societies have religion and politics – which means they all have myths and ideologies. In this book terms such as 'myth' and 'ideology' recur. However they are never used in a pejorative sense, but rather as an objective label for specific forms of ideas.

To summarise what will be explored in greater detail later, ideologies can be thought of as the 'deep structures' of a society. Myths can be thought of as ideologies plus narrative. However myths are rarely retold as complete stories. Rather we encounter them as mythic fragments which allude to larger narratives. So mythic phrases such as 'the war on terror' allude to much larger, complex and poorly understood ideologies which manifest in a wide variety of political and military statements and actions.

Interestingly, as the later chapters of this book will explore in detail, both human language and our cognitive processes (only a small part of which we are consciously aware) are also based on narrative fragments too. Mini stories based on bodily and spatial experience are innate to our perception. Our more abstract thoughts are developed from these 'primary' narrative fragments. This means our fundamental cognitive processes are more mythic than rational. Our languages and cognitive processes also make considerable use of metaphors.

Myths are, ultimately, metaphors as well as narratives. Because cognitive metaphors and narrative fragments are *primary* to our cognitive processes, this helps to explain why mythic fragments – also comprising of metaphors and narrative – come 'in under the radar' of our more conscious thinking. So, for example, referring to something or someone as 'evil' rarely leads to any analysis of how the distinctions between 'good' and 'evil' were constructed as part of the Catholic Inquisition, and have been adopted and adapted by high-minded moralists since.

The ideologies and underlying beliefs communicated by mythic fragments are readily incorporated into our 'spontaneous' thoughts, without the opportunity for rational analysis. This allows the ideologies and dogmas of religion, politics and other belief systems to be regarded as more fundamental than 'rational' thinking.

However we should not think in terms of static ideas and systems. Individuals and social groups are not static. A continual process of self-renewal is necessary. Because radical changes are rare these processes of self-renewal are based upon individual and collective recollections and memories – and such recollections and memories are invariably based around narratives, often narrative fragments that allude to more encompassing events. As individuals we rely on our memories to maintain a sense of self identity which conventionally encompasses all the events in our lives. Social groups likewise rely on the sharing and reliving of key ideas and 'rituals' to retain their identity.

Thinking of processes rather than a combination of objects and events is largely alien to western thinking – despite Heraclitus's astute observation around 2,500 years ago that we cannot step into the same river twice. However the concept of a river – and indeed of the person who stepped into the river – is sustained, despite the river and also the person being ever-changing.

Taoist and Buddhist philosophies (whose origins are roughly contemporary with Heraclitus) remain distinct from mainstream western scientific materialist traditions by regarding process as primary rather than secondary. From the perspective of social existence rather than science, concept is more significant than substance. So, while the substance of a person cannot step into the substance of the same river twice, the concept of a person can indeed step twice into the concept of a river. However concepts do not have an independent existence – rather, they are like the whirlpools in a river that are continually recreated by the flow of the water.

This idea of processes of continually (re)created concepts as a primary aspect of the way we construct reality recurs throughout this book. Another recurring idea is the process of making a distinction. This extends from our cognitive processes – where the act of distinguishing a sensation or idea is among the most primary of our mental processes – through to social groups, which (as, for example, nations) characteristically define themselves by who they are *not* rather than by a clearly understood sense of what they have in common.

The distinction between 'thing' and 'not thing' (or 'thing' and 'other') is again part of a process of inter-dependent creation. So this is less about static dualisms rather than active dialectical processes.

On the one hand a vast network of such distinctions determine each of our thoughts and also determine the complex ideas and ideologies that make up social groups and cultures. This complexity is discussed in the main chapters of this book. However, on the other hand this leads in the opposite direction to the notion of an undifferentiated 'primordial' human condition that was lost as societies constructed ever more complex cultural concepts. At first glance this might be construed as akin to a mystical sense of unity between self and not-self. However 'undifferentiated' is not the same as 'unity', or even the same as 'homogeneity' – just as a bowl of minestrone soup still has lots of different ingredients, even if (apart from perhaps the person who cooked it) thinking of it as 'undifferentiated' soup is simpler.

Those familiar with Taoist thinking will think of two sections of the *Tao te Ching*: 'The Tao that can be told is not the absolute Tao; The name that can be named is not the eternal name' and 'The Tao begot unity. Unity begot two. Two begot three. And three begot the ten thousand things.' In other words, the Tao is the undifferentiated – and therefore intrinsically unnameable – 'soup' from which we construct reality.

Those familiar with the less mystical world of the social sciences will more readily understand the notion of the social construction of reality, first proposed in the 1960s. The social construction of reality is the process – or, more accurately, a large number of interwoven complex processes – by which the world of meanings and significance are created and sustained. The term 'social construction' can be misleading if the word 'construction' is taken too literally and not regarded as a metaphor. Intriguingly, few who originally embraced the social construction of reality thesis considered the processes by which this 'construction' actually takes place; only in recent years have linguists adapted this thesis to reveal in detail how languages are socially constructed and also serve as a key factor in the wider construction of reality.

In this book I develop earlier ideas about the social construction of reality by specifically looking at processes whereby 'narrative fragments' are transmitted via both the mass media and by person-to-person communication to enable an ongoing process of reaffirming and adapting the underlying meaning and significance – the 'deep structures' – which define and bond social groups.

Just in case there are any doubts, the social construction of reality thesis is far removed from the flakey New Age notions that 'we can create our own realities'. The emphasis in this book is very much on the social processes which continually recreate the 'deep structures' on which all social groups are based. I accept that the title of this book – *The Myths of Reality* – could be dismissed as misleading. Had it been written for an academic readership *The Social Construction of Symbolic Reality* may have been more appropriate. Or even *Agency and the Social Construction of Symbolic Reality,* as my recognition of the role of mythic fragments and person-to-person communication equates to the abstract concept of 'agency' beloved of some contemporary theorists.

Such cumbersome titles are, however, inappropriate as the approach of this book is most certainly not academic. I attempt to summarise an immense breadth and depth of contentious thinking. Many of the ideas are deeply challenging to western assumptions about what is 'normal' and 'real'. To achieve this wide-ranging summary my remarks are kept as brief as possible – although this risks making them too concentrated to be easily digested.

I am well aware of a large number of self-referential traps. By and large I have simply ignored such paradoxes and ironies. Likewise I have deliberately avoided, so much as is possible, situating myself in my writing and reflexively commenting on my own relationship with what, why and how I am writing. Such issues fascinate me but stand in the way of the main aim of this book, which is to provide a concise exposition of complex and challenging concepts. Suffice to say that I fully concur with Todd Dufresne when he wrote that 'Knowledge becomes a matter of conveying one's desire to another.'

Assuming you are not already familiar with most or all of the ideas presented in this book then reading it is likely to lead to one of two outcomes. Either you simply won't 'get it' as your prevailing belief systems will not allow you to 'step outside' and see things from a broader perspective. Or you will be deeply challenged by some (maybe all) of the ideas. What you thought was 'certain' about the world and social relationships will begin to seem very fluid and arbitrary. Only you can decide which of your previous beliefs – or indeed newly-acquired beliefs – about different aspects of reality are interesting, important and meaningful. For this reason several 'health warnings' are important.

Firstly, this book is intended to pull the rug from underneath everything you ever thought was certain. If you do not feel this is the right time in your life to cope with such a challenge then I strongly suggest you save it for another time. If you start reading and find yourself deeply disturbed by any of the ideas then it's time to take a good long break, go off and do something very different.

Secondly, it is not possible to study the myths of reality and regard some aspects – such as god, life after death, political beliefs, etc – as 'off limits'. If you approach this book from 'inside' a belief system you will either find it extremely difficult to 'get' what I am saying, or you will find yourself seriously challenging your beliefs. As religious and political convictions come bundled with friendships and family ties, and these friendships and ties can be very important in times of personal crisis, you may wish to defer reading this book until such times as you are emotionally independent of such people.

Thirdly, the later chapters blow very large holes in how we conventionally think we think and how we create our sense of self. If you have a well-developed sense of self then you will probably find that life is easier and more positive when some of the false assumptions are blown away. But if you are already aware that you have problems with your sense of self identity then this book is not for you, or at least not unless you have a very clear idea of who you could turn to for effective support.

## Sources:

Dufresne 2003: 152; Giradot 1983; Hacking 1999; Hall 1982a; Kramer and Alstad 1993: 3–4; Puhvel 1987: 2

The aspects of things that are most important to us are hidden because of their simplicity and familiarity. (One is unable to notice something – because it is always before one's eyes.) The real foundations of his enquiry do not strike a man at all. Unless *that* fact has at some time struck him. – And this means: we fail to see what, once seen, is most striking and powerful.
Ludwig Wittgenstein *Philosophical Investigations* section 129


We do not see things the way they are but as we are.
Jewish proverb


We are all prisoners of our minds. This realisation is the first step on the journey to freedom.
Ram Dass


'Reality' is some kind of ontological silly-putty.
Robert Anton Wilson


If we understand the mechanism and motives of the group mind, it is now possible to control and regiment the masses according to our will without their knowing it...
Edward Bernays


The Matrix is everywhere,' informs Morpheus, 'It is all around us. It is the world that has been pulled over your eyes to blind you to the truth...
*The Matrix* (Wachowski brothers)

# Chapter 1

# The illusion of reality

> We are what we think. All that we are arises with
> our thoughts. With our thoughts, we make the world.
> Buddha

The release of *The Matrix* in 1999 created a widespread awareness that what we think of as 'reality' may not be all it seems. The Wachowski brothers used the modern metaphor of computer-generated virtual reality in a novel and ironic way. Not only is *The Matrix* (along with a many other films in recent years) a product of computer-generated graphics, but the 'real world' is also considered to be a similar construct.

Various events in the script reveal that the Wachowski brothers are well aware that there are a number of precedents to such an ambiguous view of 'reality'. These range from philosophers such as Jean Baudrillard to various authors of sci-fi novels. The oldest of these precedents are references to Buddhism – 'quoted' in *The Matrix* in the guise of the spoon-bending child 'monk' in the anteroom to the Oracle.

While the notion that reality is – in some way or another – an illusion is fairly radical to most western people, such a notion is deeply familiar to all Buddhists. Indeed one of the main goals of Buddhist training is to recognise that the world is *mara* or maya – or 'illusion' (a doctrine known as samsara).

By regarding the world as maya Buddhists do not mean that the world is deprived of all reality, but rather that it is not what it appears to us. 'Reality' is more akin to what we see in a dream. However this does not mean that reality is 'unreal', neither is it arbitrary or meaningless. What we think of as the world – which includes how we think of our individual selves as part of that world – is constructed according to

2

well-established structures. However such 'structures' are only very partial ways of approaching the more universal and less illusory aspects of reality.

Regarding maya as a purely unwanted illusion is over-simplistic, however. In a deeper sense maya is the creative aspect of reality – the cause of illusions but not the illusion itself. Maya leads deeper and deeper into the realm of matter and differentiation – whereas knowledge (*prajna*) liberates us from such illusions (the state of samsara). The state of recognition of maya is known as moksha. Moksha requires a non-dualistic way of thinking; this is something which will be explored further in Chapter 14.

Other Eastern religions have a similar awareness of the ambiguity of the world. Hindus and Jains also use the term maya for a closely-related way of regarding material reality as an illusion; Taoism also aspires to non-dualistic and non-differentiated ways of thinking about 'ultimate' reality.

If Eastern religions seem exotic, then one of the foremost quantum physicists of his generation David Böhm (1917–94) describes what he terms the 'implicate' and the 'explicate' order of reality. According to the nuclear physicist and Hindu scholar Bansi Pandit, what Böhm calls the 'implicate order' equates to what Hindu scriptures call *brahman*, and Böhm' 'explicate order' is Hindu's samsara.

> The implicate order, as Böhm explains, is the unbroken undifferentiated wholeness in which there are no differences or distinctions, and where everything is connected to everything else. At the implicate level everything is made of the same substance. The explicate order is the world of objects with name and form, which we perceive with our mind and the senses. At the explicate level, a plant or a tree is seen different from an animal, and a person is perceived distinct from everything else. At the implicate level, all matter, whether here on Earth or in outer space, is involved in the eternal dance of energy, in which particles are created, destroyed, and recreated in an endless network of interactions. At the explicate level, the dance of creation and destruction goes on through the daily rhythm of birth, death, and rebirth.
> (Pandit 2005)

Modern physics and centuries-old Hindu literature converge in an equally 'exotic' model of reality which is entirely in accord with the overall approach of this book.

3

## everyday reality

In our day to day lives we simply do not think of 'reality' from such mystical or exotic perspectives. 'Reality' as it is lived is seemingly more about friends, relations (either by blood or marriage), bringing up children, work, money, taxes, government legislation, shopping, sport (either as a spectator or participant), pastimes and parties than it is about physical objects such as houses, chairs, cars or even food – and still less about what a physicist would call 'reality', which to most people seem rather unreal theories about matter, force, time, sub-atomic particles and such like.

'Reality' is less about the physical objects – houses, furniture, food – than the significance and meaning that we invest in physical objects – even though such aspects of 'reality' are both weightless and invisible. So houses can be desirably 'upmarket' or direly 'downmarket', with many variations in between. Furniture can be cheap and practical, recycled from skips, from a famous designer, a family heirloom, an 'investment' antique too valuable to be used, a much-loved sofa, a despised built-in unit too expensive to replace, and such like. Food – what we eat, with whom, where and when – is an even richer source of significance and meaning. From intentional selection of 'organic' produce to the wilful indulgence in 'junk' food, from snacks in front of the TV, or elaborate dinner parties, to the almost-defunct formality of family Sunday lunches, we construct our social identity from what, where and with whom we eat. 'We are what we eat' extends well beyond the nutritional content – not to mention the aspect of 'We are who we eat with.'

Some of these values that we give to the physical world are so 'implicit' in that we rarely speak about them consciously. But, even though we rarely analyse such remarks, our adjectives and adverbs partly disseminate the subtle concepts by which we judge the world – 'cool', 'cute', 'smart', 'handy' and all the more derogatory counterparts. Our material culture – from bank notes, cars and toilets – is a complex interplay of physical reality and conceptual reality. Yet we are so accustomed to them that money, vehicles and bathrooms seem more real than rivers, trees and stones. The complexities of social reality are mostly learnt unselfconsciously – we grow up learning how to behave correctly in different situations, such as eating with the family, attending school, ordering a drink in a café, making polite conversation, fitting into the conventions of employment, attempting to seduce someone, and so on and so on.

## reality is both things and their ever-changing meanings

Take this just a few steps further and we begin to realise that *most* of what we think of as 'real' is, instead, more about the meaning and significance we give to objects and social relationships. It is as much what things and people *symbolise* (or signify) as what they *are* that is important. To a much greater extent than we normally realise, 'reality' is mostly experienced through words, images and narratives. None of these are accurate 'mirrors' of reality but, rather, reflect the conventions of our society or culture. We are seldom consciously aware of these conventions – they are so deeply ingrained we are unlikely to be aware that they are largely arbitrary.

Reality is the combination of things and the varied and ever-changing meanings we give to things – the 'social reality' of our culture. Or, more accurately, the various social realities of the various sub-cultures we are part of. While traditional cultures tended to have simple stratifications and be reasonably stable through any one person's lifetime, in the modern world most people are exposed to a wide range of cultures and sub-cultures, most of which are changing fairly rapidly.

This book explores how the full range of our social activities creates and sustains this shared sense of everyday reality. I will refer to this as the 'social construction of reality', although it is also referred to by other writers as the 'symbolic order' or 'symbolic reality'.

## social construction of reality

The term 'social construction of reality' arose when a book of this name written by Peter Berger and Thomas Luckmann was published in 1966. Arguably *The Social Construction of Reality* changed sociology more than any book since. The primary concern of the authors is with the kind of everyday knowledge that enables us to know where we are, what we are doing, who we are, where we are going, how we are going to get there, what time it is, and such like. However, underlying such 'everyday knowledge' is a taken-for-granted understanding of what is counted as knowledge within any given society, culture or sub-culture.

Such prior assumptions about what is 'knowable' provide the framework for interpreting whatever is not yet known within this society. More specifically, it allows the 'unreal' to be defined, ensuring that the 'marginal reality' of dreams and fantasies to be distinguished from what is considered to be 'really real'. In this way the world-views of traditional people were regarded as 'myths' and dismissed as unreal by western minds.

The 'official' version of what is real is legitimised and maintained by various 'experts'. The main challenges to such experts are usually intellectuals and artists as other 'experts' simply differ within an agreed 'framework' – so doctors may differ about the best way of diagnosing a specific illness, but would never challenge the 'reality' of the way the medicine has been professionalised in a manner that makes 'illnesses' into all but independent entities, with little consideration of, say, psychosomatic or socio-economic aspects of afflictions.

Berger and Luckmann's ideas have been greatly developed in subsequent decades. Two different but equally inspirational books that expand on their ideas are John R. Searle's *The Social Construction of Reality* (Searle 1995) and Jonathan Potter's *Representing Reality* (Potter 1996); both have influenced this book.

## social construction of self

The one common factor between the various 'social realities' and 'physical' realities is our self – or, more pedantically, our bodies and our sense of self identity. Indeed, one of the key aspects of 'reality' is how we distinguish ourselves as individuals from the 'rest of the world', especially other people.

There are two key aspects to this. One is how individuals create and maintain a sense of self-identity. The other is how a specific person is identified by others. Both these senses of identity are sustained by the ways our memories are based on narratives, although typically identity is sustained by fragmentary references or allusions to an 'overall' narrative. This is explored further in the next chapter.

With luck there will be a reasonable agreement between a person's self-identity and the identities other people create for that person. However, I suspect the majority of people feel that they are different to how most people think of them. This can evolve into major problems if two people in a close relationship (whether domestic, occupational or recreational) begin to differ significantly in these senses of identity. In some cases a person's self-identity may differ substantially from the way most people see them. They risk being considered 'mad' as there is no sharing of realities with those who legitimise 'reality'. Interestingly, many artists, comedians and charismatic religious figures challenge 'reality' in ways similar to those who are deemed 'mad'. Accepting that some artists are deemed 'mad' (for at least some phase of their lives) the social acceptance of what is deemed 'art' and the rejection of what is deemed 'madness' is a key distinction for consensus reality to make and sustain, even though the boundary may be continually contested and subtly change.

## reality can be re-made

Conscious awareness of our cultural conventions is doubly difficult in the west because 'our' worldview has been insidiously promoted as the 'best', most 'evolved' and the dominant worldview by which all others are judged. The western ideology regards reality as essentially unchanging – something that exists independently of the ways of describing it.

Thinking of reality as having an unchanging independent existence is the essential foundation to a further ideological stance. By asserting its unchanging nature such implicit ideologies deny that reality is 'constructed', manufactured like a car or skyscraper. And, if we do not think of reality as something which is 'made', then we will not begin to think of reality as something which can be 're-made'.

Once we begin to realise that 'reality' can be taken apart into its 'component parts' then we can also begin to realise that each of these 'component parts' offers deep insights into the largely unconscious ideologies of our society. Such insights include an awareness of who creates these ideologies, who controls the ideologies which become 'dominant', and how these fit into world-wide political and economic agendas. Such an approach to reality is behind Jean Baudrillard's challenging view of modern America:

> Disneyland exists in order to hide the fact that it is the 'real' country, all of 'real' America, that is Disneyland (a bit like prisons are there to hide that it is the social in its entirety, in its banal omnipresence, that is imprisoning). Disneyland is presented as imaginary in order to make us believe that the rest is real, whereas all of Los Angeles and the America that surrounds it are no longer real, but belong to the hyperreal order and to the order of simulation.

## 'Fasten your seatbelts, it's going to be a bumpy night'

In this book I attempt to explore in more detail the ideas outlined above and to show how all ideas about 'reality' are constructed according to pre-existing cultural and linguistic structures. Two ideas – 'mythic fragments' and 'folkloric processes' – will be introduced as key aspects of the processes by which reality is 'socially constructed'. Later

7

chapters will seriously threaten our presumptions about how we think we think and how we think we are individuals. I can only do my best to navigate a smooth route through this bumpy terrain: '... buckle your seatbelt, Dorothy, 'cause Kansas is going bye-bye.'

## sources

Baudrillard 1994: 12; Berger and Luckmann 1967; Cavallaro 2001: p40–1; Danser 2004; Ford 2003: 164, 169; Govinda 1960 esp. p215–19; Hine 1989; Lacan 2001; Pandit 2005: Ch.4; Potter 1996; Thondup Rinpoche 1986: 22; Searle 1995; Thompson 2003; Watts 1957 p58–60; Zizek 1989

# Chapter 2

# The meaning of myth

> Myth can only be understood mythically.
> Jean Rudhart

> When I use a word, it means just what I choose it to mean, neither more nor less.
> Humpty Dumpty, in Lewis Carroll's *Through the Looking Glass*

Confession time. My use of the word 'myth' might seem Humpty Dumpty-ish to some people. The original sense of the Greek word *mythoi* was to refer to something untrue, a 'tall story'. Indeed, the word 'myth' is commonly used in a derogatory sense that implies something is untrue.

Yet 'myth' also has the sense of much deeper significance. We get a glimpse of this in the truism 'Other people have myths, we have religion', or the suggestion that 'Religion is what happens when you take myths too seriously.' Nevertheless, while is it easy to label other peoples' beliefs as 'myths' and thereby dismiss them as untrue, there is something about 'myths' that is deeper than their apparent content.

There is more to myths than larger-than-life characters and stories based on their activities. Myths are not just 'any old stories' – otherwise we would call them stories, legends or tales. Myths may be thought of as akin to the lenses of spectacles. When we are wearing spectacles we do not see the lenses. We see *with them*. In the same way myths impart a worldview that is taken for granted. Only when we take off a pair of spectacles do we see the lenses. Only when we step back and think about myths can we begin to see how they shape what we think of as reality. The underlying 'assumptions' and structures presented (and, more typically, challenged and redefined) in myths provide the 'deep structures' underpinning the thinking of a society, or culture, or subculture.

Such 'deep structures' have nothing to do with Freudian or Jungian concepts of consciousness (although, confusingly, Freud and Jung both used traditional myths as inspiration for their own myths about consciousness). One of the deepest of these deep structures is language – this will be explored in Chapter 10. Many of these deep structures are the systems of thought underlying politics, economics, religion and 'social norms' – what we usually think of as political and religious ideologies.

Children have a remarkable ability to intuitively develop a strong sense of reality and social norms. These are learned – although rarely in a conscious way – from parents and guardians, teachers, and during play activities. What emerges are shared definitions of reality (at the level of deep structures and ideologies) and ways of behaving which become taken-for-granted as 'reality'. Through a wide variety of social interactions – arguably, indeed *all* social interactions – this constructed sense of reality is shared, repeated and confirmed. Such shared structures simultaneously *enable* and *constrain* social activities.

We cannot exist without these structures. Each of us develops within a specific combination of such social, cultural and historic structures. This provides us with a range of possibilities to adopt, develop, challenge and transform. Our sense of identity is contained within our concepts of social reality. We identify with ideas of what we are expected to be much more than what we wish to be. And even our wishes are intimately linked with cultural expectations. We desire what we think other people desire (and mass media moguls are only too happy to collaborate with the advertisers who sustain them and bombard us with details of what celebrities and lifestyle gurus seemingly crave). All too often individuals create a 'reality' which is a defective version of an illusory ideal; and their sense of self is constrained by these illusions. This is one reason why 'socially agreed reality is akin to a bleak Monday morning', as Alan Watts put it nearly fifty years ago. (The myth of individuality is a topic which will be explored further in Chapter 12.)

Our sense of reality persists only if it is continuously renewed by those we share it with. However, the underlying ideologies, accepted patterns of behaviour, and all that make up this 'socially constructed reality' *appear* to exist independently. We begin to think that this constructed reality really is 'real'. Few of us are aware of, still less examine, the 'spectacles' (i.e. myths) which create this illusion.

However this book, as the title states, is specifically about such myths of reality.

## the power of metaphors

> **'It is easier and less costly to change the way people think about reality than it is to change reality.'**
> Morris Wolfe

We name objects and ideas to fit pre-existing mental concepts. The benefit of this is to give reality coherent structure. The downside is that we continue to think in terms of the implicit metaphor. That metaphor may then limit how we think about the topic. So, if we are seeking solutions to a problem, then re-thinking the metaphor may open up ideas for new solutions.

For example, English speakers often think of life as a purposeful journey. As part of this journey we think of learning in terms of 'routes' and 'journeys' and thereby learners become seen as individual 'travellers' who decide their own destinations, directions and pace. However if we change the metaphor and regard learning as part of a 'web' where ideas are *mutually* constructed through the exchange of ideas with 'passive' sources (such as books) and 'interactive' sources (such as tutors, fellow students and email correspondents) then the learner becomes less of an individual 'receiving' knowledge and instead part of the social construction of understanding (which is a far more appropriate metaphor than the notion of an individual traveller).

Similarly debate and argument are frequently wrapped up in the metaphors derived from warfare. You may disagree with ideas in this book and 'attack my position', suggest my claims are 'indefensible', and want to 'demolish' my arguments. I may end up 'shot down in flames'. Such divisive metaphors underlying debates are less likely to lead to constructive exchanges than discussions based on metaphors of exchange or collaborative building.

Metaphors are not simply rhetorical devices to add impact to our remarks. Rather, metaphors are *primary* and unavoidable aspects of how we think. Metaphors are how we think about more 'abstract' aspects of the world and ourselves. Some metaphors are so dominant with a culture they seem literal – although stepping outside that culture would quickly reveal their allegorical status.

To use the power of metaphor to discuss the power of metaphor, we might think of metaphors hunting in packs lead by a controlling 'alpha metaphor'. Or of organic systems of metaphor that grow from a root metaphor. Replace the alpha of the pack, or graft onto new root stock, and the remainder of the metaphor system will change, subtly or significantly, thereby changing how we understand the whole system. Changing the metaphor changes how we think and how we act. Learning how to recognise implicit and underlying metaphors is the first step towards being able to change them. Recognising and replacing implicit metaphors is immensely powerful. Intriguingly few educators seek to empower their students in such ways, and the exceptions are mostly in 'arts' subjects rather than technological or vocational ones. Some belief systems need to be maintained, illusions and all...

## the power of ideologies

Metaphors are one aspect of the various ideologies which provide the 'deep structures' that simultaneously construct, reaffirm, explain and evaluate shared social reality. They implicitly (and sometimes explicitly) contrast specific events and circumstances with 'how the world ought to be'. They seek to reduce ambiguities and 'grey areas' to clear-cut distinctions. Indeed, myths and ideologies are to the fore when the topic is a contentious one – such as defining who is 'mad' and who is not; what types of behaviour and images are regarded by a society as 'obscene'; whether judicial executions are acceptable; whether abortion is morally justifiable; and so on.

Ideologies offer a semblance of security by making 'reality' intelligible and meaningful, often to the advantage of those who hold the power in politics, commerce and religion. They also create and maintain an individual's sense of identity within this social reality. Above all they create a strong sense of 'other' – everyone and every idea excluded from the socially-accepted ideals. Defining the 'other' – what is *not* us – is the main way we define ourselves and our social group. The 'other' is created by creating ideological categories which are promptly demonised. In recent decades in Britain politicians and tabloid newspaper editors have provided us with 'hooligans', 'muggers', 'travellers', 'welfare scroungers', 'paedophiles' and many more such pejorative generalisations.

Because there needs to be a reasonably high level of continuity within a group, changes within cultures and subcultures are usually fairly subtle and evolutionary. Almost inevitably deeper challenges will produce intense debate and risk splitting the original group in factions. Nevertheless ideologies – and the self- and group-identities that go with them – are fluid over time. Likewise specific ideologies and identities can be nested within broader belief systems.

Because of the media, reading books, or surfing the Internet, most individuals today are aware of the ideologies of many radically different subcultures. The frequent reaction is mostly to deem others' ideologies as excessively deviant – 'daft', 'stupid', 'weird', 'nuts', or worse. However sometimes the challenges of radically different worldviews are regarded as sufficiently interesting to attract our attention, although we often think of other peoples' interests as exotic or even transgressive from the perspective of our 'normal' ideologies.

We all have ideologies. Social groups cannot exist without them – although this certainly does not mean that all ideologies are equal. Anyone who claims not to have an ideology is unwittingly expressing an aspect of liberal ideology. This claim is a good example of how people adopt the ideas embedded in an ideology without being aware of the entirety of the belief system from which it derives. Although someone expressing fragments of an ideology may not be an adherent of the overlying ideology, such beliefs *are* ideologically determined.

The inability to recognise that in the western world we all have ideologies derives from deeply-rooted Christian preconceptions. Underlying these is the belief that all aspects of the world, especially human activities, are ruled and controlled by God, whose intentions are inscrutable and beyond human comprehension. If everything is ultimately the will of God, there is little point into looking too far into the underlying causes of events. Despite the increasing atheism and secularisation of the last 150-or-so years, most people still regard the underlying causes of the world to be 'externally' created, absolutes which are 'given' rather than created, indeed rather inscrutable and beyond comprehension.

How do ideologies get to be so powerful, so inescapably pervasive? Through the incessant use of 'mythic fragments' that allude to ideologies of the 'source' myth. Intriguingly, because we usually remain unaware of the 'complete' myth to which the fragments allude, we remain unaware of the full extent of the ideologies which the fragments suggest, making the fragments especially effective at transmitting these ideologies unnoticed.

## ideology plus narrative

Myths are narratives, a sequence of connected events presented as a story. There are usually many variants of the 'same' myth, and all these variants may be closely related to a much larger family of myths in a society, as well as having recognisable counterparts in other societies. Where myths have been recorded over a substantial period of time then considerable evolution may be revealed. Sometimes myths 'degenerate' into legends, songs, or become reduced to 'superstitions' or just nostalgic references. But historical records, when available, show that these are derived from an identifiable but now-lost narrative.

Once myths have become established for any significant period of time, they will be expressed in many variants. No versions will be identical. A particular myth is not so much a well-defined story as a theme, or themes, which recur in a number of narratives. In other words, a myth is more-or-less the same sequence of events, involving roughly the same principal characters, with a similar implied meaning (i.e. ideology), circulating among a social group (and usually, although not necessarily, helping to define and bond that group).

One approach to myths is to think of them as ideology plus narrative. Indeed, this is the main way myths are regarded in the rest of the book. One way of thinking about ideologies is as a group of metaphors based around an alpha or root metaphor. Add this together and there is a spectrum of concepts that begins with the metaphorical concepts embedded in our cognitive processes (more about these in Chapter 11) and moves through metaphors and 'sets' of metaphors. These in turn develop into ideologies, which develop into narrative fragments, with fully-developed (although rarely-encountered) myths at the far end of this conceptual spectrum.

## mythic fragments

While there is a narrative 'theme' to all myths, myths most certainly do not have to be retold in their entirety. Indeed, in the modern world myths are almost always encountered in fragmentary form. In the realm of politics they can be evoked by slogans ('the war on terror', 'economic growth', 'free trade') and allusions ('9-11'). Even single words such as 'communism' or 'democracy' shoulder an immense range of ideological associations.

In modern society mythic fragments are more often aspects of political and scientific ideologies than more overtly religious notions. Indeed, in today's secular world political myth has almost as much authority as sacred myths once had. 'Political myths' and 'sacred myths' have a close affinity, in that they are essentially narrative forms of ideology, transmitted in fragmentary references.

Furthermore, mythic fragments are not restricted to words. In political and religious rituals and ceremonies spoken ideas can be combined with actions, specific modes of dress, particular locations and settings, iconic objects such as banners, as well as music and song. Static visual images, with or without words, such as paintings, drawings, illustrations, posters, and commercial advertisements all convey ideological ideas, as can entire exhibitions or even museums. Clearly, the same is true for the dynamic images in television and film.

Photographs, cinema and the in-built presuppositions of journalism all claim to be providing an accurate representation of the world. Far from it. They communicate to us only because of shared ideologies; indeed they are the main way in which underlying ideologies are reflected back as 'reality'.

In the midst of the first Gulf War in January 1991 the philosopher George Lakoff opened a lecture with the words:

> Metaphors can kill. The discourse over whether to go to war in the Gulf was a panorama of metaphor. Secretary of State Baker saw Saddam Hussein as 'sitting on our economic lifeline.' President Bush portrayed him as having a 'stranglehold' on our economy. General Schwarzkopf characterized the occupation of Kuwait as a 'rape' that was ongoing. The President said that the US was in the Gulf to 'protect freedom, protect our future, and protect the innocent', and that we had to 'push Saddam Hussein back.' Saddam Hussein was painted as a Hitler. It is vital, literally vital, to understand just what role metaphorical thought played in bringing us into this war.

The remainder of the lecture (Lakoff 1991) included discussions of such metaphors as 'just war', and the metaphorical 'profits' associated with the 'risks' of war. Lakoff's analysis remains a rare example of a detailed analysis of the way metaphors not only express but fundamentally structure political statements and actions.

Further examples of the way metaphors are deeply embedded into politics include politicians referring to the state as is it was a person, or spokespersons for protest groups claiming to speak on behalf of members, or even 'all sensible people'.

In modern societies the citizen is constantly subjected to ideological messages and fragments from an immensely prolific and diverse range of sources. Nearly all the examples of myths which will be explored in the rest of this book are such 'mythic fragments'. The processes by which they are transmitted will be discussed in more detail in the next chapter.

# myths as hidden persuaders

The narrative form of myths distinguish them from 'logical' arguments. This is for at least two reasons. Firstly, myths are learnt through repeated exposure (almost always in fragmentary versions) rather than by any intentional or conscious learning processes. This means myths come in 'under the radar' of our usual intuitive ways of evaluating information and ideas. For example, mythic fragments are often based on unstated 'alpha metaphors' but, because there is no explicit reference to this metaphor, the fragment has the semblance of 'actuality'.

Secondly, myths create the 'templates' which shape our perceptions of the world. In other words, myths create the basis on which we evaluate other ideas. So, to revert to the metaphor introduced in the previous chapter, myths are like the lenses of spectacles in that we look *through* them rather than *at* them, and they shape our perceptions. Or to use other previously-introduced metaphors, myths incorporate an 'alpha metaphor' or 'root metaphor' which controls subsidiary metaphors.

While we can fairly easily recognise other cultures' myths, only with extreme difficulty can we consciously recognise the myths that create our own lives. Furthermore we can only escape from one mythic ideology into another.

For these reasons, beliefs and social structures conveyed by myths are largely immune to argument and even contrary evidence. Furthermore myths are the core convictions that bond together a culture or subculture. If we fail to agree on such fundamentals then we cease to share a common social group. 'They' are 'daft' or 'mad'. Or maybe it is us who has become the 'outsider', perhaps to the extent of infringing laws which underline the conventions of acceptable behaviour.

To a very great extent, myths cannot be refuted. Within a given society or culture it is the myths that define and bond the group. As the mythologist Jaan Puhvel accurately observed 'By myth man has lived, died and – all too often – killed.'

## sources

Bennett 1980; Cavallaro 2001: xiii, 75–85; Eliade 1958: 431; Flood 1996; Grey 2000; Goodwin 1992: 29; Lacan, cited in Cavallaro 2000: 39; Lakoff 1991; Ortony 1979; Puhvel 1987: 2; Rudhart 1980; Schön 1993; Sorel 1961 esp. p50, 52; Storey 1999; Storey 2003: x; Taverniers 2002; Trubshaw 2003a; 2003c; Watts 1958.

# Chapter 3

# Transmitting mythic fragments

History is the version of past events that people have decided to agree upon.

Attributed to Napoleon Bonaparte

In traditional societies myths were usually performed in a ritual or ceremonial context. Reciting myths was usually the role of specific people and different from other forms of storytelling and narration. Even the language was sometimes distinct from everyday speech, perhaps a more archaic form.

In complete contrast, the myths of western society during the last few hundred years have been passed down through written, usually printed, forms. The language may be formal, or occasionally even archaic – such as the King James' version of the Bible – but these texts are read rather than re-created anew with each performance.

Nowadays TV and film are the prevalent modes for myths. Sometimes the subject matter is quite overtly based on traditional myths – from *Lord of the Rings* to *Shrek* – in other cases the mythic quality is implicit within the conventions of the genre – for example, the stereotypical hero of Hollywood action movies.

In other cases the mythic aspects are even more subtle, as with the way news is made into 'stories' which revolve around specific personalities, who are almost invariably made to conform to pre-existing stereotypes. Selection and distortion are endemic in news reporting. A 'spin' ultimately sympathetic to dominant (i.e. usually American) values is put on events. For instance, media coverage of the anti-capitalism protests of 2000 and 2001 focussed on the 'anarchists' and justifying the heavy-handed policing rather than on the issues behind the protests. This follows a time-honoured tradition that goes back 200 years of infiltrating and inflaming anti-capitalist movements. Likewise, the Israeli invasion of Palestine in Spring 2002 became focussed on the 'issue' of the Palestine leader, Yasser Arafat, rather than the drastic American-sponsored military action by the Israelis.

As Daniel Chandler has cogently observed:

> The newsreader is presented as a 'neutral' observer. By reading the scripted news, the newsreader, dressed with sober formality in an orderly studio, and seated behind a desk (which reduces their body language), appears to speak 'the objective discourse of "the truth"'. Newsreaders have a sense of permanency: they are always there when the programme begins: they are never seen to arrive, and they don't move about during the programme. And yet we are directed by the newsreader. Our gaze follows the newsreader's gaze when he or she looks off screen. Everything seen seems to support what the newsreader says. Although the content may be far from reassuring, the newsreader's manner is always friendly, reliable and reassuring. The 'tail piece' offers a happy ending. Even the weather presenters have become cheerful figures.

TV news 'stories' do not present a coherent narrative based on historical connections. Instead they make a series of disparate associations (many of which are visual – recent 'news clips', archival footage, maps, histograms and diagrams). Simple images are used to denote complex issues. There are clearly identified victims. As with any fairy story or sit-com, news stories have principal and minor characters (some of which are heroes –*hurrah!* – and others are villains – *hiss!* – although, as with all good pantomimes, heroes and villains often mutate as the plots unfold), and a dependence on frequently used plots with beginnings, middles and ends. The only key difference from drama and comedy is that the news presenter makes eye contact with the camera (and, by extension, the viewer) thereby seemingly removing the news story from the realm of fiction.

For all the emphasis on constructing news 'stories', they are mostly compiled from secondary sources such as news agencies, press conferences and spokespeople. Indeed, comments made by prominent people may be presented as a self-contained news story. The more-or-less overt biases of these sources are rarely mentioned. A limited number of well-known 'experts' appear regularly to reinforce the hegemony, countered (if at all) only by token 'eccentrics'.

The fragmented structure of TV news means viewers can only make sense of the information by relying on pre-existing ideological assumptions, or by tacitly accepting the ideological framework within which the mass media 'news industry' operates. In the UK and USA, and most other western countries, this 'news industry' promotes views which tend to support the political right (i.e. the status quo), leavened with a little liberalism. Ideas contrary to the hegemony (for example, anything verging towards the political left) are typically ignored, presented as a problem and/or as the views of 'a small minority', or simply denied, demonised, trivialised or ridiculed.

So strikes are regarded as a bad thing. News presenters assume their viewers are on the same side as the management; the unions are 'other'. The use of language is distorted, so union leaders are reported to 'demand' while management 'offers'. Specific events are presented as examples of already established myths – another example of 'left wing infiltrators', 'declining moral standards' or 'Islamic fundamentalists'.

## Mass media and other media

Predictably enough the mass media are the predominant transmitters of myths in the modern world. Indeed most of the content of the mass media is mythic, at least in the sense that it is made up of vast quantities of 'mythic fragments' (see Chapter 2). But mass media is not the only way that mythic ideas are expressed. And some of the other ways actually turn out to be more interesting.

To more fully understand the different ways in which myths are transmitted in modern society I want to explore the differences between 'mediated' means of communication and what, for convenience, I will call 'folkloric' transmission of ideas.

First let's look more closely at the mass media. Essentially this refers to newspapers, magazines, TV and radio. Many people would also include books, cinema and pop music in the list of mass media. Indeed, to a certain extent this is sensible. But only *some* books and *some* films and *some* pop music really conform to the label of 'mass' media. A great many books, films and musical genres are of limited appeal and are not promoted with anything like the marketing budgets of blockbuster novels, Hollywood features or the 'hit factory' mentality. How we get to know about 'cult' books, independent films and obscure genres of music usually depends on being part of a specific social group – whether it is the 'formal' mailing list of an arts centre or an 'informal' association of people on an obscure email discussion list.

Such comparatively specialist productions as cult films and indie bands are nevertheless 'mediated' by the subtle (or otherwise) influence of editors, publishers and the processes of generating awareness. However they are less likely to have a mass influence. More specifically, awareness of such specialist books, films and music comes largely from folkloric transmission of ideas and not from the mass media. Therefore, in my opinion, such comparatively little-known aspects of culture do not deserve to be included in 'mass media', even though they share the same media (e.g. books, magazines, films, music) with what is more genuinely mass media.

So, unless otherwise indicated, my use of the term 'mass media' refers only to newspapers, magazines, TV and radio, plus best-selling books and high-profile films ('Top 40' genres of popular music are, from this specific perspective, effectively a synergy between TV, radio and tabloid newspapers). In other words 'mass media' are the media used to present a 'mediated' range of ideas and products to 'the masses'. From time to time in later chapters of this book I will refer to both mass media and more specialist media in contrast to 'aural' and 'folkloric' transmission (these latter two terms will be discussed later in this chapter).

As an aside, big budget advertising quickly caught on to the way the Internet transmits new fashions by folkloric transmission, although they refer to it by a different name – 'viral marketing'. But the essence is the same – create a 'cool' enough Web site and encourage as many people as possible to email their friends about it. While most attempts to set up such viral marketing fall by the wayside, the few successful attempts can be dramatically successful. One of the earliest success stories for viral marketing was the pre-release promotion for the low-budget *Blair Witch Project* film in 1999, so much so that the film had achieved 'cult status' even before its release.

## mass media and popular culture

Considerable interest has been devoted by academics from various disciplines – notably cultural studies – to the way popular thinking is influenced by ideas transmitted by the mass media. (For an easily digested overview of cultural studies see Brooker 1998; for a more detailed discussion of ideas especially relevant to this chapter see Storey 2003.)

The culture promoted through mass media is referred to by various terms, notably 'mass culture' and 'popular culture'. However both of these are problematical. For example, we do not think of ourselves as one of the 'mass', so the term 'mass culture' is an arbitrary term that only makes sense from some 'external' perspective. Likewise 'popular culture' implies an 'un-popular culture' or, more accurately, a 'high culture'. Here is not the place to discuss how 'high culture' was invented in the second half of the nineteenth century and actively promoted throughout most of the twentieth century as in some way better, more 'sophisticated', more 'evolved', than popular culture (see Storey 2003: 32–40 for a summary).

## Unpacking 'popular culture'

The reality is that in any one society there are a great number of overlapping 'popular cultures'. Individuals are unlikely to be involved in more than a small proportion of all of them but are likely to be involved in a range of such subcultures in any one month (unless they snobbishly restrict themselves to 'high culture') and very likely to adopt and subsequently drop an even greater range of cultural interests during the course of their lives.

Within this wide range of subcultures there is a variable relationship with the mass media. Football fans theoretically could fulfil their interests with little or no input from the mass media. Indeed supporters of a local non-league team do just that. They turn up at the matches, then meet with fellow fans to vent their thoughts about what they would have done if they were playing, refereeing or managing. However the large majority of football fans support Premiership teams. Their games are televised, when well-established pundits air their thoughts about what they would have done if they were playing, refereeing or managing. The most famous players are subjects of a media circus that follows any significant aspects of their professional lives and, rather too often, less significant aspects of their personal lives.

Followers of sports and leisure pursuits which are seldom televised – such as golf, angling, cycling, playing computer games – are served by a range of specialist magazines that more-or-less subtly persuade the reader that the latest products are essential for them to fulfil their enjoyment. However, at least until recent years, the main way ideas are shared is through face-to-face social activities, however informal. The Internet has added a further opportunity for sharing ideas which falls part-way between the informality of face-to-face discussion and the greater formality of published periodicals.

Some leisure activities have little in the way of specialist magazines, Web sites or email discussion groups (or, more specifically, if these exist they are seen by very few of the people who pursue the activity). Darts players and bowls teams are good examples of subcultures that effectively exist only during a match and the associated drinking at the bar.

A similar spectrum of subcultures exist with fans of different types of music. Some styles of music – such as that associated with the Top 40 – are inextricably interwoven with the popular daily press and specialist music magazines. Other styles of music intentionally distance themselves from such 'media hype', although there are probably several specialist monthly magazines reviewing recent recordings and gigs, and providing interviews with notable performers. Again, there will be followers of local bands and genres for whom word of mouth and the Internet are the only ways of sharing information.

A quite different example of groups which exist without any input from mass media are the groups of people who work together. In medium and large companies there will be several subgroups, usually based around age, seniority or job function. Chats around the coffee machine and circulating emails are the main opportunities for these groups to bond, although there may be shared social activities out of working hours.

But the most prevalent groups which nearly all of us belong to are families. They have a shared lore and culture. This includes what we do at birthdays, Christmas, weddings, where we go on holiday and what we do when we get there, and even the customarily weekly routine of shopping, domestic chores and spending time with other family members.

However people who work together and live together are not entirely separate from mass media. The chit-chat that bonds the members of the group together is quite commonly based on television programmes (especially 'soaps'), Premiership football, notable adverts, and (depending on age group) pop music. More crucially, ideas advanced by the mass media subtly influence family and work behaviour. Few offices in Britain have been the same since *The Office* brilliantly parodied archetypal characters. More subtly still, all 'soaps' influence how people think about contentious topics. The scripts of all British-made soaps such as *Eastenders*, *Brookside* through to *Hollyoaks* introduce controversial characters and situations. In recent years even the once-conservative *Coronation Street* has become a sequence of contentious crises. Whereas teenage pregnancy was once all but beyond the pale, now a transsexual character is mundane.

While the script writers of soaps do not tell the audience *what* to think, they create a framework for *how* viewers should respond. The contrasting attitudes taken by fictional characters effectively define the limits of possible attitudes. Needless to say, these options exist within a given mythic structure – soaps are not intended to challenge the deeper assumptions of modern society, but simply provide the illusion of debate.

This 'illusion of debate' – limited possible options within 'invisible' bounds created by an implicit belief system – is a well-tested technique in education. It is most blatant in religious study groups, where the limits of debate are constrained by the religious belief system. It is more subtle yet insidious in the curricula of state education for children. In higher education the illusion has long been maintained in science and social science faculties; worryingly it is being increasingly encountered in the humanities and arts too.

## folkloric transmission of mythic fragments

As discussed in the previous chapter, the deep structures which underlie our thinking are transmitted mostly in fragmentary form.

The mass media is most certainly responsible for promoting some of these mythic fragments but, in many cases, the media have only an indirect impact on the underlying belief systems of a social group. Such groups include families, people who work together or share leisure pursuits.

Folklorists have termed such groups 'folk groups' and one of them, Alan Dundes, has defined them as:

> ... any group of people whatsoever who share at least one common factor. It does not matter what the linking factor is – it could be a common occupation, language or religion – but what is important is that a group formed for whatever reason will have some traditions which it calls its own.

Groups can be as few as two people or as large as a nation. Not everyone in a group need know all the other members, but they will know the common core traditions belonging to the group. This 'common core tradition' is often a major component of the group identity. 'Large scale' examples of common traditions creating group identity include national identity – although all too often the highly emotionally-charged 'traditions' have little historical depth or accuracy.

From this perspective, we are all folk. Indeed, unless we are exceptionally reclusive, we are all 'lots of folk', as we shift from one group to another. The traditional way of exchanging ideas among the members of a folk group has been through face-to-face conversations. However technology has broadened this, first of all, telephone conversations and, more recently, the Internet. 'Web communities', chat rooms, Usenet groups, 'blogs' and the vast number of email discussion groups reveal that social groups can now be created and sustained without any physical encounters.

Such Internet groups often share information – such as what folklorists term 'contemporary legends' – in ways directly analogous to previous non-technological ways. Whereas previously these legends were typically passed on over, say, a drink in a pub, now they are shared electronically. Likewise the sort of cartoons and humorous aphorisms that at one time were photocopied and circulated around offices – so-called 'xerox lore' – have also transferred to the Internet.

Just a brief aside on terminology. Pioneer folklorists in the eighteenth and nineteenth century collected songs, tales and lore by writing down what their so-called 'informants' were singing or saying. For reasonably logical reasons this was referred to as 'oral transmission', i.e. 'by mouth'. In the early twentieth century the invention of the gramophone confused things as such lore and – more especially – songs could now be passed on by recordings, including the finer nuances of performance. The folklorists started calling this 'aural transmission' (i.e. 'by sound'), a rather nifty substitution of one term by another which sounds the same. However many aspects of Internet communications are directly comparable to aural transmission. Folklorists have yet to come up with a widely-established terminology which encompasses both aural and Internet transmission. In the rest of this book I will use the term 'folkloric' to refer to these processes, except where it is more appropriate to use the terms 'oral' or 'aural'.

## defining, bonding and excluding

The retelling of tales and jokes helps define and bond folk groups. Ever-evolving 'in jokes' help bond and define who is in a specific group (or sub-group) and who is not. Among the most prevalent jokes are nicknames, both ones known to their 'owner' and scurrilous ones used only behind their back. Context is often critical. Many of the tales or jokes that bond groups may be considered crude or obscene if heard out of context. Tolerating or condoning humour that would be taboo in other contexts helps to define the folk group. So, the type of joke shared between 'the lads' after watching a football match would probably not be appropriate for a social evening to raise funds for a religious group. The extent to which sexist jokes have been prevalent among some sections of the British armed forces, and racist jokes among some constabularies, shows that 'taboo' jokes may be an inevitable part of bonding groups, but conflict with acceptable behaviour can lead to the blurring or transgression of 'real world' boundaries.

Families are excellent examples of folk groups. A considerable number of tales and jokes are shared at family gatherings – usually framed by opening words such as 'Remember the time at Alan's wedding when… ' or derogatory references to absent members of the group with unfortunate habits, such as 'Don't do an Aunt Beth!'. Nobody in the family needs to be told any more – this fragmentary reference is sufficient. Anyone who is not 'family' is immediately excluded; the circumstances when one or more of these tales is told more-or-less in its entirety are, to all intents and purposes, 'initiation ceremonies' into the group, even if there is rarely anything premeditated or formal about such 'initiations'.

Stories, jokes and conventional activities become 'traditional'. But, to any long-standing group member, they can be seen to have steadily changed over the years. The changes are often subtle – perhaps the bringing together of two different family traditions when people get married – and rarely noticed consciously. Only occasionally are the changes noticed, perhaps when someone contentiously breaks with the 'done thing'.

The in jokes and shared lore of the various types of 'folk groups' – whether they be families, people who work together, or those who share a common leisure interest – function in exactly the same way as 'mythic fragments' convey the more broadly shared 'deep structures' or ideologies of politics, religion, science and commerce (see previous chapter).

As already stated, folk groups can be as few as two people or as large as a nation. Indeed the whole concept of 'folk groups' comes from folklorists and folklorists invented the concept of 'folk lore' as part and parcel of emergent nationalism in the late eighteenth and early nineteenth century.

## nationalism and the invention of folklore

> The life of nations no less than that of men is lived largely in the imagination.
> Enoch Powell

By the early nineteenth century the idea of a nation was becoming associated with its people and their 'popular culture' – the idea of the 'folk' (rural peasants who in some undefined way epitomised the national image) had been invented and the notions of 'folklore' and 'folk customs' developed soon after. Initially the emphasis was on poetry – especially epic songs – as being the voice of the people. German, Russian, Swedish, Serbian and Finnish songs were collected and arranged to form epics between 1806 and 1835.

Significantly, interest in national epic poems and the subsequent interest in folklore developed first in Germany, Finland, the Baltic states and Ireland. At the time these countries were ruled over by other nations. Even in Spain, the fashion for popular culture during the late eighteenth century was a way of expressing opposition to the French-led Enlightenment. Anti-French attitudes in Germany also led to less interest in the Enlightenment there too. Similar concerns in eighteenth century Britain resulted in anti-English sentiments fuelling Scottish, Welsh and Irish nationalism. (For a discussion of the invention of Scottish and Welsh nationality see *The Invention of Tradition* (Hobsbawm and Ranger 1983); and the largely-invented notions of Scotland, Wales and Ireland having a shared 'Celtic' culture see *The Atlantic Celts* (James 1999).)

By the later part of the nineteenth century the study of mythology had developed and this too began to be used to support nationalist agendas. One clear example of how an apparently 'abstract' mythic motif, that of sacred central places, has become intimately implicated in politics is the way that academic interest (while on the surface quite dispassionate) has focussed on one specific (and exceptionally contentious) example of such sacred centres – the Holy Land and Jerusalem.

# folk 'lore' and ideology

All folk groups – from nations to couples – share some common 'lore'. This lore helps to bond and define the group. Very often it does so less by intentional inclusion than by subtle exclusion – if you don't understand the in jokes, or are offended by their taboo themes, then you're not 'one of us'. The jests can even be focussed around fictional activities, such as the subplots of TV soaps, or the recurrent jokes and subtle references of sit-coms and cartoons. If you're not a fan of the show then you will be excluded from the witticisms. *The Simpsons* is a good example, as much of the humour relies on sly cross-references to previous episodes or to a wide range of novels, films and other TV shows.

Usually such jokes and references make fragmentary references to a broader narrative and implicit ideologies. Different groups will vary in the extent to which mass media, the Internet and face-to-face conversations help to spread and influence ideas.

We always have a positive image of our 'in group' – and all 'out groups' are *always* inferior. Some interesting experiments by social psychologists have shown that assigning volunteers to arbitrary groups still creates this 'we are better' scenario. In the real world this can readily be used to create narratives that define groups as 'communities of fear'. The last hundred years abounds with deadly examples of such myth making, from the First World War British propaganda about despicable 'Huns' and 'Krauts', Adolf Hitler's anti-Jewish polemics, Cold War scare mongering, through to the current 'war on terror' (which 'coincidentally' demonises Islam).

However the ideological and mythic aspects of the lore that bonds the groups together will rarely be recognised. Even within political and religious groups which are by their nature essentially ideological, the recognition of such ideologies is restricted to a comparatively superficial depth and never looks at underlying assumptions and deeper beliefs. This is partly because groups' ideas are shared in fragmentary form rather than the 'complete' myth, and partly because belief systems are 'internally reflecting' and have no in-built ability to recognise ideas that fall outside of their own boundaries. Indeed, in the realms of commerce and science there is explicit denial that there are any assumptions and beliefs beyond the boundaries set by their belief systems. Such an internally-reflecting doctrine allows proponents to claim that their beliefs are The Truth.

## cultural consensus and hegemony

This sense of a shared (but usually unrecognised) lore bonds people into societies, cultures, subcultures and groups. Part of the bonding is sharing *implicit* values, belief systems and other 'deep structures'. This sharing of implicit ideas is one of the key ideas of this book and subsequent chapters explore in more detail how these manifest in the modern day. Suffice for now to say that this bonding and sharing may involve ideas which are transmitted initially through the mass media. However, whether or not the mass media is significant initially, the key processes of bonding and sharing take place through what I have termed 'folkloric processes', whether face-to-face or via the Internet.

The combination of mass media and folkloric transmission enables cultures and sub-cultures to achieve a consensus of ideas, and for those ideas to evolve and adapt over time. In the arenas of commerce, politics and religion dominant people and organisations will actively seek to support their continued leadership. The ways in which such dominant ideologies and implicit myths are promulgated are many and various. However there is a concise way of referring to rather complex ideas. This is the word 'hegemony', a complex and prevalent concept which deserves a chapter all of its own before we start to explore in more detail the modern day myths that make up reality.

### sources

Blackmore 1999; Brooker 1998; Chandler no date (quoting Fiske 1987: 288); Cocchiara 1981; Danser 2003; Daekins 1976; Dundes 1980: 6–7; Hobsbawm and Ranger 1983; Irwin and Lombardo: 2001: 89–90; James 1999; Koven 2003; Lewis 1991; Powell 1946 (cited in Wiener 1981: v); Storey 1999, 2003; Thompson 1980; Trubshaw 2003c.

The Foamy Custard Web site (www.indigogroup.co.uk/foamycustard/) contains a number of articles which discuss the overlaps between folklore, mythology, cultural studies and related disciplines.

# Chapter 4

# Hegemony:
# Mythic fragments by another name?

Hegemony is a term first introduced into twentieth century thinking during the 1920s and 30s by the Marxist sociologist Antonio Gramsci (1891–1937). Although pronounced in various ways, *he'gemo'ny* is most consistent with the Greek origins of the word.

To the Classical Greeks 'hegemony' implied leadership by one state of a confederacy, making that ruling or 'supreme' state 'hegemonic' over the others. In contrast Gramsci used the word hegemony to refer to societies where:

> ... the rule of one class over another does not depend on economic or physical power alone but rather on persuading the ruled to accept the system of beliefs of the ruling class and to share their social, cultural, and moral values
> (cited in Joll 1997: 8)

If a social group can be persuaded to accept the ideology (cultural, social and moral) of another group then hegemony is established and the 'hegemonic group' will be able to dominate or control the other group. Hegemony can be established either by coercion or more subtly by what are usually termed 'consensual' processes. These all-but invisible processes of domination are made to seem 'natural', so that the oppressed consent to their subjection. The transmission of 'mythic fragments' as discussed in the previous chapters provides just such an all but invisible processes of domination.

According to Gramsci, those wishing to establish hegemonic control benefit from gaining the consent of those they wish to control (as American politicians have recently rediscovered in Iraq – without consent there can only be coercion). Gramsci understands hegemony as cultural and ideological, for it is the process whereby dominant groups sustain their dominion by gaining the informal consent of lesser groups. The modern day hegemony comprises of the actions of certain groups and institutions within capitalism; for example, the state, popular culture, the family and the mass media.

In the 1960s and 70s the pioneer British cultural studies researcher Stuart Hall picked up on Gramsci's ideas of hegemony. Whereas Gramsci had seen hegemony as the power struggles between a state and its inhabitants, Hall broadened hegemony to encompass the whole domain of social and cultural life. Hall also looked specifically at the ways hegemonic domination could be uncertain and contested by 'oppositional' alternative interpretations of mass culture.

## Contesting the hegemony

More interestingly, at least from the perspective of this book, the Marxist social historian E.P. Thompson looked specifically at how popular culture – such as 'folk customs' – contested the hegemony of the eighteenth century British gentry. The parallels for contesting modern day hegemonies are interesting as they suggest that, despite the potential for 'oppositional' alternative interpretations of mass culture, the real opportunities are with those areas of popular culture that are not primarily transmitted by mass culture and might be better regarded as 'folk customs' and 'folk lore'. (This of course links back to the concluding section of the previous chapter).

Although Gramsci, Hall and Thompson all adopted a Marxist approach, in recent years the concept of hegemony has become detached from its Marxist roots. Among the first of the non-Marxist writers to adopt the notion of hegemony was Roland Barthes. In the 1960s he was the first to recognise how the 'power of myth' helped to make hegemonic imbalances seem to be 'common sense'. Cunning, rather than force, enables the 'powers that be' to nullify subversive elements.

## denial, demonisation and trivialisation

The standard reaction of any ideology to a challenge that undermines its underlying belief system is either to ignore it or, if pushed for a response, dismiss it as 'nonsense'. Indeed, from the perspective of the belief system this is exactly how such a challenge appears. So, homeopathy is 'nonsense' to the belief system of allopathic pharmacists. Clairvoyance is nonsense to a material rationalist. State ownership of public utilities is little more than nonsense to the world view of free enterprise capitalism. The right for all nations to determine their own destiny is nonsense to American and British foreign policy makers. And so on and so on.

If denigration, dismissal and denial do not work (though they often suffice) then another commonly-used technique is to label undesired behaviour as 'deviant'. Over the years this way of categorising has been applied to homosexuals, victims of psychiatric illnesses, muggers, football hooligans (even the terminology used is emotive), and – more recently – so-called 'anti-capitalist' protesters. An even more emotive categorisation, with its associated myth-making, is the term 'terrorist'.

Implicit in this process of excluding beliefs from what is acceptable – and, as already mentioned, groups define themselves by who they exclude, who are deemed 'transgressive' – is a process of demonisation. The time-honoured tradition of Christian proselytisers is to describe the followers of other religions as 'Devil worshippers'. This is an especially curious accusation to make, as only Christians believe in the Devil, so by definition followers of other religions can never be Devil worshippers. Accusations of Devil worship may be nonsense to those outside the Christian belief system, but the logic is seemingly impeccable to those within its confines.

A further technique is to absorb subversive threats into the mainstream culture by trivialisation. British TV sitcoms have a long track record, starting with *Till Death Us Do Part*'s still-powerful parody of racism, *The Good Life*'s frivolous perceptions of self-sufficiency, and *The Young Ones'* parody of youth cultures of the 1970s. Around 1977 the British tabloid papers set out to make punk seem 'cosy'; indeed the Sex Pistols' rendition of *God Save the Queen* is now thoroughly absorbed into 70s nostalgia. In the late 1980s black rap music was promptly made safe by pretty white boys such as Vanilla Ice and Duran Duran. This process was started by Elvis Presley's 'acceptable face' of black rock'n'roll, continued with the Rolling Stones' appropriation of black r'n'b, and Eric Clapton's appropriation of the nuances of black blues musicians such as Otis Rush. More recent examples of such trivialisation include Ali G's parodies of black street culture and the way the drum-and-bass style of music created by black street culture entered the mainstream in the mid-1990s via the far-from-threatening guise of backing tracks for TV commercials selling various brands of upmarket cars.

# mass media and hegemony

In recent years the increasing concentration of economic power in the hands of interwoven multi-national businesses has seen all the major mass media interests being concentrated into a remarkably small number of owners. Such multinational businesses have vast resources to promote the 'benefits' of particular forms of consumerism and capitalism as the 'only possible way'. As politicians can only reach the voters by using the mass media controlled by these same global businesses there are strong grounds for regarding the western political system not as a democracy (in any meaningful sense of the word) but as a hegemony.

For example, Al Gore was quoted in the *New York Observer* during November 2002 saying:

> Fox News Network, The Washington Times, Rush Limbaugh – there's a bunch of them, and some of them are financed by wealthy ultra-conservative billionaires who make political deals with Republican administrations and the rest of the media... . Most of the media [has] been slow to recognize the pervasive impact of this fifth column in their ranks – that is, day after day, injecting the daily Republican talking points into the definition of what's objective as stated by the news media as a whole.

For British parallels think of Rupert Murdoch's sustained stance of being more important than the British Prime Minister. After bolstering support for Margaret Thatcher ('It's *The Sun* wot won it' was his overstated claim in 1992) he famously swapped sides – '*The Sun* backs Blair' – just before the General Election of 1997. Most recently, in early 2004, this political meddling has manifested by inviting Michael Howard, Leader of the Opposition, to 'audition' for Murdoch's support at a meeting of the directors of his Newscorp.

All multi-nationals, not least the mass media operations, are extremely adept at using hegemonic processes to nullify alternative viewpoints – and this certainly includes the ability to nullify political parties and leaders who do not agree with their objectives. Dissent is rarely entirely silenced but merely reduced to tokenism – a few individuals are permitted who are presented as talented 'eccentrics' (for example George Monbiot and John Pilger are currently tolerated/patronised in such a manner by the British media).

Journalists write the sort of stories that from experience they know their editors are most likely to publish. The other option is to look for another job. Editors appoint foreign correspondents from journalists who accept the assumptions of imperialism. According to Reese Erlich, who was in Baghdad during early 2003 as the second Gulf War unfolded:

> I didn't meet a single foreign reporter who disagreed with the notion that the US and Britain have the right to overthrow the Iraqi government by force. They disagreed only about timing, whether the action should be unilateral, and whether a long-term occupation is practical.

Erlich also provides an excellent insider's view of the way media journalists unselfconsciously self-censor their stories, concluding that 'Reporters quickly learn to self-censor, or they're taken off the beat. US and Iraqi media policies have more in common than the leaders of either country would care to admit.'

## democracy or hegemony?

**Once a newspaper touches a story, the facts are lost forever, even to the protagonists**
Norman Mailer

The combined tactics of denial, demonisation, trivialisation and unselfconscious self-censoring all ensure that ideas conveyed via the mass media are well and truly 'mediated' to reflect the dominant political, economic and religious ideologies. Corporate businesses, modern government 'spin doctoring' and the mass media (plus, at least in America, the powerful voices of conservative Christian pressure groups) create a deeply-intertwined hegemonic partnership.

This hegemony ensures that in the USA and UK there is no alternative to political parties that are (a) dismantling social equality; (b) refusing to plan effectively for the future; (c) taking the side of corporate businesses at the expense of the populace. The western world is better described as a hegemony rather than a democracy, at least in any meaningful sense of the word.

Simultaneously major western governments have also removed – indeed inverted – the main reason a populace benefits from a democracy. Where democracies should score over monarchies and oligarchies is by providing private individuals with a way of exerting power over corporate businesses. By this definition US and UK government can be regarded as democracies in name only, as the powers of government are now forced through the hoops set for them by corporate lobbyists. Few if any of the 'pressure groups' based around private individuals can muster more than a small percentage of the budgets devoted to parliamentary lobbying and funding by commerce and industry (and if these prodigious sums of money weren't bringing in the right sort of 'returns' then these budgets would have been cut a long time ago). Mythic fragments may be born equal but some have the benefit of much bigger bank balances...

What western political leaders regard as ideal 'democracies' are hegemonies where the rights of nationals are subservient to lobbying by transnational corporations. Modern so-called 'democracies' must allow Monsanto to successfully lobby for the 'right' to grow genetically-modified crops and at the same time the right of citizens to insist on efficient welfare, health and education services must be fatally weakened.

The preoccupation with the belief that there is no sensible alternative to democracy is a recent one. Bear in mind that not so long ago democracy was a decidedly revolutionary concept:

> Two hundred and fifty years ago the words 'democracy' or 'democrat' were used primarily as an insult. It was not easy to call yourself a democrat without careful apology, explanation or self-deprecation. When the poet Wordsworth wrote privately to a friend in 1794, 'I am of that odious class of men called "democrats",' he wrote as a defiant young man inspired by the French revolution, but 'democrat' nevertheless it was a difficult word for him to use. Even the intellectuals in France before the revolution rarely used to 'democracy' in a positive way.
> (Goldhill 2004: 164)

Bear in mind also that 'democracy' originally meant something different again when it was invented in Athens two and half thousand years ago. Athenian democracy was about participation in public duties. When the Athens Assembly voted for war (as they did almost every year in the fifth century BCE) they were voting themselves and their sons into battle. The original sense of 'fighting for democracy' was a personal commitment, not something you voted other peoples' sons to perform. This is in total contrast to the famous scene in the film

*Fahrenheit 9/11* (2003) where members of Congress ducked Michael Moore when he asked them to enlist their children for the war in Iraq.

## opposition to hegemonies

However the electorate is becoming harder to convince despite (indeed perhaps almost because of) the 'spin' put out by such hegemonic processes. Partly this is because the Internet makes alternative opinions available to those who seek them – either online or by drawing attention to 'offline' sources (and this book ranks as a typical 'offline' example). In Britain (but less so in America) the ideological variation within society is more diverse than ever before. Also the more educated and perhaps more influential members of the population have travelled overseas; millions more have relatives and friends who live abroad. The ethics underlying foreign policy are increasingly challenged by the politically active. And simplistic propaganda – such as the Bush/Blair 'good versus evil' rhetoric – invites scorn from many different areas of British culture (although is an unquestioned aspect of the Judaeo-Christian ideology that pervades American politics).

As ever, everything changes. Within a year of the invasion of Iraq, the Bush-Blair rhetoric has come under sustained criticism. The abbreviation WMD has come to stand less for 'weapons of mass destruction' than 'widespread mass deception'. What Bush, Blair and their advisers seem not to have fully realised is that 'spin' and 'perception management' are increasingly difficult when the Internet circulates critical views quickly. Whereas 'folkloric' transmission of oppositional attitudes could only be circulated by word of mouth or specialist magazines and books, now far more widespread circulation is instantly available. However, the threat to the hegemony is so far essentially superficial rather than fundamental because, predictably enough, those driving the hegemony have well-established strategies for minimising opposition, and they are still well to the fore in modern day Britain and America.

## intentional ignorance

The main strategy, well-established early in the nineteenth century, was to ensure that the 'masses' were educated only to a sufficient standard to perform useful work for the capitalist system, and be left with too little time to discuss wider issues. 'The Devil makes work for idle hands' has long been part of Protestant ideology. However, as idle hands mean that the mind is free to think and talk, the danger is less what the hands might be up to as the tongue. Thankfully for many centuries the populace did not need to be able to read to do its work. Early in the eighteenth century Bernard Mandeville wrote:

> To make the Society Happy and People Easy under the meanest of Circumstances, it is requisite that great numbers of them should be Ignorant as well as Poor... The more a Shepherd, a Plowman or any other Peasant knows of the World, and the things that are Foreign to his Labour or Employment, the less fit he'll be to go through the Fatigues and Hardships of it with Cheerfulness and Content.
> *The Fable of the Bees*

Mandeville went on to write:

> It is impossible that a Society can long subsist and suffer many of its Members to live in Idleness, and enjoy all the Ease and Pleasure they can invent, without having at the same time great multitudes of People that make good this effect, will condescend to be quite the Reverse, and by use and patience inure their Bodies to Work for others and themselves besides.

Since Mandeville's day the full impact of the Industrial Revolution, various socialist and communist revolutions (and their demises), and the rise of a global economy have given his words a significance that now extends well beyond Europe. In recent decades the number of Members who live in Idleness has diminished in number (although certainly not in combined wealth) and the Bodies who Work (with their consequent Fatigues and Hardships, and rarely for more than two dollars a day) now comprise most of the Third World.

Mandeville was explicitly arguing against the lower classes being taught literacy and numeracy. In the nineteenth century one of the attractions of the nonconformist churches in Britain was that they offered Sunday Schools. Quite unlike the Sunday Schools of a century later, when Sunday School meant Bible stories, these provided a basic education in the 'Three 'Rs' for a significant proportion of the population that would otherwise have remained uneducated.

Although perhaps hard to imagine now, encouraging working people to read was politically radical. The intent was one of explicit dissent – empowering the lower classes with the ability to read 'improving books' (not only the Bible) and newspapers, thereby entering fully into the political debates of the day. The fathers of these Sunday School children could be found discussing recent political events in village reading rooms and at self-help 'institutes' and the formative trade unions. Indeed, the conversation in the local 'tap room' was likely to be far more politicised than it ever has been in the last hundred years.

## if you can't silence them then distract them

The dangers of self-educated people talking politics in the pubs were self-evident to the powers-that-be. Rather than try to tell the 'have nots' what to think, the 'haves' very successfully suggested what the 'have nots' should *think about*. In the closing decades of the nineteenth century spectator sports such as football and cricket were promoted. A few decades later Americans were sold baseball, US football and basketball. The notion of watching sport rather than doing it is itself rather ridiculous, but something even more ridiculous resulted – men and boys spent a large proportion of their leisure time talking about what they had watched, or were hoping to watch the next weekend. The natural human instinct to put the world to rights was successfully superseded by putting the team manager to rights.

Newspapers pioneered ways of distracting the 'common man' from potentially seditious conversations. Recognising that men's leisure interests are mostly a continuation of their boyhood, this propaganda was very usefully sown in boy's story papers such as *Hotspur* and *Rover*. Tabloid newspapers and television have now made such distractions a part of 'normal life'. Such endless and peculiarly pointless conversations have evolved into an industry of epic proportions selling people over-priced clothing (produced in the usual Third World sweatshops) to be worn while 'supporting' this smoke-screen sustained by the hegemonic processes.

The wives of the 'common man' had to wait for TV soaps before their leisure time was equally subverted. In the mean time the middle classes were offered distracting 'pass times' such as golf and motoring. From the 1920s onwards *Country Life* magazine (together with guide books, such as those produced by Shell and the series written by Arthur Mee) promoted an invented rural idyll that not only still pervades modern day notions of the British countryside but is generally regarded as 'real'. From the 1960s onwards air travel and package holidays enabled more exotic places (such as the beaches of the Mediterranean coast) to be marketed as enticing distractions. By the 1980s British culture had become a mesmerising pick-and-mix of marketing messages offering neatly packaged 'life styles' which, surprise surprise, required the appropriate equipment and clothes to be bought, and usually involved travelling to the appropriate place for the specific pastime. Two key goals of the hegemony – consumption and distraction – had been simultaneously achieved.

## hegemony as a process

Numerous metaphors can be used regarding the concept of hegemony. For example, it can be referred to as if it was a unified entity, in a similar way that nation states are sometimes spoken of as if they are individuals. Earlier in this chapter I referred to politics, economics and the mass media as a 'deeply-intertwined hegemonic partnership'. However such partnerships are never static. This means a better way to think of hegemonies is as ongoing *processes*.

Such hegemonic processes are transmitted mostly through mythic fragments, with changes in emphasis usually being intentional top-down 'spin doctoring'. However challenges to hegemonic ideas are typically instigated through folkloric processes, either face-to-face or via the Internet. As the later chapters of this book unfold the significance of thinking about hegemonies as a 'process' will become more apparent. In the meantime in the next chapter we will explore some specific myths of the modern world.

### sources

This chapter borrows extensively from Danser 2003 and Trubshaw 2003b. Other sources are Brooker 1998: 67; Easton 2003: 11; Goldhill 2004; Joll 1997; Mailer 1964; Mandeville 1970: 191, 292–3; Rampton and Stauber 2003; Solomon and Erlich 2003: 12, 20, 22, 47; Storey 1999; Thompson 1980; 1993: Ch.2 esp. 74–5, 87; Trubshaw 2003c.

# Chapter 5

# Myths in the modern world

The modern myth is that there are no myths
Attributed to Frank Muir

In my opinion, the greatest single failure of
American education is that students come away
unable to distinguish between a symbol and the
thing the symbol stands for. ...most 'educated'
people cannot tell the difference between a fact and
an idea, the most common confusion of symbol and
thing.
Paul Lutus

Myths are usually associated with societies distant in space and/or
time. Indeed, most mythology has been the study of such myths,
especially as they relate to religious beliefs. But myths are just as alive
and thriving in modern day cultures. In modern society myths are more
often aspects of political and scientific ideologies as much as more
overtly religious notions.

Indeed, in today's secular world political myth has almost as much
authority as sacred myths once had. And the most authoritative mythic
system in modern society is the scientific worldview. And the most
pervasive, and intentionally persuasive, are the myths of commerce.
Taking a broad view of science, commerce, politics and religion we
can recognise a shared spectrum of non-narrative thoughts – 'facts',
beliefs and truncated references – that come together as mythic

40

narratives. For example, the 'facts' of science (e.g. hydrogen is the most common element in the universe) and 'beliefs' (e.g. the universe is infinite) are distinct from more narrative 'interpretations' (e.g. the Big Bang theory) which are essentially mythic.

From this perspective, the Big Bang theory is as much a sacred cosmology for modern western societies as Genesis is for Christians, the dreamtime for Australians, or the writing of *Das Kapital* for Marxists. Similar distinctions between facts, beliefs and narrative myths can also be made in the realms of religion, commerce and politics.

> In the secularised modern world politics is often more relevant than religion – indeed 'Green', far Left and far Right politics tend to be associated with personal beliefs that are to all intents and purposes sacred creeds. Mainstream Western politics attempts to stand apart from the underlying Protestant Christian ideologies. But, while British Prime Ministers and American Presidents may rarely proclaim that 'God is on our side', their opponents – whether the Catholic IRA or the Moslem Al'Qaeda – most certainly regard religion as integral to the political spectrum.
> (Trubshaw 2003a: 169)

One of the myths of science is that scientific rationalism has claimed cultural supremacy over earlier religious worldviews. And yet during the time this book was being written both candidates in the American presidential election attempted to appease bigoted Christian beliefs, and a vastly expensive (both in terms of money and human suffering) war was being waged on the back of mutually-intolerant fundamentalist religious attitudes. So much for the myth claiming the cultural supremacy of rationalism in the western world...

Commerce and science, every bit as much as religion and politics, have their foundations in ideologies, which fulfil a variety of functions. These ideologies provide the 'structures of thought' which filter perceptions, and also shape and motivate individual and group activities. These structures are so deeply embedded in the cognitive processes that they underlie more conscious thoughts, utterances and actions.

People in modern societies are continually presented with ideological messages, many of which also contain 'mythic fragments' which allude to a wider narrative. The ideological content may be more overt, as in the cases of party-political broadcasts, campaigns by pressure groups, or partisan newspaper editorials. But usually the ideology is more hidden, as it is when political analysts put forward arguments which purport to be unbiased or journalists and TV documentaries claim to be reporting reality; or in the writings and teachings of educators, parents' words to their children; and so on and so on.

Most people in the west have considerable difficulty in recognising that their beliefs and ideologies are not 'givens', and that theirs is only one worldview among many. The modern western liberal idea of persons being autonomous and having inalienable rights is a specific ideological stance. Concepts such as 'freedom' and 'human rights' are not simply timeless entities that have hitherto been concealed by countervailing ideas. They are part of a deep ideological stance which was invented in the last few hundred years and have been substantially adapted in recent decades.

## the myths of nationalism

One example of a larger ideological myth usually only encountered in mythic fragments concerns nationalism. Nation states, by their nature, relate to a specific geographical territory, often referred to by such emotive metaphors as 'the homeland' or 'mother land'. The mythic fragments that define and bond groups of people who believe they share a specific identity are transmitted in all possible ways – from intentional propaganda, through the hegemonic processes of mass media, to informal folkloric communication. In reality families and communities have only a notional fit with such myths and ideologies. People have continually migrated so that cultural, political and religious differences do not 'map' onto the physical world. 'Nations' and 'homelands' are essentially myths, only 'making sense' in the imagination.

But any threats to the accepted notion of this identity or territory are guaranteed to inflame passions. The consequences of threats to these mythic notions of nationality are anything but imaginary. The twenty-first century has opened with the legacy of 'ethnic cleansing' in the Balkans and the continuation of over 2000 years of conflicting myths of rights to territory between Palestinians and Israelis. Two world wars and numerous 'local' and civil wars characterised the twentieth century. Most, at least in part, were attempts to resolve conflicting territorial claims. However ideological issues and myths were invariably used to support these territorial claims. In a few cases – the American involvement in Vietnam for example – ideological issues were the sole justification.

Nations as much as individuals define themselves by what they are not. Such phrases as 'the west' and 'the free world' require there to be non-western nations and un-free worlds – although such simplistic dualisms exist more in the mind than as accurate distinctions between different ideologies. During the forty-four years of the Cold War western 'democracy' polarised itself in contrast with totalitarian communism. With the dismantling of the Berlin Wall and the USSR, which commenced in November 1989, the west has found it more difficult to define itself in opposition to communism. In its stead George W. Bush's 'war on terror' has created essentially mythical adversaries which reflect Judaeo-Christian disdain for Islam. America – and by extension the west – once again has found an 'other' which is excluded in a deceitful attempt to define itself.

The 'war on terror' is, so far, less about terrorism or even territory than the even more mythical notions of 'good' versus 'evil', and a convenient smokescreen for taking control of important sources of oil. As the erudite Eric Hobsbawm observed '… I cannot think of one time when the USA went to war exclusively to do good… '

Attempts by presidential spin doctors to demonise the 'other' share the rhetoric of the least-imaginative medieval preachers. Such propaganda fails to recognise that people can be regarded as 'other' in an infinite number of ways; we (collectively and individually) are often 'other' to a great many others.

Britain has its own territorial/ideological conflict in Ireland, and has made significant political changes to defuse radical nationalism in Scotland and Wales, which in turn has stimulated a movement for Cornish independence. The mythology and folklore associated with the nationalism of these parts of the British Isles is largely invented and draws upon a very heavily 'filtered' account of events over the last three millennia. This is of course quite characteristic – the conflict between Israel and Palestine is 'justified' by events of one to two thousand years ago with little attention to the various major changes that have intervened.

In some continents, such as America and Africa, historical claims to territorial rights are confused as the various traditional 'tribes' had been steadily migrating over the centuries. The occupants of a particular territory at the time of colonisation typically were relative 'newcomers' to their region (although, nevertheless, had well-established myths that justified their presence there and, in many cases, claimed that they had always been there). The fine detail of such migrations can only be established by archaeology; the apparent simplicity of events offered by myths is illusory.

> ... historical monuments may be claimed by nations far removed in culture or time from the peoples originally concerned with them. In Africa the one-time European colonies of Dahomey, Gold Coast, and French Sudan adopted after independence the names Benin, Ghana, and Mali, respectively – all once powerful precolonial empires – and Zimbabwe in southern Africa is named after the great ruined medieval city of Great Zimbabwe. Such names helped to instil a sense of unity within culturally disparate states whose artificially drawn frontiers rarely took account of pre-existing ethnic, cultural, or linguistic boundaries.
> (Molyneaux and Vitebsky 2001: 215)

Kenya likewise drew its 'origins myths' from a politically-aware version of traditional myths written in 1938 (see Bernardi 1987).

## the invention of history

In contrast to politically-promoted views of the past, history is not directly dependent on what really happened in the past but on how it is remembered or, more pedantically, how it is repeatedly recreated in the present. Our so-called 'common sense' creates illusory causes for events by using hindsight to see 'inevitable' connections. However, at the time the events were being played out there were a vast number of possible 'outcomes'. Only in retrospect is what actually happened seen as 'inevitable'. The past was once the indeterminate future; our attempts to understand the past should therefore be equally indeterminate. Attempts to filter the past into specific historic narratives are no more than ideological myths.

In the last few decades this reconstruction of the past has acquired a whole new emphasis. Deeply embedded into present day culture are complex constructions of 'nostalgia'. Places and artefacts of historic interest no longer have any practical importance but make mythic references to the past. Such nostalgia is pervasive but far from homogenous. The place or object, while only ever existing in the present moment, signifies the cultural reconstruction of the past. Such 'cultural reconstructions' are termed by Jean Baudrillard 'simulations'; the same place or object can evoke a wide variety of simulations of the past, mostly dependent on prior knowledge and belief systems. (Fans of The Matrix will know that early in the film the hero – yet to be reborn as Neo – sells some dodgy software kept hidden in a hollow copy of Baudrillard's *Simulacra and Simulation,* suggesting that this book is the 'key' to hacking into *The Matrix.*)

In Britain anyone under the age of about 40 has been brought up within a culture largely fabricated from notions of nostalgia and simulation, mostly woven by commercial concerns and the whims of mass media, into which tourism and heritage are thoroughly intertwined. The heritage industry has long been creating such nostalgic simulations of the past, notably in regard to country houses and stately homes although the 'visitor centre syndrome' has increasingly infected prehistoric sites too. Visiting an English stately home is more akin to a trip to Disneyland than most tourists appreciate.

Film and TV frequently seek to blur the borderline between fiction, fact and speculation. From Sergei Eisenstein's *October* (1928), through Oliver Stone's *JFK* (1992), to recent TV biographies of famous leaders as diverse as Napoleon, Churchill and Ghandi, all mythologise real-life individuals and political events. TV programmes increasingly use vague, stylised re-enactments to 'represent' a period or episode. Innumerable historical novels and plays provide even more scope for mythologising the past, whether the finery of Victorian Britain, the perils of the American West, or the escapades of war.

The way in which novels and films use stories that involve similar types of characters and similar situations to historically real events enables narrative and ideology to be seamlessly interwoven. As Hollywood and the moguls behind television are fully aware, such scriptwriting is one of the best ways to subtly communicate ideological beliefs. As 'innocent' a genre as 1950s cowboy films are populated with racist stereotypes and, in hindsight, are as much about myths of white supremacy as propaganda films put out by the Third Reich.

## the myths of consumerism

Nationalistic myths date back as far as the emergence of nation states in the eighteenth century (although, by the very nature of such myths, usually implicate the myths of much older cultures). Along with political and religious myths (with which they were often intimately interwoven), they comprised the main forms of myths encountered. Then, about fifty years ago, a major change began. Consumerism increasingly became an important aspect of western society. And since the 1980s the machinations of multi-national commerce have actively promoted individualistic life styles to consumers. Each of these is attractively packaged with its own mythic fragments and specific ideologies. At any one time any number of 'life styles' can be adopted, each of which quickly changes. If the classic definition of culture is 'the product of humanity acting within an environment', humanity now acts not so much in the natural environment but in a consumption-based environment.

The mass media are often responsible for promoting these subcultures. Style pundits might argue that it is still teenagers who dictate what is fashionable, yet style magazines and their advertisers seem to exert sufficient influence to justify their existence. Any high street newsagent now offers a plethora of 'life style' magazines aimed at all age groups, all of them promoting specific types of consumption either by overt advertising or the slightly more subtle antics of journalists and experts.

By the 1950s consumerism was promoted by adopting René Girard's ideas of 'mimetic desire', by which he means that we copy our desires from other people. 'Media personalities' seemingly open up their private lives in the popular press so we can desire the clothes, cars, furnishings, gadgets, holidays that they lend their personae to. The purveyors of the hegemonic process have every reason to be happy with way the mass media works.

However, the mass media are not essential for promoting subcultures. Subcultures have become so prevalent in modern society that major marketing exercises are no longer needed to create or promote them. So an immense range of specialist publications also circulate to share and promote the ideas of specific subcultures (although not all of these carry advertising or even promote the consumption of anything more than books, music or DVDs). Additionally, all subcultures also share ideas through the more folkloric processes of the Internet and face-to-face conversations.

The consequence has been more than just a pluralism of styles and their associated values. Frequently-changing fashions mask, indeed in some cases replace, the more deeply-rooted traditions that shape and give a historical depth to a culture. Modern societies fragment into myriad ever-changing sub-cultures.

The first person to look at myth-making in modern consumer society was the French critic Roland Barthes (1915–80). He made himself into something of a myth with his 1973 book *Mythologies*. This looks at the underlying myths and ideologies associated with topics as diverse as wine, wrestling, steak and chips, striptease, haircuts in Hollywood films, Greta Garbo's face, and Citroen cars. From Barthes' viewpoint, adverts are 'mythological universes'. Barthes' counterpart in Italy,

Umberto Eco (best known for his novels *In the Name of the Rose* and *Foucault's Pendulum*) wrote a number of essays analysing the symbolism underlying modern culture for Italian 'popular' periodicals between 1967–86; these are best known in English from a collection titled *Travels in Hyper-reality*.

The prevalence of modern day myths is self-evident to any parent or teacher. They are well aware of how the enormous expansion of the mass media – especially television cartoons, commercials and magazines – competes for influence over children's imaginations. The myths of modern society are increasingly being reinterpreted through non-written media such as films, TV programmes, computer games and popular music (both the lyrics and visual iconography).

Television allows us to view the world mythically while apparently presenting us with reality. 'Seeing is believing' – yet we forget that first of all who and what appears in front of the camera is carefully selected by the director, then the camera lies by picking and choosing what we see, and finally the editor picks and chooses what is included (and, more crucially, what is excluded) and in which order we see events.

> The tacit aim of television... is to keep us from catching a glimpse of the world in which we actually live, the world in which real pain, real love, actual death, loss and despair, real struggle and conflict, economic and social deprivation play such a prominent part. Instead, television feeds our passive torpor by permitting us to sink into the semi-conscious world of our most primitive dreams and fantasies, in which we may indulge the half-formed urges for personal, tribal and sexual conquest which slosh about in the sumps of our minds. Any visiting Martian anthropologist intent on gauging our values from the way we spend our spare time would surely be appalled at what television reveals as our major preoccupations.
> (Smail 1984: 117)

The visiting Martian would note that violence and death are by far our major preoccupation. Violence has seeped from Hollywood action films into soaps. Death is the dominant topic of a vast output of crime investigation programmes, which in turn blur into the 'reality' of news programmes and documentaries. The parallels with the gladiatorial contests of the Roman empire are clear, and explicitly so with films such as *Spartacus* and *Gladiator*.

… war is just another TV program. Not so, of course, to the soldiers themselves or to the civilians maimed and killed by American missiles, but to the television audience. And although the vivid television coverage of Vietnam stirred up anti-war opposition, the coverage of the first Gulf War, with its greenish flickering images and explosions of phosphorescence, famously resembled a video game rather than a battlefield.

(Hamilton 2004)

## role playing and zapping

One new genre greatly outstrips even television for incessant violence – computer games. However not all computer games are simplistic splat-fests as traditional folkloric and mythic narratives have spilled over from literature, film and TV into role-playing games and their computer-based successors. *Dungeons and Dragons*, created in 1974 by Gary Gygax and Dave Arneson, is regarded as the father of role-playing games. Vast armies of fantasy figurines were inspired by its rather Tolkienesque characters and mythology (although purists consider that *Dungeons and Dragons* owes more to Fritz Lieber's *Grey Mouser* series than it does to Tolkien).

The success of these board-based fantasy games has been greatly exceeded by computer-based games. Some are close to the *Dungeons and Dragons* model but most draw rather loosely on mythology to beget hosts of macho phantasms to be 'zapped' with the joystick's fire button. Other games, known as 'adventure games', require the player to solve arcane puzzles. They started out in the 1980s as text-only computer games but by the 1990s had acquired simple graphics too. One of the pioneering graphical adventure games, *Myst* (1994), set a high standard of visual design. The puzzles centre around 'mystical symbols' in a sort-of-Classical 'grove' and Myst Island has many mythical qualities, although few overt references to traditional myths.

The next generation of games, such as *Tomb Raider* (1996), blended action and adventure genres so there was exploration, puzzle solving and combat. *Tomb Raider* invoked some of the imagery of the films featuring the swashbuckling archaeologist Indiana Jones (*Raiders of the Lost Ark* (1981); *Indiana Jones and the Temple of Doom* (1984); *Indiana Jones and the Last Crusade* (1989)). Indiana Jones, as manifest by Harrison Ford, managed to combine the attributes of an action hero with aspects of a learned academic – although he has also been seen as a cross between the Greek hero Odysseus and comic strip hero Tintin.

*Tomb Raider* adapted the Indiana Jones myths by creating more complex gender interactions with the players. The bimboesque physique and action-loving lifestyle of the heroine, Lara Croft, undoubtedly appealed to the adolescent attitudes of boys of all ages. More significantly, Lara gave *Tomb Raider* an appeal to girls in a way that the macho male characters of other action games had not. One female fan, Loren Petrich, wrote about Lara Croft on her Web site:

> The personality she projects in the game reminds me of how the classical Greek deity Artemis was depicted – always single, roaming the wilderness, and with a bow and arrow (what her worshippers were familiar with). Ms. Croft, of course, packs some more recent heat. And when Artemis was seen bathing in a stream by the hunter Actaeon, she turned him into a deer, whereupon he was attacked by his dogs. The ending of *Tomb Raider 2* seems reminiscent of that story. (www.petrich.com/games/tombraider/tombraider.html)

The 'mythology' of *Tomb Raider* includes the fifteen 'levels' which Lara explores. These include Vilcabamba, a civilisation that flourished for hundreds of years in the Peruvian rainforests of South America. Lara battled wolves, bears, raptors and bats in a lost Incan city. Another level of the game is set in a labyrinth in Classical Greece. Here Lara must fight lions, alligators and crazed monkeys. A different level of *Tomb Raider* takes place among the pyramids of ancient Egypt; another of the levels is also set in a pyramid, but this time on Atlantis. According to one Web review,

> Like Indiana Jones, Lara is not just a tourist, she is seeing the mythical, esoteric dream locations that are the stuff of legend.

The rational materialism of western culture is proving to be an avid consumer of irrational fantasy and myth as presented in computer games. However consumers quickly become creators because games such as *Dungeons and Dragons*, *Tomb Raider*, and their many imitators and successors have spawned a vast number of Web pages from fans, a number of whom act as historians and analysts. The boundaries between these games-related sites and an even vaster number of fantasy-fuelled Web sites can be blurred at times, making for very fluid interactions between 'traditional' mythic motifs and the constantly-evolving contemporary manifestations of these motifs.

In the case of *Enter the Matrix* the boundaries become even more blurred, as this game (one of the most technically advanced so far) shares scenes filmed at the same time as the movies, and shares the profoundly post-modernist mythic conjectures that characterise *The Matrix* trilogy, and thence with the unprecedented amount of both popular comment and more academic analysis that these films quickly generated.

## modern monsters and heroes

Multi-cultural societies, political correctness and growing awareness of the illusory nature of such distinctions has made it more difficult to define ourselves by excluding other races. The 'other' is no longer Arabic, Asian, still less Hispanic or Jewish, as people from all these cultures now live in western countries. Furthermore, to a greater or lesser extent, these races have adopted or aspire to western values in their own countries. So we have invented science fiction monsters as 'other'. Some, such as the Daleks of *Dr Who,* effectively dramatise the menace of autonomous machines who are no more human than their distorted speech. Others are palaeontologically-plausible, such as those 'cloned' for Steven Spielberg's film *Jurassic Park* (1993). But the monsters of sci-fi are dominated by imaginative aliens which have a semblance of human physiology or psychology.

Modern popular culture holds sway over monsters in ways which are far less sophisticated than traditional myths. Rather disturbingly, the monsters which abound in modern popular culture such as films and video games are there as little more than cannon fodder. What this says loud and clear is that if you're not one of us, if you are 'other', then you're dead – preferably with a violent, blood-splattering demise. Or in the spin of political speech writers, with 'shock and awe'. Modern culture seemingly lacks the sophistication to look beyond the dualisms of 'us' and 'other' and see that both heroes and monsters are aspects of a larger belief system. The clearest recent example of this is that a surprisingly high proportion of Americans (and rather too many Britons and Europeans) were, initially at least, taken in by George W. Bush's seriously unsophisticated rhetoric of 'good' versus 'evil'.

These naïve concepts of monsters correspond to uneasiness about how we construct our heroes and heroines too. Real-life people are increasingly reified by the media as hero-like – film stars, sports players and pop stars are all presented as heroic role models on very thin pretexts, mostly to arouse their readers' desires to share their wealth, looks, self-esteem, status, life style and so forth. What we expect of such heroes has indeed become super-human, not least in their 'private' lives. So American presidents, members of the British royal family, and any number of the famous-for-being-famous have found that perfectly human sexual peccadilloes become front page news, displacing stories of sustained corporate greed, unnecessary wars, human rights abuses, and a vast number of other topics of far greater significance.

## the myths of gender

The same sectors of the media that perpetrate the cult of celebrity also construct our prevalent myths of sexuality. Whether we look at TV's soap operas or lifestyle magazines such as *Cosmopolitan* or *Loaded*, sexuality is deeply mythologised. Women are polarised into whores and angels, conquests and victims. They are situated tussling between macho exploitation and tokens of feminist ideologies of correctness. Male characterisation is confined to roles that likewise restrict rather than reflect the complexities of reality. And then there is the way in which transgressive sexuality, such as homosexuality, has spawned its own cultural norms which in turn create further transgressive subcultures. These are prime examples of modern myth making. For instance, the way gay icons are perceived often has more in common with mythical heroes and deities than their flesh-and-blood entities.

We make sense of the world from a heterosexual perspective and assume that this is both the 'natural' and 'ideal' way of things. Other sexualities are transgressive, deviant or 'queer'. As ever, what seems 'natural' and 'ideal' is constructed. In the case of sexuality what is deemed normal is the outcome of ever-increasing attempts to define what is *not* normal. For example, not until about 1870 was the concept of homosexuality created, with implications of it being deviant, a sin, a crime and a form of sickness. Prior to that same-sex relationships between men had no doubt flourished, but without arousing the negative connotations of this newly-invented cultural concept, to which individuals could be categorised, or could identify with. And only many decades later were same-sex relationships between women 'formalised' into the concept of lesbianism.

Modern cultural concepts make it difficult to understand the sexual concepts of a different culture. Even seemingly impartial words such as 'reproduction', 'role', and 'sexuality' are part of the language and ideology of modern pseudo-objectivity.

The feminist debates of the 1970s onwards developed their own origin myths and heroines (whether flesh and blood females elevated to iconic status, such as Germaine Greer, or 'reclaimations' of mythical figures, such as pagan goddesses). Indeed, radical feminism entered a richly mythopoetic phase when it 'reclaimed' the Neolithic period of European prehistory as a matrifocal, goddess-worshipping utopia. The processes of this mythmaking is fascinating, as the feminists based their ideas on the work of academic archaeologists – especially the work of Marija Gimbutas – with little or no awareness that these ideas were not generally accepted by other archaeologists. For instance, while feminists make much of stylised female figurines from the Neolithic, this is not a reliable indicator of goddess worship (just as the vast number of Barbie dolls around today are equally stylised but are rarely associated with goddess worship).

## lost wisdom

The Mother Goddess mythos borrows in part from wider modern myths of a lost 'golden age'. A plethora of popular books argue for a lost wisdom revealed by the author's exegesis of archaeology and early literature. Celtic, Arthurian, Mayan and Egyptian flavours predominate. As already noted in Chapter 5, there is a seemingly widespread human need to create the image of an ideal cosmos or utopia. Because such an ideal is recognised as unattainable it is commonly placed in the past (except in sci-fi writing where it may be in the future or on another planet). Traditional myths promptly introduced 'the fall', a specific mythic event such as the expulsion from the Garden of Eden. Modern myth-makers simply accept the deeply-rooted notion that the processes of industrialisation steadily led to a loss of this idealised wisdom.

Apart from any other considerations, such books claiming to reveal aspects of this lost wisdom also reveal a significant desire to read – and create – such modern myths. What sort of people consider these at least plausible, if not true? Indeed, why are myths and mythological figures generally so compelling today? The answer lies with writers such as Sir James Frazer (1854–1941), Carl Jung (1875–1961) and Joseph Campbell (1904–87). These three figures have one other characteristic in common – their ideas were never accepted by academic mythologists but nevertheless their books became widely read. (See Trubshaw 2003a: Ch.1 for a detailed discussion of these now discredited pioneers.)

However most of the myths we live by – and, remarkably often in the twentieth and twenty-first centuries, we are prepared to kill for – have not yet been sufficiently well-studied. The legacy of the major mythographers simply does not provide an adequate basis on which to embark on such 'mission critical' assignments. We urgently need more understanding of modern day myths and the ways they enhance identity and impart ideologies.

## soaps as myth making

As already noted in Chapter 3, TV soaps influence how people think about contentious topics introducing controversial characters and situations, creating a framework for viewers' responses, while limiting the range of possible attitudes to those adopted by the soap's characters. As a result soaps provide the illusion of debate without challenging the deeper ideologies.

Domestic soaps now blur into emergency services soaps, which in turn blur on one hand into TV drama series (*The Bill; Frost; Midsomer Murders*) and on the other hand into docusoaps and documentaries about the police, fire and ambulance services.

In hospital soaps the health care staff are idealised. Wards are never endemically short-staffed, no one complains about being overwhelmed by paperwork (indeed, how often is anyone seen doing paperwork, except at the opening of a sequence before someone else walks up and starts talking to them?), the plots rarely depict the frustration of bureaucratic hold ups, no one ever complains about under-funding or the lack of equipment. The myth that 'medicine cures people' is perpetrated without question, despite the many challenges to this questionable belief which date back to Ivan Illich's books of the 1970s.

More implicitly, if viewers become more obsessed about their personal health they have think less time to think about wiser social issues. Political debates about the National Health Service compete for media time with wider political debates – indeed there have been some decidedly cynical attempts by British health ministers to 'bury' less favourable announcements about the NHS at times when international terrorism is grabbing the headlines.

## the convenient myths of the blue flashing lights

Alongside the relentless offerings of soaps, TV moguls provide us with a culture of violence and blue flashing lights. Hollywood has long portrayed a society in which guns and violent crime are inescapable, giving the illusion that such behaviour is, if not legal, at least normal.

Little wonder then that people are afraid of violent crime, even though the per capita incidence has (outside of the drug dealing underworld) diminished in Britain during recent years. Despite public perceptions, violent crime perpetrated by strangers on young children, women or the elderly is very much an exception. In Britain during the late 1990s crime statistics reveal that only one percent of people ever experience violent crime. Of this one percent only two percent are elderly people. The greatest proportion of attacks take place in the home, not on the street. The victims of attacks which take place in the street are predominately young males; few victims are female. Contrary to media stereotyping, attackers have rarely taken illegal drugs – but are often drunk, and are mostly known to the victim.

> Despite the scepticism of parents, [British] murder figures look relatively reassuring. Between 1983 and 1993, on average 86 children under 16 were killed each year in England and Wales, mostly by their parents and minders. But the number murdered by strangers has been tiny, averaging five a year...
> (*Sunday Times* 6th September 1995)

Although five a year is five too many, in the late 1990s 20 children *each day* were killed or seriously injured in UK road accidents...

Police forces need TV programmes such as *Crimewatch* not so much to solve specific crimes but to create a general fear of crime, so that the financial budgets for police forces are considered necessary. What the public do not realise is that little of the budget is spent detecting or even preventing crimes against persons or property (figures released early in 2004 suggest that the British 'Bobby' spends only about 20 percent of his or her time doing activities that the public would recognise as 'being on the beat'), but increasingly on administrative 'paper-chases' and keeping up with the ever-increasing legislation which moves us ever-closer to the situation where, if it is not compulsory to do something then it is illegal to do it.

Whereas not too many years ago the eye-catching visual impact of blue flashing lights on TV was almost entirely associated with police cars, increasingly TV dramas have involved the other emergency services. Hospital-based soaps risk outnumbering domestic soaps – and the boundaries have become increasingly blurred as many of the old style soaps have evolved to include intense dramas that also make great use of emergencies, extended hospital treatment, not to mention police interviews and court cases.

The overall result of watching TV in Britain on a typical weekday evening is that a great many people are meeting violent deaths. Certainly many more people die on screen each night than are likely to be conceived by all the on-screen sex acts – most of which are seemingly not about procreation anyway. But not to worry, our society cocoons you with this illusion of eminently professional paramedics, police and fire fighters. Blue flashing lights are there to reassure you, they are the visual lullabies of night time TV. Sleep tight, society is under control, even the unpleasant bits.

Constant exposure to this myth conveniently ensures that no one questions whether or not a significant proportion of our taxes should sustain a 'nanny state' of largely unaccountable, and most certainly intractable, self-appointed 'professionals' whose real life skills are often greatly inferior to their onscreen counterparts, and run by administration systems with a reputation for being appallingly bad at core organisational and people-management functions. The blue flashing lights of TV perpetrate some highly convenient distractions.

## from the Wild West to the final frontier

These convenient myths reflect back and construct reality. From the 1960s to the 80s the space race was an inseparable aspect of the Cold War. The activities of NASA became, to all intents and purposes, a US soap opera and the astronauts became among the most celebrated of superheroes for the national ethos. Predictably Hollywood was happy to reinforce all the mythic ideologies and stereotypes being constructed and cultivated by NASA. Just as America had originally forged its identity in the mythos of the Wild West, so space was the new frontier.

In the mid-60s Gene Roddenberry decided that this would be a good basis for a TV script and touted the script for *Wagon Train to the Stars.* Somewhere along the way the South African name for wagon trains was suggested and *Star Trek* was born. Early *Star Trek* episodes indeed had a Western frontier feel to them. This was sci-fi with irresistible optimism. Roddenberry's scripts reflect the liberal-humanist idealism of that era. Despite this being the height of the Cold War, with the Vietnam conflict escalating, he offered a radical vision which cast aside national and racial differences. Although a little hard to imagine now, back in 1965 *Star Trek* was an aspirational vision of how America might evolve. There was also a Russian, Mr Chekov, on the bridge. More radically, a black person was included in this vision of future America. OK, she was little more than a switchboard operator, but young black Americans at the time picked up on this as important. And, in a small but significant step for mankind, the first inter-racial kiss shown on American network TV was that between Captain Kirk and Uhura.

In contrast Stanley Kubrick's *2001: A Space Odyssey* (released in 1968) had the look and feel of white, modernist purity. The technological vision of *2001* was made to seem just around the corner, just 30 years ahead. Like *Star Trek*, the ideology of *2001* was self-conscious myth-making.

One up and coming director, George Lucas, saw even greater potential and intentionally deepened the mythic content of such science fiction by involving the maverick mythologist Joseph Campbell. *Star Wars* (released in 1977) combined the 'final frontier' with interstellar imperialism. Despite the galactic dimensions of the action, the combat in one-man fighters is reminiscent of gunfights outside Western saloons, or of Second World War dogfighting.

## myth reflects back as myth

Twenty years on from the invention of *Star Trek* and *Star Wars* the Cold War had thawed. Space exploration may have been hip in the 60s but was now rather dull. NASA had ceased to be a miracle factory and had become something of a long-distance haulage outfit, albeit longer-distance than any Earth-bound equivalent. Like all high-mileage trucks, the older they get they more likely they are to fail. Few NASA-watchers were surprised that the oldest of their 'trucks', Challenger, failed all too spectacularly.

In the 1960s both *Star Trek* and *2001* piggybacked on the success of NASA. Thirty-odd years on NASA now piggybacks on *Star Trek* by employing one of the actors to front press conferences, or by naming projects using a Star Trek sounding-name to capture the public's imagination.

Myths become dangerous and insidious when metaphors are mistaken for reality, and fictional stories become incorporated into ideologies. The actions of recent American Presidents – notably George W. Bush – can easily be confused with Hollywood myths about superheroes. Ronald Reagan famously blurred the boundaries between myth and truth – or, according to the spin provided at the time of his funeral, 'Reagan stood at the intersection where dreams and reality meet' (Rather 2004), whereby 'misinformation' becomes replaced with 'dreams" and, instead of blurring the boundary between fantasy and fact, Reagan stands at their 'intersection'.

The antics of the Lone Ranger now seem to be the main inspiration for the 'scriptwriters' of the world's gung-ho superpower, with the president as the embodiment of the mythic Hollywood superhero. Politics and warfare are now, more than ever before, inspired by fictions and invented rationales which have become deeply embedded into the mythology underpinning modern day culture.

Just as most traditional myths use violence and/or a heightened sense of the erotic for dramatic effect, so waging war is one way that the myths of real world politics heighten their 'dramatic effect'. Real violence is a highly effective 'smokescreen' which greatly hinders the evaluation of the ideologies and political posturing that are brought to bear to justify armed conflict. Phrases such as the 'war on terror' are turbocharged with such spin. Given the prevalence of Hollywood's action films and associated superhero myths, not surprisingly most of the public cannot distinguish cinematic fantasy from political fantasy. Indeed, it seems most politicians, including several American presidents, are either incapable of making such distinctions or intentionally choose not to.

For the last 25 years the clichés of cinematic heroes have provided role models for American presidents, not least George W. Bush who was seemingly reliving countless cowboy movies when announcing in September 2001 he wanted Osama bin Laden 'dead or alive'. Then, towards the conclusion of the supposed 'liberation' of Iraq in May 2003, he arrived on the deck of an aircraft carrier in a fighter jet as if re-enacting a scene from the film *Independence Day* (1996) which has a fictional American president piloting combat aircraft against incoming alien attacks.

Likewise in the film *Air Force One* (1997) the actor Harrison Ford (famous for playing swashbuckling adventure heroes such as Indiana Jones) brought intentional role-transference into the movie and took on the role of a fictional American president who bucks political protocol and tells all the terrorists of the world 'It's your turn to be afraid', later to be the thinly-veiled message of Bush's 'war on terror'. However Ford's fictional president is a Vietnam veteran who kills four or five adversaries in the course of the film, one with his bare hands. Along the way he reconfigures the fuel system, commands missile attacks and pilots a tension-filled rescue mission. Such action-packed derring-do usually requires the wearing of tights and capes and is in marked contrast with the military record of President Bill Clinton, who was in office at the time these films were released. Nevertheless such myth-making enters popular consciousness so it is little surprise that the military accomplishments – or lack of – by George W. Bush and John the myths of reality

Kerry were the focus of attention in the 2004 presidential election campaign.

Unless we are personal friends with American presidents they are imaginary beings because, as with all major politicians, we know them only as characters created by journalists. To a large extent we accept the mythic personae the media provide. We then expect these mythical entities to live out the myths that have been created for them. Like a kaleidoscope of reflections, the mythmaking of politics reflects back on itself. To a larger extent that most people feel comfortable accepting, the world's most important countries are governed and ruled by imaginary entities.

## the threat from within

The underlying theme of heroes protecting 'us' (usually the 'US' of the USA) from an alien 'other' has been explored in popular culture in the form of myths that have migrated from a Wild West that was largely a fantasy (although the deep racism was most certainly not fantasy), through a romanticised World War II or Vietnam, and then to extraterrestrial encounters.

While perhaps epitomising the yearnings of the Reagan and first George Bush eras, the 'final frontier' metaphors of *Star Wars* now seem less relevant. 'Us' and 'them' distinctions have become progressively more blurred. In *ET* (1982), a less-than-threatening homesick alien takes up residence within an archetypal American home. With *Alien* (1979), the alien is born from a human womb, but on a spaceship remote from Earth. When the birth of an alien from a human recurs in *Men in Black* (1997) the threat is more sinister. Not only does this take place in America, but the distinction between human secret agents and their extra-terrestrial counterparts are blurred by sharing the eponymous dress sense.

Paranoia and phobia thrive in the fuzzy frontier zones of identity. One theme found in movies and TV dramas but even more prevalent in contemporary legends is contamination. From reptiles, spiders or insects invading someone's body; through snakes or tarantulas lurking unseen in clothes, plants or household goods, to the most abiding of all these themes – the contamination of foodstuffs. The latest variants tell of a man who picks up a woman in a local bar, sleeps with her, and awakens to find the message 'Welcome to the world of AIDs' scrawled in lipstick on the nearest mirror.

There are clear parallels here with the fears of 'invasion' and 'contamination' underlying the widespread popular interest in UFOs and close encounters with aliens, itself only an extraterrestrial extension of the xenophobia and racism lurking rather too close to the surface of western societies. In-depth training in psychology is not needed to spot the insecurities about our physical and social boundaries which these scenarios feed upon. The motifs of these contemporary legends were the basis of scripts for *The X-Files* and their endless permutations are tracked in such magazines as *Fortean Times*.

## trauma and drama

Clear examples of the way we make sense of reality through myths arise when people are subjected to unexpected trauma. After the attack on the World Trade Centre on 11th September 2001, witnesses repeatedly said 'It was like a movie', 'It was like *Independence Day*', 'It was like *Die Hard*', 'No, *Die Hard 2*'. In Britain we still use expressions like 'It was like the Blitz', even though the people using the expression are too young to have experienced the German air raids personally – the Blitz has become a mythic concept, reinforced by brief film clips broadcast on TV.

Almost exactly the same responses were seen in the aftermath of the devastating tsunami of 26 December 2004, with the inevitable comparisons to the disaster movie *The Day After Tomorrow*, released in May 2004, or *Deep Impact* (1998).

Such mythic 'transference' of traumatic events is not in itself a modern development as traditional religions have their own corresponding 'disaster' myths, such as the Book of Revelation in the Bible or equally apocalyptic visions of the end of time in Scandinavian mythology, and corresponding Hindu myths in *Shatapatha Brahmana*.

## living in a mythical world

This chapter has been rather like fast-forwarding a video through a film with a vastly complicated plot, but has hopefully illustrated just how extensively Hollywood and TV creates the myths which create the 'reality' of politics, nationalism, terrorism, consumerism, sexuality, heroes, monsters, presidents and aliens.

Time now to slow down and press 'Play' to look more closely at two especially influential modern day myths: those of commerce and science.

## sources

This chapter borrows extensively from Trubshaw 2003a Ch.14. Other sources are Armstrong 2004; Barthes 1973; Baudrillard 1983, 1990; Bernardi 1987; Cavallaro 2001: 121–3, 129–30; Dean 2003; Doniger 2005; Eco 1987; Flood 1996: 16–17; Hamilton 2004; Hine 1998; Hobsbawm 2000: 17; Illich 1976; 1983; James 1999; Kapell and Doty 2004; King 2002; Lawrence and Jewett 2002; Lutus 2001; Meskell 1995; Molyneaux and Vitebsky 2001; Rather 2004, cited in Hamilton 2004; Simmons 2004; Smail 1984: p116–22; Taylor 1989; 1999: 143–4; Trubshaw 2003a; 2003c; 2005 Ch.1; Woolley: 1996 3.1–3.6 and 5.1–5.4.

# Chapter 6

# Myths of commerce

> Humans cannot live without illusion. For the men and women of today, an irrational faith in progress may be the only antidote to nihilism.
> John Gray

> The secret of life is honesty and fair dealing. If you can fake that, you've got it made.
> Groucho Marx

> … in the universe [of advertisement makers] the truth is ultimately what the client wants the world to think is true
> Edward Bernays

> The conscious and intelligent manipulation of the organized habits and opinions of the masses is an important element in democratic society.
> Edward Bernays

The most pervasive myth of recent decades, the one which generates mythic fragments that populate nearly every aspect of western daily lives, is the ideology of capitalist commerce. This has four key components:

- The overriding ideal is growth.
- Quantity is more important than quality; power always lies in numbers.

- The main motivation is self-interest.
- Ideas are communicated in numbers and visual images.

Implicit in the overriding notion of growth is a crude Darwinian notion of evolution, survival of the fittest, and 'progress'. The underlying myth is that centuries of progress have developed a self-improving system and, rationally, there is no alternative. 'Progress', 'improvement', 'rationally' – all ideologically overloaded words. 'There is no alternative!' – a dictum drummed into the British sensibility by Margaret Thatcher, whether it was justifying testing out the latest generation of military technology against retreating Argentinean battleships; ensuring the political processes in Ulster remained in stalemate to provide the Parachute Regiment with sufficient live firing target practice; or encouraging an ethos of greed and unchecked self-interest in the City of London. 'There is no alternative!' still resounds in the rhetoric of New Labour, especially when following at the heels of US foreign policy, or the demands of multinational corporations. Indeed, with no political opposition to capitalist commerce in Britain and America, there is indeed no obvious alternative.

As already noted, history is created according to how you filter the evidence. So, by joining up the dots in a specific way the illusion of 'progress' is created and sustained. This chimera is contrived by excluding the less-than-progressive effects on the non-western world, from the impact of the slave trade on western Africa, the loss of indigenous peoples' territorial rights throughout the American and Australian continents, repeated de-stabilisation of political leaders and regimes considered inimical by western leaders, the imposition of disastrous trade terms, pharmaceuticals priced beyond the reach of Third World citizens, and so on and so on, quite literally *ad nauseum*.

The self-reinforcing myth of 'progress' allows western technology to assert greater and greater impact. After all, isn't the overall aim to make the world a better place? Given enough progress the whole world can have pleasure without any pain, health without sickness, wealth without poverty. This illusion simultaneously requires and justifies such progress as intensive farming, widespread use of pesticides, development of genetically-modified foods, nuclear energy, accelerating depletion of fossil fuels, ever-more complex methods of communication, and a vast plethora of legislation ensuring that everybody is 'good' and 'healthy'.

Every one of these activities disrupts complex ecological and social systems about which we have little understanding. Inevitably, sooner or later, such large-scale and heavy-handed human interventions make matters worse rather than better. So, to sustain the illusion of progress, further technological or legislative interventions are made. The myth of 'progress' is the façade which masks the fallacy of trying to control systems we do not adequately comprehend.

The typical metaphors of the myth of western progress abound with militaristic and competitive terminology, such as 'targets' and 'goals'. In contrast, traditional cultures 'go with the grain' and understand the cyclic nature of growth and decay, whether the short-term seasons of the year or the lifetimes of animals and humans. Non-western metaphors of progress are often more akin to wind-powered sailing which, to be successful, requires a skilled understanding of winds, currents, tides, stellar navigation and much else. Such traditional skills are supplanted by transnational control freaks unaware of their profound ignorance.

## distractions and desires

Just as western colonisation required the myths and cultures of the traditional peoples to be denigrated and trivialised, so too the myth of western progress requires our own traditions to be trivialised. Disney has thoroughly trivialised a wide range of once-vigorous childhood literature. By removing or sweetening the conflicts of the traditional versions of folktales, Disney versions perpetrate simplistic and entirely different ideological messages compatible with conservative 'family values'. Disney's *Snow White* is presented as a model housewife, dusting and cleaning for her men folk. *Cinderella* and *Sleeping Beauty* both encourage women to believe that some day their prince will come. And, whereas once different variants of a folktale circulated, now the truncated Disney film is regarded as the 'true' version from which other versions, if any are known, are regarded as 'deviant'.

Likewise the heritage industry has re-invented the past in a suitably sweetened manner that cuts out the prevalent ill health and the near-slavery of large numbers of working people. Visiting a National Trust stately home has more in common with a trip to Disneyworld than most visitors care to suspect.

The imaginations and machinations of marketing men have largely taken over from myths and storytellers. TV jingles are the nursery rhymes of modern childhood. TV adverts are prolific breeding grounds for story motifs that hitherto were most commonly found in fairy tales, and advertisers frequently appeal to the 'magical' properties of their products. We are encouraged to develop fantasies based around idealised products. By obtaining these we will simultaneously fulfil our desires and express our social identities

> Advertising, the media and the information industry capitalise on the translation of people's subjective desires, emotions and fantasies into images of ideal and desirable products. Such images bypass individual tastes and preferences by being presented as universally appealing. They thus create a curious notion of commonality, based on the assumption that belonging to a culture amounts to desiring the same commodities desired by virtually any other individual inhabiting that culture. In this illusory community, people are often little more than anonymous strangers to one another: all that connects them is an abstract network of representations.
> (Cavallaro 2000: x)

These illusory desires are the driving force of capitalist consumerism. Just as any suggestion that agriculture is still a key factor in western economies is laughable, so too within the next few decades any suggestion that industrial production is a key factor will become equally laughable. Indeed production has long since ceased to be as important to national economies as consumption.

And what is it we are mostly consuming? Distractions and desires. We desire – and therefore consume – what we think other people desire. And frankly, we desire just about anything that will distract us from boredom. We consume anything novel, especially if it has a sense of the exotic. Having consumed it, the novelty and the exoticism are gone and we need new antidotes to boredom. The promised fulfilment of the desire is never attained. The resulting relentless consumption drives the economy onwards.

Except the physical result – from a new CD to a foreign holiday – is less important than the meaning and significance we give to it. We relentlessly consume the *idea* the 'reality' signifies. So, in the same way reading that a cookery book will never overcome starvation, so our desires for largely interchangeable symbols of status, sex appeal, and conformity to specific subcultures, are no more than distractions.

The culture of consumption began with the physical object being important – and, indeed, in the 1950s ownership of a fridge, a washing machine, a telephone, a car and such like were all significant 'status symbols'. However this has now changed. 'Everyone' now owns a wealth of 'essential' appliances along with any number of gadgets and gizmos. It is not the object itself which is now important but rather its symbolic significance, whether it is an item of clothing, furniture, a car, computer or a pet. Even the type of food we buy – and where we buy it from – is a 'lifestyle statement'. In this confusion of functions and fantasies symbolic significance is more real than 'reality'.

By the time we elevate eating to a culinary art then immense strata of cultural meaning have accumulated, such as the perceived exoticness of ingredients, the techniques of preparation, types of cooking utensils, varieties of serving vessels, the room décor, the table setting, why we are eating in this manner, and who we are sharing the meal with. None of this has anything to do with how the food tastes, still less its nutritional value. We are consuming our cultural myths more than we are satisfying our visceral needs. We never simply eat. Eating is always a ritual, a re-enactment of profound cultural concepts.

We consume all physical products mostly for their meaning and significance. As a result our 'reality' is awash with an excess of meanings. And, lest it has not already crossed your mind, these meanings are created and developed by the mass media, specialist cult media and the folkloric processes. The way they are communicated is as 'mythic fragments'. Anything from cars to alcoholic drinks are promoted by associating the products with images of apparently affluent lifestyles and with people who are acting out 'independent' lifestyles and having 'fun'. We all know they are actors working to cleverly-written scripts yet we are still seduced by the desires the adverts arise, rather than disgusted by deep cynicism about manufacturers who peddle products with nothing more to offer than deceptive fantasies.

The advertising agencies who dream up these advertisements are experts at weaving the complex symbolism which passes for the 'reality' of the modern western world. With products aimed at young adults, they often weave in intentional and subtle ironies which 'nests' the viewers' abilities to 'deconstruct' the imagery of advertising into a flattering but ultimately condescending message which decodes as 'this product is aimed at people like you who think they are "cool" because they can spot the irony in the advertising'. One clever (and overtly ironic) metaphor enables another level of metaphorical ideology to pass by undetected.

Indeed, of all the mythic fragments discussed in this book, the mythic meanings we attribute to 'everyday' products are among the most inescapable and also most difficult to bring to conscious recognition. They are effectively the mental equivalents of the air we breathe.

## consumption and production of meanings and myths

There is another level of complexity too. The processes of consumption and production reflect back on themselves because those who are doing the *consuming* are often the same as those who are *producing* (more usually by developing rather than inventing) the 'mythic' meanings and significance given to the objects within specific groups and subcultures. 'Culture' can be thought of as the dynamic processes of consumption and production, neither of which exists independently. Even when a mass-produced product is bought we may well give it personal significance and meaning – in the same way children gain comfort from favourite soft toys, so adults become fixated by 'their' wristwatch, mobile phone or PDA. Subcultures consume mainstream culture while 're-producing' it with different meanings – and this applies to cultures as diverse as the Bhangra culture of British-born South Asians and straight divas such as Judy Garland and Shirley Bassey becoming icons for camp gay men.

## enter the anti's

With huge irony we even produce and consume anti-consumerism products – books such as *No Logo,* magazines such as *Adbusters,* films such as *American Beauty* and *Fight Club.* However there is much more to this attitude, this subculture, than anti-consumerism. Since breaking into wider awareness in 1999 with the 'Carnival against Capitalism' in June and the 'Battle of Seattle' in November, a fairly wide-ranging protest movement has been labelled 'anti-capitalism' or 'anti-globalisation'. As with all labels that are 'anti-' anything (or, indeed, 'post-' or 'pre-' something) they stand or fall relative to whatever they are dialectically contrasted with. The self-definitions of anti-capitalist protestors lead me to think that their objectives might just as aptly be termed 'anti-hegemony' or 'post-capitalism'. However, if only to fit with the more-or-less established tradition, it is simplest to refer to 'anti-capitalism', even if this should not be used to narrowly define the wider concerns expressed by protestors.

One anti-capitalist Web site states:

> Anti-capitalism isn't Communism or Marxism – the last communist nations on earth practice capitalism today. It isn't anarchism – it says nothing about government or freedom. It isn't nihilism – it's about improvement and change, not total destruction.

Anti-capitalism: modern theory and historical origins;
www.personal.psu.edu/users/w/x/wxk116/antic/

Despite this assertion the mass media will always emphasise Marxist or anarchic tendencies, knowing that they are essentially alien to middle class ideologies. Without well-established mythic fragments of its own, combined with the wide scope of its ideological objections, anti-capitalism is also wide open for opponents to play the old games of divide and trivialise.

The result of this hegemonic spin is that, even if the 'apathetic' and apolitical middle classes of the USA and the UK may have some sympathies with the extent to which modern governments too often support the interests of corporate businesses and not the interests of the electorate, the 'anti-capitalist' movement is perceived as far too 'other'.

Corporations, trans-national and otherwise, are themselves mythic entities, albeit ones capable of serious consequences for the material world.

## the illusion of corporations

What would you call beings which:

a)   don't have physical bodies
b)   seem relatively crafty, and
c)   appear to be immortal?

A tulpa, a djinn, or a familiar? Ghosts? Spirits? Gods? Demons? How about *corporations*?
(Nathan 2004)

Paco Xander Nathan's witty take on the substance-less legal entities we call corporations and limited companies is followed by a wickedly accurate definition of their essence: 'Externalize risk and perpetuate wealth for shareholders.' And this is exactly what a 'limited company' is all about – transferring the risk of debts from the company to external investors. Put simply, if individuals such as you or I lose money in a big way we risk losing our assets and even going to prison. But corporations cannot be put in prison, and western commercial law ensures that directors are offered plenty of ways of avoiding risking their personal wealth. That's what's limited about limited companies – the financial liability of any person associated with them.

Companies and corporations are legally intangible. They are entities created by an act of imagination – what Yiddish-speakers would call a 'golem' and what Tibetans allegedly refer to as a 'tulpa'. Ritual magicians use the term 'servitors' for such entities. What golems, tulpas and servitors have in common with corporations is that the more we think about them and interact with them, the more 'substantial' they become. Indeed the word 'corporation' was invented in the sixteenth century from a Latin word *incopratus*, used by alchemists to refer to the process of embodiment or giving material form.

What servitors and corporations also have in common is that just as servitors are invoked by sigils – magical symbols, beloved of alchemists, that act as shorthand for the essence of each entity – so too corporations are invoked by their logos and trademarks.

A further link with alchemy arises when we consider their use of the Latin word *egregor* to mean a self-perpetuating belief structure. Indeed, while corporations can be thought of as servitor-like (or simply demons conjured up by appropriate 'spells' and rituals) they are most certainly based on self-perpetuating beliefs. (Indeed, the whole of social reality also has *egregor*-like aspects, linking directly to the prevailing theme of *The Myths of Reality*; had I wanted to cloak this book in a shroud of exoticism, it could have been called *Egregria et Incorporatus*.)

## Mammon – the modern day almighty

With the increasing secularisation of western society the belief systems which support a sense of 'divine inspiration' have also been secularised. So belief systems such as economics use the same call to a 'greater force' but do so without invoking a sense of divinity, still less of an anthropomorphic entity. There are calls to the 'greater good', 'common sense', 'the natural order of things' and similar omnipresent yet invisible and intangible entities.

The consequence is a subtle but effective one. Whereas calls to Mammon would conflict with prior religious beliefs or be resisted by the secular-minded, such impersonal evocations of an otherworldly idealised order can be sustained. The driving force of western society – mass consumption – is sustained by secular rhetoric. However the end results would be similar if we called shopping malls 'Temples to Mammon', Christmas a celebration of Mammon's renewal, and the budget speech a celebratory liturgy.

## the myth of money

Compare and contrast the following two sentences:

> Bank notes are the medium of exchange because they are valuable.

> Bank notes are valuable because they are the medium of exchange.

If you take a ten pound note into a bank and point to the words that say 'I promise to pay the bearer on demand the sum of ten pounds' what will they give you in exchange? A different ten pound note? Ten one pound coins with a metal content worth substantially less than ten pounds? Such promissory notes have long since ceased to have counterparts in valuable commodities such as gold. There is simply far too little gold in national reserves to honour such promises. Indeed American bank notes dropped the promise to pay the bearer. Our belief in the value of money is sustained because we believe money is valuable. If that belief fails, at it did during the worst financial crises of 1930s Germany and 1990s Moscow, bank notes cease to provide a medium of exchange and are replaced by cigarettes.

Money is the manifest aspect of complex social beliefs and myths. Indeed money hides some complex – and usually exploitative – social scenarios. We use money to buy goods and services. Popping to a shop to buy a pint of milk and a loaf of bread makes us the beneficiaries of the time and effort of the shop keeper, the delivery driver, the dairy and bakery staff, the produce wholesalers and their transport workers, the packaging manufacturers, the farmers, and *ad infinitum* to all their suppliers, not to mention the more abstract 'suppliers' who demand rates, rent, taxes and such like from all these contributors.

In the final analysis 'wealth' is about the ability to benefit from other peoples' time and effort, though few people make that analysis because the First World is wealthy largely through the blatant exploitation of Third World labour. In our 'reality' (although not in imaginable alternatives) one person's wealth is achieved by making many other people poor. The invention of money was key to hiding this profound imbalance.

A different analysis is that every producer of products and services requires sufficiently wealthy consumers. Marketing hype is fairly transparent when it is promoting gadgets and gizmos, and even when it is persuading us to pay for purchasing popular music and other 'inessential' items. The hype becomes much more subtle when, say, it is part of the dubious ethics of the pharmaceutical and medical industries. These also need sufficiently wealthy consumers (although the 'wealth' may come impersonally via the National Health Service from national taxation).

Statistically we are likely to consume more drugs and healthcare products in the last few months of our lives than the rest of our lives put together. Euthanasia is anathema less on moral grounds than because it would deny the healthcare industries a substantial part of their income. We need to die long lingering deaths to ensure shareholders are paid dividends.

Likewise making low cost generic drugs available to the Third World would risk undermining the complex way in which massive profits from current pharmaceutical products fund research into possible future money spinners. This is far from farfetched – the stock market value of the major drug producers is based on what patents are expected to become profitable in the near future. Stock market values drop off sharply when key patents are due to lapse.

## conscious and intelligent manipulation

If you have any doubts that the consumerist capitalist system manipulates consumers then the following pronouncements by Edward Bernays may quash them:

> The conscious and intelligent manipulation of the organized habits and opinions of the masses is an important element in democratic society. Those who manipulate this unseen mechanism of society constitute an invisible government which is the true ruling power of our country. ... We are governed, our minds are molded, our tastes formed, our ideas suggested, largely by men we have never heard of. This is a logical result of the way in which our democratic society is organized. Vast numbers of human beings must cooperate in this manner if they are to live together as a smoothly functioning society. ... In almost every act of our daily lives, whether in the sphere of politics or business, in our social conduct or our ethical thinking, we are dominated by the relatively small number of persons ... who understand the mental processes and social patterns of the masses. It is they who pull the wires which control the public mind.

[…] If we understand the mechanism and motives of the group mind, it is now possible to control and regiment the masses according to our will without their knowing it…

Bernays is not some modern anti-globalisation agitator penning an over-stated parody. Bernays was the hugely influential inventor of what we now think of as 'public relations', 'marketing' and 'spin' – although his own term was 'the engineering of consent'. These quotes come from a book he wrote in 1928 called *Propaganda* (the word 'propaganda' had yet to take on the irredeemably negative connotations it acquired when, for example, Bernays' ideas were taken up in the next decade by Joseph Göbbels to promote anti-Semitism).

By 1928 Bernays had already completed numerous successful acts of propaganda. One of his first coups was, at the request of the American Tobacco Company, to overcome the taboo against women smoking, especially in public. He persuaded rich debutantes to light up cigarettes in public and made the press aware of these events in advance. This was followed by a group of suffragettes lighting up cigarettes in public – and the Bernay's emotive catch phrase 'Torches of Freedom' made the front pages of the newspapers. Bernays created the idea that if a woman smoked it made her more powerful and independent. This myth is still very much with us as today more women light up their illusory 'torches of freedom' than men suck on surrogate nipples (or should that be penises?). The counterparts to cigarette smoking debutantes are very much with us every day in the pages of the tabloid press, where people famous-for-being-famous wear 'the' brand of clothing, or are photographed about town driving whatever type of car has been provided for them at the promoter's expense.

Bernays' techniques for manipulating public opinion favoured 'third party authorities'. For example to promote bacon sales he conducted a survey of doctors asking if people would benefit from eating substantial breakfasts. Fairly predictably they responded positively. He then sent the results of the survey to 5,000 physicians – together with publicity promoting bacon and eggs for breakfast, even though bacon had not been mentioned in the survey.

Bernays's 1920s clients also included Proctor and Gamble, CBS, General Electric, Dodge Motors – and President Calvin Coolidge (who held office 1923–28 and had to devote considerable effort to restore public confidence after scandals associated with the previous president). A notable self-publicist (or 'braggart' to his detractors),

Bernays also tirelessly promoted the ideas of one of his uncles, including paying for the translation and publication of his books. That uncle was Sigmund Freud...

Bernays' propaganda for the United Fruit Company (now United Brands) in Guatemala sustained a corrupt regime (the original 'banana republic') which used virtual slave labour to produce bananas sold very profitably in the USA. When a politically-moderate opposition party sought control, Bernays created a media campaign that derided these reformists as communists. This led directly to the CIA-led overthrow of the elected government and the consequent forced migration, torture and death of many thousands of the impoverished Maya Indian majority. US 'intervention' in all other south American countries has followed this 'success', and the Middle East is currently being disrupted by essentially similar propaganda combined with CIA-sponsored intervention, military equipment and training, and, if all else fails, invasion.

Since the Second World War, international conflicts have become more and more explicitly about the growth of American imperialism. The western economic system is foisted on developing and Third World countries, making the world safe for Mammon. Coincidentally (perhaps!) since the 1920s the only American President to resist Bernays' manipulation of the populace was Franklin D. Roosevelt – in office between 1933–45, i.e. the build-up to and duration of the Second World War). By the Nixon era (1969–74) any compulsions against the 'engineering of consent' were forgotten; manipulation and 'spin' became the predominant techniques of American Presidential politics, with Britain quickly playing catch-up when Margaret Thatcher (the most fulsome acolyte of Mammon this country has so far had to endure) took office in 1979. To understand politics since the 1970s requires understanding Bernays' legacy of media manipulation. Indeed, since his death in 1995, the 'engineering of consent' has become an increasingly aspect of American and British politics, to the extent it is difficult to recognise any significant political issues which are not cloaked in impenetrable 'spin'.

## the ultimate threat of non-violence

Opposition to manipulative politics has been through 'protest movements'. These have been with us since the 1950s when the Campaign for Nuclear Disarmament took to the streets. A decade later anti-Vietnam war protests threatened public order in both Britain and America, and women's liberation groups also organised several high-profile demonstrations. In America 'black consciousness' emerged through riots and demonstrations.

Protest movements present themselves as non-violent 'demonstrations'. Their opponents – who pull most of the strings in the media – know that support for the protestors will diminish if there are well-publicised incidents of violence. The forces of 'law and order' are therefore provocative and heavy-handed, especially if there are some TV camera crews in the vicinity to record the events (editors can be relied upon to make it appear that the violence appears to have been instigated by the protestors, either by omission or – as with the miners' protests of the 1970s – by intentionally reversing the chronology of key events).

A pre-eminent example of violent subversion of non-violent protest was seen in the 1950s and 60s, when Martin Luther King junior (1929–68) severely disrupted the local economy in Alabama by instigating a non-violent boycott of the transport system. The peaceful protests were opposed by heavily-armed white police officers who did their best to ensure the outcome was not peaceful; indeed some were probably implicated in King's assassination. But the ensuing support for the protestors brought long-overdue changes to the legalised racism in that state.

Soon after, hippies and students armed with no more than flowers helped erode support for the Vietnam war, although some of these most peaceful of protestors paid with their lives when the forces of law and order opened fire at Ohio State University.

The long-standing British tradition of infiltrating anti-establishment organisations with *agentes provocateurs* to promote violent confrontation rather than peaceful protests was maintained under the British Labour government at this time. When they were succeeded by Margaret Thatcher things became less subtle. The Metropolitan police force, Ministry of Defence police, and British Transport police were equipped with 'protective' riot gear and retrained as a private army of heavies. They were let loose successively on unionised miners (at Orgreave and elsewhere), unionised print workers (at Wapping), the most conspicuous part of alternative counterculture, which the media sneeringly dubbed 'New Age travellers' (at the Battle of the Beanfield near Cholderton, on the border of Wiltshire), and subsequently at the Poll Tax protests in London. Needless to say, in all these instances the violence came from those who were employed to maintain 'law and order'. Contradiction and hypocrisy at the whim of the Iron Lady of Mammon.

# the ultimate threat of non-consumption

For all the rhetoric about the war on terror the main risk to the American-led capitalist consumer belief system has, for the last fifty years, been a simple one. It is the threat that no one dares to mention. It does not involve anything so substantial as a virus from a biological attack, or even radioactive particles from a 'dirty' bomb. It requires quite literally nothing. Neither does it require anybody to do anything. This insidious, invisible threat which would quickly bring the western economy to its knees simply requires that a small proportion of the population of western countries does nothing. That's right, *nothing*. No protests, no speeches, no boycotting this in favour of that. It is the threat that the global world order dare not contemplate as they have no countermeasure – they can hardly put a gun to everyone's heads to insist we *consume*.

Far more effective than buying organic produce, buying energy-saving light bulbs, buying cars with better petrol consumption, the real threat is that we buy nothing; or more specifically we buy either secondhand items or via fully independent chains of supply. If between ten to twenty percent of the population of America and Britain stopped buying new cars, new clothes, new gizmos, mass entertainment, food from fast food chains, and minimised the amount of food they bought from supermarket conglomerates then within a year the profit margins of the manufacturers would be hit sufficiently hard for them to sit up and take notice. While not everyone wants or is able to grow their own food, make their own clothes, or keep old cars on the road economically, sensible use of independent retailers, charity shops, car boot sales, auctions and secondhand dealers will meet most everyday needs. Just as atheists see no reason to worship in church, so those whose disbelief extends to economic myths have no reason to pay the customary observances to Mammon.

This strategy means ignoring the desires for novelty and status-enhancement created by the media and the advertisers who support them. But, as the boycotting of Shell petrol a few years ago amply demonstrated, only a relatively small drop in sales can damage profits disproportionately. Non-consumption is undemocratic in that it does not require a majority of the population to support it for the effects to be devastating. As such it is well-placed to counter party politics, where undemocratic minorities also have disproportionate influences. For example about forty percent of the vote (which, allowing for non-voters, probably equates to not much more than twenty percent of the adult population) can produce overwhelming majorities in the House of Commons or the House of Representatives. By comparison, if about thirty percent of the American population did nothing in this strategic way there would be a worldwide economic catastrophe (in reality the percentage is distorted because a significant proportion of the American population is already living in poverty and not properly fulfilling their duties of unnecessary consumption). In practice a far smaller number of people strategically non-consuming would have far more effect than the most concerted political lobbying could ever achieve.

The simple act of not consuming is the ultimate threat to the economic belief system. It is so powerful that it is never mentioned in the media because those in power (who are well aware of the fragility of national and world economies) do not want anyone to realise that there is an alternative to conventional political conflict, where little changes, least of all the balance of power in the hands of the same small minority. They promote a status quo which requires protest to be overt, manifest, confrontational and violent – the sort of things that can be contested in the media and escalated by the forces of law and order.

## government and the capitalist hegemony

By focussing on specific icons – the World Bank, the IMF, MacDonalds, and the like – the anti-capitalists are trying to work at the level of specifics, where 'mythic fragments' work best. However sometimes it is not sufficient to look only at the trees. Sometimes the wood needs attention too. For example, seeking specific ecological changes without tackling globalisation is like trying to protecting a species without looking at its environments. Trans-national corporations (TNCs) are the environment in which issues such as ecology are just 'species', specific issues. Without changing the TNC environment then attempts to protect specific ecological issues are likely to be futile.

It is not simply the specific weaknesses of capitalism that are the problem but the absence of effective political opposition to the capitalist hegemony. The major political parties in the USA and the UK have got into power by offering sweeteners to the floating voters while peddling essentially the same flavour of middle-right corporate subservience. Political policy making has been replaced by responses to the short-term concerns of focus groups (on a BBC2 programme aired Spring 2002, one of the Labour government's own spin doctors, Derek Draper, reported that party policy in the late 1990s had been determined by 'groups of eight people sipping wine in Kettering').

Over the last decade democratic capitalism has proved to be poor at both social equality and planning for the future. These are exactly the two areas that capitalist commerce is never going to address without government coercion. In the USA and UK all other political matters are seemingly secondary to ensuring the electorate consumes avidly and uncritically. Rising poverty levels in these countries and the increasingly removal of welfare (and the consequent increases in crime and prison populations) have little impact on the 'groups of eight people sipping wine in Kettering' so become politically invisible. The effect of 'domestic' political policies on Third World economies are completely beyond the awareness of focus groups and so, like the sweat-shop economies that sustain the international brands, far greater problems can be intensified without any risk of affecting political popularity.

## comfortable and conforming middle classes

As long ago as 1977, as R.J. Morris has noted, one aim of hegemony is to create 'the near impossibility of the working class or organized sections of that class being able to generate radical... ideas independent of the dominant ideology.' These days the hegemonic aim is to keep people in Kettering sipping wine and using the Internet for shopping and trivial emails, so they do not feel inclined to visit Web sites containing ideas independent of the dominant ideology.

As discussed in the previous chapter, a plethora of lifestyle magazines and TV programmes increasingly provided topics for trivial conversations. As ever the hegemonic forces do not overtly tell people what to think, just what they should *think about*. These days going into a typical pub and starting a conversation about politics rather than football, golf or cars is now the mark of an eccentric, someone who is rather too zealous to be 'one of us'.

How much has changed in the three hundred years since Bernard Mandeville promoted the necessity of keeping the population in Ignorance? Notably the modern industrialised world needs a workforce with basic literacy and numeracy, together with the vocational skills that the education system strives to provide. However Mandeville was wrong to think that literacy creates the risk of seditious conversations in the pubs; the mass media very successfully fill our 'idle time' with trivia. In this way Mandeville's desired Ignorance is maintained.

## contesting the hegemony

Hegemonies work most effectively when the dominant few have only indirect contact with the source of their wealth. E.P. Thompson has described how this created a three-tier system in the eighteenth century, where the landowning gentry mediated their power through a middle layer of stewards, bailiffs, tenant farmers, dealers and other 'middlemen'.

This meant that the landless labourers by and large, 'did not confront the gentry as employers, nor were the gentry seen to be in any direct sense responsible for their conditions of life... [so] When the price of food rose, popular rage fell not on the landowners but upon middlemen, forestallers, millers. The gentry might profit from the sale of wool, but they were not seen to be in a direct exploitative relation to the clothing workers.' The gentry 'met the lower sort of people mainly on their own terms, and when these were clients for their favours; in the formalities of the bench [i.e. for infringements of the legal system]; or on calculated occasions of popular patronage.'

Parallels for the 'real powers' (and wealth accumulators) of the modern world also operating through a middle layer are clear, with politicians and senior media executives the more conspicuous examples of this middling sort. Indeed the main difference between the élites of the eighteenth century and those of the twenty-first century is that they are now totally invisible to the populace. Unlike 'media celebrities', the lives of these prosperous few do not feature in the press. Apart from *Fortune* magazine's annual list of the world's wealthiest people, such folk rarely get their names into print or even, and this is perhaps more surprising, onto the pages of anti-capitalist Web sites. They are most certainly unlikely to have any social interactions with the sort of people who might take part in an anti-capitalist protest.

The anger of anti-capitalists can only be directed at the 'middle tier', while the 'real powers' have their anonymity protected by their middlemen running the mass media. As in the eighteenth century, the focus of attention is more on the middle tier than on the individuals who benefit most from the hegemonic system.

Nevertheless Thompson manages to keep an optimistic outlook:

> But while cultural hegemony may define the limits of what is possible, and inhibit the growth of alternative horizons and expectations, there is nothing determined or automatic about this process. Such hegemony can be sustained by the rulers

only by the constant exercise of skill, of theatre and of concession. Second, such hegemony, even when imposed successfully, does not impose an all-embracing view of life; rather it imposes blinkers, which inhibit vision in certain directions while leaving it clear in others. It can co-exist (as it did co-exist in eighteenth-century England) with a very vigorous self-activating culture of the people, derived from their own experience and resources. This culture, which may be resistant at many points to any form of exterior domination, constitutes an ever-present threat to official descriptions of reality...

Although this seems a long way removed from what the anti-capitalist movement has so far achieved, here's to ever more vigorous self-activating counter-cultures.

## arenas for contest

But where does one look for 'self-activating counter-cultures'? And how do they become 'vigorous'? The answers lie with what I term 'folkloric transmission' – the otherwise unnamed category of ideas and activities that are exchanged and developed between people who socialise or work together.

Clearly, only a small part of these ideas and activities will contest hegemonic ideas (indeed some groups, for example those who play golf together, are most likely to reinforce hegemonic values). In Britain the most politicised of such groups have long been the members of trade unions and the Workers' Educational Association. Other more-or-less conspicuous examples of British counter-culture include 1960s folk singers, Mods and Rockers, hippies, skinheads, punks, hip hop and rap music, so-called 'New Age travellers' and the whole free festival 'scene', rave culture, neo-paganism, and British Asian bhangra music.

With the exception of hippies and hip hop, which were essentially imported from America, the others are, to all intents and purposes, 'home grown' British popular cultures. Their formative phases were in no way mediated by TV or newspapers (although the mass media were quick enough to subject them to the usual hegemonic processes of trivialisation as soon as they were recognised as subversive threats; see Hebdige 1979 and Brooker 1998: 66–8). Interestingly, bhangra is the only one of these examples that has not been trivialised, perhaps because it is not regarded as subversive, although diluted versions of 'Bollywood' (one of bhangra's 'roots') have been extensively promoted by the media recently.

Thompson's optimism is based on the presence of 'a very vigorous self-activating culture of the people, derived from their own experience and resources' – exactly what the British counter-culture has repeatedly created. The hegemonic processes will continue to make full use of the media and the education system to restrict awareness and impose an uncontested world view of subordination and powerlessness. Nevertheless such blinkers can be removed and the hegemonies then recognised and contested. This chapter has attempted to recognise the way the hegemonic processes promote hugely influential myths about commerce. The next chapter attempts to recognise equally influential myths about science.

## sources

This chapter borrows extensively from Danser 2003. Various books by Noam Chomsky and John Pilger have influenced my underlying thoughts about the myths of commerce. Other sources are *The Century of the Self* (four one-hour programmes directed by Adam Curtis and broadcast on BBC2 Spring 2002); Baudrillard 1994; Bernays 1928: 23; Brooker 1998: 66–8; Cavallaro 2000: x; 2001: 209–10; Cutlip 1994; Dégh 1994; Ewen 1996; Fauconnier and Turner 2002: 202–3; Flowers 2000; Gray 2002: 29, 162–3; Heath and Potter 2002; Hebdige 1979; Hertz 2001; Kick 2001, 2002; Kilbourne 1999; Koven 2004; Miller 1987; Morris 1977; Russo 1992; Schalit 2002; Searle 1995: 41–3; Stauber and Rampton, 1995; Storey 1999 esp. 161–2, 170; Thompson 1993: 43–5, 86–7; Tye 1998; Worthington 2004.

# Chapter 7

# Myths of science

The difference between reality and fiction is that
fiction has to make sense.
Tom Clancy

Nothing surprises me. I'm a scientist.
Indiana Jones

... scientific theories may have a great deal in
common with Amazonian myths.
Adam Kuper

Knowledge of nature (science) and actions
performed in accordance with that knowledge
(technology) are both infected by a Faustian quest
for power.
David L. Hall

We feel that even when all possible scientific
questions have been answered, the problems of life
remain completely untouched.
Ludwig Wittgenstein

This chapter is about science. Despite widespread confusion, science is not the same as technology. Science is essentially concerned with systematic observation of phenomena, especially those concerned with the material and functions of the physical world. By a process of metaphorical association we get constructions such as 'natural sciences' and 'social sciences'. Technology is the application of scientific knowledge. However the word 'science' is widely considered to have more kudos than 'technology' – except for the rhetoric of the opponents to the myth of technological 'progress' who tend to demonise 'scientists' (even though they are often maligning people who would be better referred to as 'technologists'). The confusion is increased by phrases such as 'science fiction' and 'science park' which are used when 'technological fiction' and 'technology park' would usually be more accurate.

Technology has proselytised itself a modern day miracle cult, offering the fulfilment of some of the most prevalent human fantasies – the abolition of sickness, ageing and poverty. For most people science-based technology is a direct counterpart to medieval religion in that it brings together notions of authority, mystery and miracles. As with medieval religion, technology accrues power from belief systems based on specialist knowledge.

That said, technology rarely comes fully armed with ideological biases – although it may quickly acquire such connotations or have any original biases seriously subverted. High explosives work equally well for quarry companies, demolition contractors, military forces and terrorists. In the same way, all the science and technology needed to create the computer on which I am writing this book, and for the equipment used to print it, is simultaneously being used by people with a wide range of different political, religious or philosophical ideologies. As ever, the problem is less to do with the technology itself than with what the technology is used for and the meaning and significance it is given. Not only is western culture unimaginable without vast amounts of technology, but western culture is largely a complex interaction of the even more immense array of meanings and significance given to different technologies and the many products, and – above all – the underlying myth of technological 'progress'.

## the ideologies of science

Although technology has ideological biases, most technologies can be used to further a wide range of ideological attitudes. In contrast, science is constructed around some deeply-rooted ideological myths –

even though scientists often perpetrate the contrary myth that science is entirely objective and the antithesis of ideology. Despite what philosophically-naïve scientists may claim, science is the modern world's most potent source of myths. (I am using here 'myth' here specifically as 'ideology plus narrative', as discussed in Chapter 2.) Some of the more important of these myths will be explored in this chapter.

Regarding science as myths is deeply problematical to many scientists. And regarding science as ideology plus narrative is even more problematical. This is in large part because scientists endeavour to downgrade narratives as ignorant and backward. However, scientific knowledge can only be presented by resorting to narratives.

Science purports to be the knowledge of events, things, or facts. This is achieved by recording what has happened in a way that provides a basis for the prediction of what should happen. Thus science is an analysis of past experience, a form of history. What science claims as universal 'truth' is an account of a singularity, stripped of its context, and expressed in 'stereotyped' language. These linguistic conventions used to formulate scientific observations are as important – perhaps more important – than the 'facts'.

By isolating, naming and classifying 'events' and 'things', such accounts of 'facts' claim to be based on objective criteria. But a moment's reflection reveals that this 'objective' record is constructed by *subjective* reflective thought processes. The seemingly 'objective' experiences are described according to established verbs and nouns. Even when some of these verbs and nouns have apparently tight scientific definitions, they ultimately derive from more generalised linguistic conventions. This means that the reality or realities which science discusses remain ultimately undefined. And in the realm of sub-atomic physics even the nomenclature is metaphorical. For example the term 'quark' is borrowed from James Joyce's *Finnegans Wake*, a masterpiece of literary allusion; and the properties of particles are whimsically designated 'charm' and 'colour'.

Compared to quarks such concepts as gravity and electricity seem straightforward. But this is illusory. Both are names given to concepts that have yet to be properly understood by scientists. While they can be measured and applied, we have yet to understand the 'how' or 'why'. We may think that an apple falling to the ground is 'explained' by the force of gravity. Indeed we think of the Earth 'attracting' smaller bodies. But it is not necessarily true. Modern physics 'explains' all matter as irregularities in ten-dimensional membranes, with gravity perhaps the 'leaking' of a strong force from a parallel universe. And that explanation is only tentative and likely to be refined or superseded. And these 'explanations' of the most fundamental aspects of 'concrete' reality are essentially only metaphors which are borrowed from elsewhere.

According to ideas put forward by scientists early in 2004, the visible universe may be only four percent of the total. The vast majority of the universe is described as 23 percent 'undetectable' (known as 'dark matter') and 73 percent 'unimaginable' (and the unimaginable is designated 'dark energy'). If what we think of as reality is 96 percent undetectable or unimaginable, clearly the universe is considerably more exotic than popular understanding admits.

More philosophically-inclined scientists have, for fifty years or more, accepted that they must work with a number of basic unknowns, signified by undefined terms. What are these 'basic unknowns'? Well, they include space, time, force and matter. Yes, you read that right. Just about everything the man in the street takes as 'reality' is a 'basic unknown'. If you find this hard to reconcile with your prior beliefs then suspend (dis)belief until later in this chapter.

## myth of time

Modern western ideas about time seem so 'obvious', so 'scientific', that it is difficult to conceive of alternative ways of understanding time. Yet these modern ideas about time have only dominated Western thinking in the last 150 years. Non-western societies, and traditional European cultures all display much wider attitudes to time. Despite the obsession with time shown by denizens of Western culture, we should not forget that such an obsession is still rather a novelty.

The modern western conception of time is so ubiquitous most people assume it is a 'given', something which is 'natural' and 'real'. But the precision and accuracy of the modern sense of time was invented in the mid-nineteenth century. The new-fangled railway network required a standard national time, whereas previously there had been numerous 'local times', which could differ by many minutes. To ensure railway passengers did not miss connections, the railways brought about a standardisation of time throughout Britain. Furthermore the new regime of factories required adherence to consistent working hours. The combined result was that, by the later part of the nineteenth century a formalised 'abstract time' had became intrinsic to most people's lives, especially those living in urban communities.

The Western notion of time is precise and essentially abstract, consisting of equal segments, endlessly repeated. Such abstract time is in marked contrast to how humans experience time. Or, more pedantically, we do not experience time *directly*. Instead, all human languages describe time metaphorically, usually through images that suggest movement through time, or time as a container. Modern societies also make increasing use of metaphors where time is a resource.

'That's all *behind* us now.'

'He has a great future *in front* of him.'

'We're looking *ahead* to the future.'

'The time will *come* when there are no more typewriters.'

'The time has long *gone* when you could post a letter for one penny.'

'The time for action has *arrived*.'

'The deadline is *approaching*.'

'Summer has *flown* by.'

'I have to *budget* my time.'

'I *spent* too much time on that.'

'That mistake caused a big *loss* of time.'

Without one variation or another of these metaphors we cannot think about time. Our way of relating to time is story-like, placing experience within a narrative context. Time as experienced is the memory of significant moments. Together these 'significant moments' comprise the relationship to the past which make up the identity of a person, group or society.

Metaphysicians debate whether time is an objective property of the universe or whether it is our subjective experience of the universe. At the deepest level trying to distinguish the two concepts of time is probably futile. However we do distinguish between concepts which are 'timeless' and those which are experienced 'in' time. However such distinctions are subjective: being deeply absorbed in some activity can result in a sense of timelessness.

Most traditional cultures represent time in ways significantly different from modern Western thinking. Regarding time as a linear progression is essentially a Judaeo-Christian innovation – almost all other worldviews think of time as cyclical. Many traditional societies also deliberately use alternative images of time to suggest differences between the mundane world and the Otherworld. For instance, storytellers often combine an 'everyday' time-scale measured in generations with a 'mythical time-scale' which is, paradoxically, timeless. Such mythical time-scales are known in every western nursery as 'Once upon a time'. The Arabic equivalent is 'It was and was not so'. The 'Dreamtime' of the Australian aborigines is likewise both always and never. Creation myths and 'end times' are frequently encountered in myths. Genesis and Revelation are far from novel, merely versions of once widespread origin and end time myths.

Such 'paradoxical' traditional ideas about time have much in common with the way theoretical physicists see time. For them, time is not an immutable forward progression but one factor in a space-time model of relativistic causality and determinism. The way physicists think about time is at least as exotic as anything encountered among traditional societies.

The way we – or indeed any society – think about time is never 'natural'. Instead it is derived from the deep-seated myths and ideologies which structure our thinking. St Augustine, who lived between 354–430 CE, summarised the dilemma succinctly: 'What is time? If no one asks me about it, I know; if I want to explain it to the one who asks, I don't know.'

## is science a myth or a religion?

The eighteenth century philosopher Immanuel Kant considered that reality requires three *a priori* categories: time, space and causality. Two hundred years on from Kant, modern physics holds that that none of these three can be regarded as *a priori*. Instead all three are illusions created by our cognitive processes, even though most of us, like Kant, regard them as fundamental to our sense of 'reality'. (The myths of causality will be discussed in Chapter 9.)

Science's quest for a materialistic and rationalist understanding of the world has come full circle to a recognition that we construct the material world according to our prior mental constructions. Space, time, force and matter are mental constructions in the same way as 'accepted' metaphysical ideas such as God. Modern day scientists going in one direction have met head on with time-honoured mystics coming the opposite way. Such scientists and mystics concur that subject and object are indistinguishable, self is also 'other', and the perceiver and the perceived combine into an idealistic unity.

From the outside looking in, science is as mystical – and ideological and mythological – as any religion. This is far from a new idea – Sir James Frazer (1854–1941) observed 'In the last analysis magic, religion and science are nothing but theories of thought.'

And, just as the scientists' ideology considers it heretical to regard science as akin to religion, so too their ideology is even more offended that science and technology can be compared to magic. Arthur C. Clarke famously observed that any sufficiently advanced form of science is considered magic. However, as Peter J. Carroll less famously observed, the obverse is more accurate – i.e. any sufficiently advanced form of magic will appear indistinguishable from science.

When magic becomes scientific fact it is adopted by relevant technologies and referred to as say computing or medicine. Furthermore science endeavours to exclude all the areas of human experience which do not fit neatly enough into the scientific scheme of things. They are dismissed as nonsense or trivialised as 'paranormal'. However, as readers of *Fortean Times* magazine and various like-minded books will be well aware, there is a large amount of human experience which lies outside the boundaries recognised by science. The term 'fortean' refers to Charles Fort (1874–1932) who spent many years researching 'inconvenient' data that scientists were ignoring, suppressing, discrediting or explaining away. Fort was sceptical of scientific explanations and was one of the first to note that scientists argue according to their own beliefs rather than the rules of evidence.

Do the paradigms and implicit ideologies of science make it effectively a modern-day religion? The answer to that question requires another question – since when was there a dialectical opposition between science and religion anyway? This distinction is a result of nineteenth century rhetoric which sought to amplify the scientific ideology of rational materialism. It may seem 'natural' to western thinking but it most certainly is not a given. It is rooted in purely ideological myth. Much of what science 'does' is about promoting ideologies with specific narratives. As already noted, myth can be thought of as ideology plus narrative, so this makes science as much a myth-making process as any religion. Science and religion are not opposed but simply different myth-making processes and, taking the broadest possible viewpoint, different myths. The very distinction between scientific and religious worldviews is part of the myth of science.

## the invention of the scientific revolution

Furthermore, the scientific world has as many 'origin myths' for the different disciplines into which the world of science has divided itself as, say, a traditional society may have for the various deities which control different aspects of their cosmos.

In the realm of scientific endeavour these 'origin myths' not only define but also effectively constrain thinking within the prior assumptions of the discipline. Only in retrospect has there been a recognised origin of the 'scientific revolution'. The notion of such a version of history slowly emerged in the later part of the nineteenth century. The term 'scientific revolution' was not invented until 1913 although, after being popularised in the 1930s by Alexander Koyré, is now taken as a 'fact'. As is so often the case with history, those who claim victory write history according to their viewpoint.

The modern quest for heroes has populated this mythic history with undue emphasis on specific individuals. So, in the field of physics Nicolaus Copernicus (1473–1543), Johannes Kepler (1571–1630) and Galileo Galilei (1564–1642) have been singled out as demi-gods. In anatomy the accolades of near-divinity are shared between Andreas Vesalius (1514–64) and William Harvey (1578–1657). Francis Bacon (1561–1626) and René Descartes (1596–1650) are considered the chief prophets of scientific enquiry. Isaac Newton (1642–1727) outscores them all in this quasi-divine line up as he gets credited for miraculous insights into physics, optics and mathematics (although curiously his far more extensive writings on the occult get passed over by the inventors of the history of science, reinforcing the previously observation that when magic becomes scientific fact we refer to it as computing or medicine.)

The problem is not simply that these demi-gods stood on the shoulders of numerous unsung heroes. The problem is that this version of history has been constructed to emphasise gradual, evolutionary change. The ideology of the steady march of progress is drummed into every aspect. It is the ideology of Jacob Bronowski's *The Ascent of Man*, a TV series and best selling book back in 1974. The triumphalism of progress (not to mention explicit sexism) is self-evident from the four words of the title.

Bronowski's approach was ideologically influenced as he was specifically countering a new upstart with quite different views. Just four years before, in 1970, Thomas Kuhn (1922–96) had set out a seemingly novel view of the history of science in this book *The*

*Structure of Scientific Revolutions*. Traditional accounts of the history of science were blind to something crucial according to Kuhn. Scientific change was *not* a rational, slow-but-steady march of progress. Rather, significant developments came about as often by accident as by rational scientific method.

The day-to-day practice of the scientific community proceeds slowly, steadily and methodically. This is science as 'puzzle solving' within an already defined set of beliefs, theories and hypotheses – even a set of agreed upon questions – which Kuhn referred to as a 'paradigm'. The paradigms of each scientific discipline are self-reinforcing because theories are taken to be 'laws'. This means that any further research is expected to reinforce the paradigm rather than contradict it. Only in exceptional circumstances do new paradigms emerge, offering new 'belief systems' for providing narratives of seemingly objective events and 'facts'.

Since 1970 Kuhn's concept of paradigms has been challenged. His use of the term 'paradigm' is poorly defined. Some scientific disciplines have never been dominated by a single paradigm at any one time. Furthermore, modern scientific research, with near-instantaneous communication of results through the Internet is subject to much more rapid changes. However key parts of Kuhn's approach remain accurate as most science is conducted within a specific and largely unchallenged ideological framework. In other words, the 'truths' of the scientific community have much in common with political and religious ideologies.

Since the 1970s the discipline of Science Studies has built on Kuhn's pioneering ideas. One concern is with the extent to which technology and science are socially and culturally determined. Another concern is the ways in which the scientific community operates in terms of 'norms, its system of rewards and sanctions, its organisation into specialities, and its patterns of communication'. Yet another aspect explores 'the process through which scientific knowledge is developed, how "facts" are created, incorporated, or resisted, and how new knowledge becomes certified as scientific or excluded as myth.' (Nelkin 1996: 32–3)

Some of the people who we now think of as key to the development of science – such as Kepler, Galileo, Newton, Einstein and their many less well-known contemporaries who shared their interests – saw themselves as living in a divinely-created world, not the materialist reductionism of modern-day science. So Kepler described anomalies in astronomy as reactions of the 'telluric soul'. Galileo saw himself as a defender of theology, not an enemy of the Church. Newton thought he was discovering the principles of divine creation; indeed he explained anomalies as traces left by God. And Einstein famously contested Walter Heisenberg's Uncertainty Principle with the retort that 'God does not play dice.' Beliefs now regarded as belonging to religion, myth and magic were central to the worldview of the people who we regard as originating the modern scientific worldview.

The impression that science emerged from magic in a clear cut way is less an accurate account of the so-called 'scientific revolution' than a decidedly spin-doctored version of history. Magic and science were once far more intimate than is comfortable for twenty-first century scientific ideology. But such hard-headed ideologies are being undermined by the leading edge of science. Theoretical physics is taking science well into the realms of 'magic'. The current models of the nature of matter, force and time suggest that the principles of the universe are more akin to sorcery than clockwork.

So, the properties of atoms are far stranger than scientific ideology originally envisaged. Atomic particles can, in some sense, be in more than one place at one time. The current theory of the universe, which has superseded the earlier 'string theory', is referred to as M-Theory which seemingly refers to 'membrane theory' but, according to several eminent physicists interviewed for a BBC *Horizon* programme broadcast in February 2002, 'Maybe M stands for mother, the mother of all strings. Maybe it's magic. Maybe it's the majesty… of a comprehensive theory of the universe.' (Michio Kaku, City University of New York). For Michael Duff (University of Michigan) the M stands for 'magic, mystery or membrane'. And for Neil Turok (Cambridge University) it denotes 'magical mystery, madness.'

So not just pioneering mythologists such as James Frazer or sci-fi authors such as Arthur C. Clarke see a blurring between science and magic. The scientists actually developing the theories see their own work in almost mystical terms.

## the myth of science is based on the myth of knowledge

So, is science really as rational as it makes out? Since Thomas Kuhn there have been many critics (especially Paul Feyerabend, Jurgen Habermas and Richard Rorty), who have observed that the social organisation and development of science have little to do with science's claims for impartial methods and the quest for objective reality. Instead they have more to do with power and consensus. Science is not disinterested. Practical issues of the organisation, purpose and practice are as important as the problems which science ostensibly addresses.

Rorty argues that science's search for secure, rational foundations of knowledge is akin to following a mirage. Scientific principles such as reason, objectivity, rationality and truth are all values and moral principles, created and adopted for a variety of historical and social reasons. This accords with Michel Foucault's observations that knowledge, truth and power are closely linked. Despite the ideology sustained and nurtured by science, truth is not 'out there' waiting to be discovered. Instead what we take to be truth is a product of multiple constraints. These constraints form a circular relationship with the systems of power which produce and sustain it.

Despite deeply held beliefs to the contrary, truth cannot be an exact mirror of reality. This is because truth is a representation or reflection of reality. And that representation or reflection derives from specific conceptual schemas (such as language) and perspectives (such as ideologies). No representation of reality can be objective. Indeed there are an indefinitely large number of conceptual schemas and points of view; which means there are an indefinitely large number of 'truths' about reality, none of which can claim to be an 'ultimate' truth.

In the final analysis scientific truths – what we think we 'know' – are ideological and sustained by conceptual processes. Contrary to science's own ideology, 'scientific knowledge' is not inherently more truthful than any other system of knowledge. Time to move on to explore the myths of knowledge.

## sources

Contributors to BBC 2 *Horizon* programme 'Parallel universes' broadcast 14 February 2002 (transcript online at www.bbc.co.uk/science/horizon/2001/parallelunitrans.shtml).

Ashman and Baringer 2001; Badiou 2003: 53; 58–68; Carroll 1987: 111; 1995: 14; Cohen 1994; Dawson 2004; Delacampagne 1996: 250-3; Fauconnier and Turner 2002: 195–8; Feyerabend 1975, 1987; *Fortean Times* 'Why Fortean?' (in all issues since 1980s); Foucault 1977; Gray 2002: 22–3, 123; Gutting 1980; Habermas 1972; Hall 1982a: 232; Kuhn 1970; Kramer and Alstad 1993:266; Kuper 1988: 13; Lakoff and Johnson 1999: 141–69; Lyotard 1984; Nelkin 1996: 32–3; Rorty 1980; Searle 1995: 175–6; Sivier 2004; Trubshaw 1997; 2003a Ch.3; Watts 1954: 58, 63; Whitworth 2003: 202.

# Chapter 8

# Myths of knowledge

A long habit of not thinking a thing wrong gives it a superficial appearance of being right.
Thomas Paine

The world is such and such or so and so only because we talk to our ourselves about its being such and such or so and so.
Carlos Casteneda

Michel Foucault regarded truth and power as closely linked. More accurately, he argued that knowledge is power. Or was it that power is knowledge? Frankly, the answer is 'both' – power and knowledge are inextricably intertwined. And that power:knowledge relationship is inseparable from its cultural circumstances. So two ideas need to be borne in mind throughout this chapter. Firstly, knowledge does not exist independently of culture. Secondly, knowledge does not exist independently of power. Clearly neither knowledge nor power are fixed, both are continually recreated and reasserted as part of cultural processes, and continually changing and adapting.

Frankly, Foucault's observation, although somewhat radical to western understanding, is old hat to Chinese culture. For many hundreds of years Chinese paintings and sculptures have depicted dragons with a pearl in one of their front paws. Chinese dragons are far more benign than Western ones and have none of the associations with 'evil'. Indeed they are best thought of as symbolic of change. The pearl symbolises both wisdom and power. Accepting the distinction between 'knowledge' and 'wisdom', this ancient Chinese symbolism is nevertheless close to Foucault's much more recent recognition that knowledge and power are two aspects of the same whole, and that knowledge:power 'whole' is a function of continual change. The Chinese dragon can be read as the processes of change 'playing' with pearl of knowledge:power.

## we create our own knowledge

In the first few years of our life we predominately learn from direct experience rather than from structured tuition. We try to make sense of our experiences of the world by repeatedly forming and testing hypotheses. As we get older our mental model of the world become more complex. This model includes not just the external world but also our relationship to it. There is a commonly used word for referring to the relationship we have with the world: our personality.

Our personality works two ways. Initially it helps us construct functional (but not necessarily 'true') hypotheses about how to interact with the world. We then see the world according to these mental models, also known as 'core constructs'. When faced with contradictory information, our mostly deeply held 'core constructs' (e.g. 'values' and 'principles') are the ones least likely to change.

As a Jewish proverb says, 'we do not see things the way they are but as we are.' More profoundly Jeremy Narby wrote: 'We see what we believe, and not just the contrary; and to change what we see, it is sometimes necessary to change what we believe.'

## knowledge structures reality

The older we get the less knowledge is acquired by direct experience. Instead it is either acquired informally – as with reading a book or watching a self-help video – or it is more formally taught. Books and videos are tightly structured. Even the most informal of teaching – say chatting with a mate about the best way to do a DIY job – requires some structuring of the total knowledge needed. More formally-recognised teaching is invariably structured to a much greater extent. There are key issues about assumptions of prior knowledge because effective learning must build in a fairly unbroken manner from previous knowledge, without undue conflict with 'core constructs'.

The overall result is that all forms of knowledge have to be organised before they can be taught. Furthermore, knowledge has to be reduced to clearly communicable chunks of information before it can be organised. The overall result is that organisation appears to be an inherent property of knowledge and thus reality is inherently organised. However, this is pure illusion: reality is exactly the opposite. Our accustomed processes of learning create an illusion of order out of the chaotic nature of reality. The bottom line is that we *make* sense, although ultimately this sense of understanding we have created is illusory.

Knowledge – and the power it accrues – is always constructed. The *author* of knowledge assumes *author*ity (even though, as Roland Barthes famously recognised back in 1977, the power is really with all readers/listeners/viewers, who assign their own specific meaning and significance according to their own cultural context). At its most obvious, this means a book published in the nineteenth century – say *Sense and Sensibility*, the first of Jane Austen's novels – has a different significance now than when it was first published. Partly because cultural norms of Austen's day are now exotic or extinct, partly because the usage of English language has evolved, and partly because Austen is now regarded as one of the canonical authors of a well-established genre of novels – although at the time of publication of *Sense and Sensibility* she was yet to become famous, and the novel was indeed 'novel'.

In a more contemporary context a given book – say the one you are reading now – is interpreted according to the reader's personal history e.g. how much prior knowledge each reader has of the subjects being discussed and what ideological biases the reader already has, together with the willingness to recognise or step outside those biases.

Not only are sense, understanding and knowledge constructed, they are also consumed. The two aspects of this apparent construction and consumption dualism are ultimately inseparable.

## constructing and consuming narratives of knowledge

There is also the whole issue of how an author creates a narrative to carry the reader through a sequence of ideas, and – perhaps even more importantly – how much an author *excludes* from his narrative. So, for example, the specific topic of the author:reader relationship has created a vast literature which I have summarised in a single paragraph; the same can be said for almost every other paragraph in this book. All authors of introductory overviews structure their ideas more by what they *exclude* than by what they include. The reader is assumed to have sufficient prior knowledge that the overtly discussed ideas have sufficient significance, yet not to need to know the more detailed 'ins and outs' of the topic (at least without following up any references, if they are given).

A great deal of popular fiction is structured and written in a style which (more or less explicitly) tells the readers how to interpret the characters, themes and situations. Other authors – and Umberto Eco is perhaps the most famous – intentionally allow multiple associations and interpretations; they assume that different readers will create different meanings. Moving from novels to the moving image, *The Matrix* likewise provides almost endless scope for individual interpretations (see Danser 2004).

## knowledge is dangerous

A little knowledge is said to be a dangerous thing. More accurately, all knowledge is best regarded as dangerous. Most of our knowledge is acquired uncritically via sources that we 'trust', although this trust is based only on prior ideological assumptions. Some of us may be on the defensive when being presented with information by someone dressed in a white lab coat (although many are not!). Others will be more critical when listening to a politician, or the leader of a religion they are unfamiliar with, or when someone presents themselves as having a 'mystical' understanding. We are least critical when presented with information by people who appear to be in accord with our prior ideological assumptions.

Little of our knowledge is gained first-hand. Rather, we live in a reality constructed from second-hand knowledge. As with material possessions, we are seldom satisfied with what we know – most people are perpetually curious, perpetually consuming ideas. So, what we once thought we knew quite comprehensively at some point turns out to be quite partial. As individuals we forget what we once knew as new knowledge comes to the fore. As societies we collectively discard old knowledge and develop new knowledge.

Yet we don't know *how* we know, any more than we 'know' how we move our hands or how we make a decision. When Alan Watts asked back in 1972, 'How can we know what we know without knowing knowing?' little did he know that over thirty years later the best minds in consciousness studies would still be as perplexed. We do not understand the neural processes associated with the simplest act of reasoning (see Chapter 11). This means the entire edifice of human knowledge – from religious mysticism to logical scientific materialism – is built on foundations about which we have no logical scientific understanding and which remain essentially outside our conscious awareness,

Just as logic cannot provide the theoretical foundations for logic, so the foundations of what we think of as knowledge are outside our current knowledge.

## we know because we distinguish

One of the most primary of cognitive processes is making a distinction. Indeed all our processes of perception are based around making distinctions of greater or lesser sophistication. Distinguishing 'light' from 'dark' or 'stationary' from 'moving' are fairly basic. Hearing the voice of the person facing you in a noisy environment requires considerable pre-conscious 'filtering'. Recognising the faces of friends in a crowd requires more complex distinctions, although these are mostly pre-conscious.

If 'making a distinction' seems a little dry and lifeless, then bear in mind that G. Spencer Brown devised a complete theory of mathematics from just this starting point – and proved it was more than just a theory by using it as the basis for a novel and complex signalling system for British Rail in the 1960s. For that matter 'making a distinction' – breaking everything up into a 'binary bit stream' – is at the heart of digital computing, the Internet and increasingly the basis of music and video recordings, broadcasting, most manufacturing processes, and much else.

However, from the perspective of this chapter I want to pursue how 'making a distinction' is intrinsic to how we construct knowledge. Most readers are probably familiar with the Taoist idea of *yin yang*, that is how the world can be thought of as comprising a wide variety of dualist distinctions, from hot/cold, dark/light, up/down, male/female, birth/death, happiness/misery, and so forth. Taoism recognises that each half of these dualisms contains the 'seed' of the other and that the pairings are relative – so that we could not see the light of the stars without the darkness of night, although the light of stars is 'dark' compared to sunlight. Taoist philosophy furthermore holds that all these dualisms are simply aspects of an all-encompassing unity, the *Tao*.

In traditional thought throughout the world similar dualisms are prevalent. Myths polarise not just the material world but also aspects of society such as gods/humans, hero/monster, servant/king, rich/poor, older/younger, male/female, chaos/order, destructive/constructive, socially approved/socially disapproved, and so forth. These dualisms are expressed directly and through widely-used metaphors.

For example, 'up/down' is an especially rich and complex metaphor in western thinking. We see the future as 'up' ('What's coming up this week?'). 'Up' is unknown ('The decision's still up in the air') and down is 'settled'. We 'wake up' and 'fall asleep'. More is up ('My pay went up') and less is down ('Sales have gone down'). Virtue is up ('She has high standards') and depravity is down ('Doing that's beneath me'). Status is high or low ('He's well up the corporate ladder'; 'They are near the bottom of the social hierarchy'). Spirituality is up ('heavenly', 'angelic') and the mundane world is 'down to earth' or – on a bad day – 'hellish', with its implications of the Underworld.

The up/down metaphor extrapolates into mythical concepts. Below the everyday world is a mythical 'other world' of fairies living in hollow hills, dragons living in underground lairs, the fires of Hell, and such like. Nothing changes much in modern day thinking – we continue to demonise the 'underworld', linking it metaphorically with criminals.

Although by their nature these dualisms link together pairs of ideas, such pairings are only aspects of much more complex dualisms. Indeed many distinctions (such as hot/cold) are relative rather than mutually exclusive (so a warm day in winter is cooler than a cold day in summer). Some are quite culturally specific, as with the distinction between sacred and profane, or between the human world and the natural world. These distinctions, natural as they seem to modern thinking, are inventions of western society in recent centuries.

For example, there have been broadly four ways of thinking about nature in Europe during the last few hundred years:

1. In medieval times 'nature' equated to the whole of God's creation, with people being an undifferentiated part of this whole.

2. By the end of the Renaissance a more secular and rational abstraction had been conceived – the idea of 'humanity', which was defined by distinction from 'nature'. The adoption of perspective by Renaissance artists undoubtedly helped foster this 'alienation' from nature, in that a landscape painting is viewed as an object, by a viewer who is entirely 'outside' the topography depicted.

3. During the eighteenth and nineteenth centuries humans increasingly intervened in 'nature', whether by agricultural improvement, science, and the various technical and social

changes of the industrial revolution, so that all aspects of nature became regarded as something akin to objects. This was the Age of the Enlightenment, where 'reason' was diametrically opposed to 'nature'.

4. Within the last three decades this way of thinking about nature as quite distinct from humanity has been moderated in various ways by the concerns of ecologists, James Havelock's 'Gaia hypothesis', and pagans who regard the Earth as a goddess.

Indeed, apart from some basic distinctions (such as static/moving) which are seemingly 'hardwired' into out cognitive processes, all dualistic distinctions are culturally created. No matter now 'natural' they seem to people brought up within a belief system, only some of these dualisms are universally recognised. So a great many such discriminations made in, say, eastern philosophy and religions do not readily translate to the different dualisms of western thought.

Distinctions can of course be nested. While urban can be paired with rural, the concept of urban contains other distinctions such as suburban/inner city, commercial/residential, upmarket/downmarket, quiet/busy, safe/threatening and a whole range of geographical distinctions based on types of businesses, varieties of recreation, and diversity of shopping environments. How we construct our concepts of city centres changes according to whether it is a workday or a weekend, and according to time of day – rush hour, lunchtime, evening, dead of night.

## we define what *is* by what it *is not*

Many distinctions are defined less by what something *is* than by what it *is not*. The concept of 'western culture' is used frequently in this book. However one of the key ways in which 'the west' defines itself is by excluding 'the east', the 'orient'. No matter that it was hard to pin down what 'the orient' really was – after all, no one ever comes along and introduces themselves by saying 'I am from the orient' – the concept came to represent what was not western. The orient was constructed as exotic, somewhat erotic, sexually transgressive (with fantasies of polygamy and sodomy), perhaps a little barbarous, fiendish or cruel. The west became fixated with *The Arabian Nights*. A whole genre of Victorian erotic novels developed, including *Three Nights in a Turkish Harem* and *The Lustful Turk* (in case you are not familiar with these, the plots revolve around the violation of British virgins who then can't stop). The eroticism continued with Rudolf Valentino's role in *The Sheik*, a silent film of 1921, and the dancing girls of such films as *The Italian Girl in Algiers* or *The Thief of Baghdad*. From the scores of mummy-monsters to *Indiana Jones and the Temple of Doom*, Hollywood's version of the orient continues to be populated by fiendishly sadistic Arabs and Asians stereotyped as 'Yellow Peril'.

## we define ourselves by what we *are not*

Not only nations identify themselves largely by who they exclude, this is true of all social groups, including the most informal of affiliations between people who work together or share a leisure interest. If you don't know the in jokes and nicknames you are effectively excluded from the group until someone 'initiates' you.

With dualistic distinctions that carry a payload of attempting to define what is acceptable, better, or just the 'done thing', then commonly we define what is preferred by defining or excluding what is unacceptable. This is a steep and slippery slope which frequently resorts to demonisation. Hooligans, muggers, travellers, devil worshippers and other such categorisation have led to a wide- range of historical and contemporary 'witch hunts'. Indeed, where would today's tabloid press be without such 'excluded others', such easily created scapegoats?

A more self-aware understanding of identity recognises that distinctions are nested. We are all 'other' to someone else, and to a wide number of social groups. Furthermore, distinctions are fluid over time. Today's 'terrorists' are mostly yesterday's CIA-backed 'freedom fighters'...

Creating distinctions by excluding what something is not is widespread. But only some of these distinctions create a more-or-less explicit sense of 'other'. And only some of these 'others' are problematical. Our sense of 'otherness' only really comes to the surface when the 'other' is in some way troubling, even if only in an enigmatic and undefined manner. Frequently this ill-defined 'troublesomeness' is considered to be a problem for the 'other' too. However, if the 'other' has any opinions at all about the supposed 'trouble', it is probably a non-problem, an illusion of the original distinction. Even if the 'other' recognises something problematical, the cultural distinctions probably see potential solutions to the problem in quite different terms. Such misidentifications of problems occur throughout human society, from people working together (so 'the management' rarely have any idea of the 'real problems' according to 'the workers') through to the foreign affairs of major countries (so

American politicians' views of the 'Middle East problem' seldom seem to have much in common with the views of government leaders in the various Middle Eastern countries).

## celebrating otherness

Early in life we must learn to separate our sense of 'self' from everything else. So, unless we learn to regard our parents as 'other', we will not progress far as humans. In adult life this sense of self and other becomes incorporated into our language, social customs and laws.

Western society has long established social constructions which regard women, homosexuals, non-white races, and disabled people as 'other'. We seem to be discriminating against those parts of our selves which are deemed incompatible with our ideals. The 'other' is the stranger within, our anxieties, fears and irrational desires. This fear readily degenerates into hatred and abuse.

The sense of other is inevitable. We could never sustain the level of political correctness needed to include all the excluded others into one homogenous sense of identity. However rather than denying difference, we can celebrate it, creating a multiplex culture in which we are all 'other' to others in some way, yet respecting the rights and views of a wide diversity of others.

## nothing exists without a distinction from what it is not

Such examples of 'otherness' in politics and culture are only complex versions of the processes of making distinctions that are integral to all our thoughts. Indeed, we cannot think of a single event or a single idea. Events, ideas, and everything else can only be identified by distinguishing them from what they are not. By identifying *something* we are simultaneously identifying what it is *not*. For those who think the world is made up of self-contained conceptual 'building blocks' such as 'facts' this is seriously disconcerting. Everything we 'know' (or, more accurately, think we know) is the result of a process of distinguishing the known from what it is not. Sometimes such distinctions appear convincing. The integer number 2 can be thought of as a whole number which is not bigger or smaller than itself. But the number 2 can also be used to denote a wider range of quantities from 1.5 to 2.4999… Already the boundaries are becoming more blurred. And most concepts are more blurry than that. While the distinction between bacon and eggs is obvious, what about bacon and gammon, or bacon and ham?

Creating dualisms such as light/dark and wet/dry is 'hardwired' into our perceptions. However more 'sophisticated' (and more-or-less arbitrary) paired distinctions are one of the characteristics that distinguish human culture from animal thinking (no prizes for spotting the self-referential ironies in that sentence!). They are fundamental to how we create and maintain the illusion of 'certainty' in the face of a reality that is far more amorphous. 'Knowledge', 'ideas' and 'facts' are a long way from being primary entities which are 'out there somewhere'. Before we can get close to the realm of 'ideas' and 'facts' we have already built of raft of dualistic distinctions based on our perceptions and cultural preconceptions. 'Knowledge' is an illusion constructed from numerous dualistic distinctions. Many of these dualistic distinctions are culturally-specific, and all are culturally constructed. We impose these distinctions on the non-dualistic continuum of existence. This continuum is ever-moving, capable of being defined and divided in as many different ways as there are viewpoints. Reality is not something that can be cut up neatly like a cake, but more like trying to slice up a bucket of water. Except that there is no bucket to define the extent of the water...

## dualisms and dialectics

Until the previous paragraph I have presented the process of making distinctions as comparatively static. However if dualisms are culturally-constructed then there must be an ongoing process of construction, with the potential for change. Indeed, rather than seeing distinctions as being static we should see them as a process. There is a well established term for such dualistic processes: dialectical thinking.

This in turn means that our systems of knowledge are based on these dialectical processes. Indeed, as will be discussed in the final chapters of this book, the myths of reality are best approached as dialectical processes. However in the meantime there are other aspects of distinctions that are relevant.

## betwixt and between

The attempt to make distinctions creates not only dualisms – 'this' and 'that' – but also a boundary area, not quite this and not quite that. Western minds often think in terms of literal boundaries – this is my house, that is your house. We like to avoid uncertain boundaries, where we are left 'sitting on the fence' or 'walking on the cracks'.

Certain 'distinctions' require special attention. The boundaries of life – both birth and death – are crucial. Birth and death certificates are the only formal documents no one in Britain can legally avoid. Achieving adulthood and getting married are usually marked by ritualised celebrations. These are life's 'rites of passage', to use the term favoured by anthropologists. Modern society brings other notable 'key stages' to life: starting school, passing exams, graduating from university, starting a new job, through to retirement. Traditional custom greatly influences the principal activities on such occasions.

Gender identity – more specifically, avoiding behaviour and dress that is not considered appropriate – can also be rigidly defined. Although transgressing such boundaries is commonly flaunted in contemporary society, such contravention is only feasible if the 'norms' are widely understood.

Where boundaries are not exact there is a 'betwixt-and-between', a transitional phase to something or somewhere else (usually, but not always, with implications of being in some way 'better'). An 'in between' (or 'liminal', from the Latin for 'threshold') time is characteristic of many traditional rites of passage. The modern honeymoon is perhaps the most developed form of this today, although it could equally be argued that all parties (especially those for weddings, 18$^{th}$ and 21$^{st}$ birthdays) are liminal events. The period between death and burial or cremation is also liminal.

We divide up time and place in rather arbitrary ways. In modern minds 'midnight' and 'noon' are reduced to timeless instants, yet (unless you make sophisticated astronomical measurements) indistinguishable from the moments before and after, whereas in traditional thinking they are less moments than transitions. The annual passage of time is also marked by 'liminal' celebrations – explicitly so with New Year parties and in more vestigial form with festivities originally based on the changing of the seasons, such as May Day and Hallowe'en.

Equally exact is the equator, or the Greenwich meridian, but there has to be a deliberate effort to mark their location. Crossing the Equator in a ship is conventionally marked by 'liminal' celebrations.

Western bureaucracy abhors ambiguous borderlines. You are either single or married, employed or unemployed, sick or healthy, sane or insane, and so on. The same abhorrence extends from individuals to nations: attempts to avoid liminality characterise military strategies and peace initiatives. At various times in the twentieth century various nations declared war on each other. Subsequently the nations signed high-profile peace treaties. The boundaries were clear. The resistance fighters on the winning side are rebranded 'guerrillas' and their opponents deemed 'terrorists'. Word play and semantics are often the only clear distinction and, as American spin doctors have shown repeatedly, if CIA-sponsored leaders and their armies do not comply with changes in US foreign policy then their attempted autonomy is rewarded with the sobriquet 'terrorist'.

Terrorism can be thought of as 'liminal warfare'. Terrorists do not declare war and are rarely constrained by peace treaties. In the minds of government leaders with hard-line attitudes to social order without 'shades of grey', the solution is seen as declaring war on terrorism, although the success of the such a stance is dependent on the improbable expectation of the terrorists agreeing to play by same rules. The terror is as much the refusal to recognise conceptual boundaries about warfare as their near-invisibility to organised armies.

## the invention of good and evil

There is one particular dualism that is especially prevalent in western thinking, which is an excellent example of how an illusory concept becomes mistaken for a 'real' distinction. Despite William Shakespeare's Hamlet advising us that 'There is nothing either good or bad, but thinking makes it so', Western culture constructs its sense of how 'good' it is by demonising what is excluded as 'evil'. In the wake of the destruction of the World Trade Centre on 11th September 2001, George W. Bush's spin doctors (and the media barons who sustain their efforts) clearly thought a large part of the American electorate could be successfully bamboozled by their 'good versus evil' rhetoric. They were right, although this rhetoric was more sceptically received in multi-cultural Europe, and totally failed to convince those who were deemed to be evil that they were anything of the sort. Indeed certain Islamic fundamentalists claim that the whole of Western culture is evil.

Good/evil dualisms predate Christianity and seem to have originated in ancient Persia and are part of Zoroastrian and Gnostic beliefs, both of which are prominent in the syncretistic soup of ideas that fed the authors of the New Testament. However not until the Inquisition was well underway in the fourteenth century do we begin to see Christianity fully developing this good/evil dualism. In their hunt for heretics the Inquisitors were not seeking a direct admission of guilt. Rather they were seeking a plea of 'Not guilty' because the accused had accidentally been led astray by the principle of evil in the divine order. 'Evil' was constructed as the *cause*. With this cause comfortably established, the specific incidence of evil could be exterminated by a triumphant process of torture.

The Christian sense of the reality of evil is strongly evident in the seemingly secular intellectual climate of today. A constant striving to 'do good' creates in its wake a sense of 'evil'. If we stopped seeking 'good' we would cease constructing 'evil'. Or, in the words of a phrase widely known in occult circles, 'The nearer the light, the larger the shadow'. It is like always turning right and ending up going round in circles. Good and evil are two sides of an illusory coin.

Nevertheless, the Christian quest for 'good' permeates present day popular culture, from the rhetoric of George W. Bush to *The Lord of the Rings,* where a Christ-like Frodo takes on and defeats all manner of evil. One of the few attempts by the mass media to portray the complexities of good and evil can be found in the *Buffy the Vampire Slayer* TV series, although the final word on this dualism has been most neatly expressed by J.K. Rowling, who puts the following words into the mouth of Quirrel (although the line is given to Harry Potter in the film script): 'There is no good and evil. There is only power.'

Indeed. All the dialectical processes that create and sustain dualisms are examples of fragmentary references to the underlying myths of a culture. These mythic dualisms impose necessary, if often arbitrary, distinctions on the undifferentiated nature of 'raw' reality in order to (quite literally) 'make' sense. The resulting illusions of structured knowledge empower those seeking to maintain the illusions created by the dialectical processes.

The recognition that 'sense' is not inherent in reality but something we culturally construct is bad news for people who like firm ground under their feet. Worse news and even shakier ground to come in the next chapter...

## sources

Barthes 1977: 142–4; Brown 1972; Carroll 1981: 27; Cavallaro 2001: 50–2, 55, 144; Danser 2004; Doty 2000: 331; Foucault 1977; Kelly 1995; Kramer and Alstad 1993: 363; Narby 1999: 140; Rowling 1997; Said 1978; Trubshaw 2003: ch.8; Watts 1957: 58–9, 1972: 414.

# Chapter 9

# Myths of causality

> Human experience only exists in the present
> moment. The past exists as memories re-experienced
> in the present. The future exists as expectations or
> fantasies, again created in the present.
>
> Peter J. Carroll

> Of course I don't believe in it. But I understand that it
> brings you luck whether you believe in it or not.
>
> Niels Bohr, pioneer atomic physicist, when asked why there
> was a horseshoe on his wall.

Western thought owes much to ideas which came to the fore in the eighteenth century as part of the 'Enlightenment'. One of these ideas has become so pervasive, so fundamental to western ideologies, that most people have great difficulty with accepting that it is not fundamental to the universe, the 'clockwork' which makes reality tick along.

What is this deep belief? That the universe operates according to material causality and is therefore rational. This belief – and it most certainly is a belief, not a 'fact' – is essential for the Enlightenment view of the world, which demands that everything is (ultimately at least) comprehensible to reason.

Given the emphasis that western education systems devote to indoctrinating pupils with this belief in material causality perhaps there is no surprise that many have difficulty recognising this as brainwashing. Thinking outside this belief system is also hampered by Western languages, which are all structured according to this cause and effect model. Our processes of logic take causality as a given. Indeed, in all fairness, most of our technology has been designed to operate according to the rules of material causality. But just because it is seemingly all-inclusive and works at the everyday level does not mean that it is only explanation, still less the 'ultimate' one. (A useful parallel is perhaps the way Newtonian mechanics is perfectly adequate for describing and predicting 'everyday' activities but, as Einstein revealed, Newton's model is only a 'subset' of the more relativistic ways the universe operates. In the same way material causality is only a 'subset' of a far less predictable model for the universe.)

Technology makes specific events more probable, but the apparent ability to cause events is an illusion created by our belief systems. Causality is a cultural construct. Or, as Gilles Fauconnier and Mark Turner helpfully elaborate:

> It takes sophisticated cognitive operations to become
> conditioned in [the manner of Pavlov's dog]… It is not trivial
> to bring cause and effect together. They have to be brought
> together in one mental space, in the right way, while being
> kept distinct in other [mental] spaces.
> (Fauconnier and Turner 2002: 76)

The construction of causality is something we learn but, because it so deeply embedded in our culture, we rarely recognise that it is not innate in reality. Just to add to the confusion, unfortunately we frequently confuse causality with correlation. Despite outward appearances, a large number of people gathering on a railway platform do not *cause* a train to appear soon afterwards. Instead the two 'events' are *correlated* with an independent causal process (railway timetables). However in our observations of many social activities – and, indeed, our observations of the way we think we think – correlations are very often regarded as causes.

'Cause' and 'effect' are of course intimately inter-linked. Indeed they are best regarded as two phases of one and the same event. We are quite used to the idea of animals having fronts and backs – there can be no 'front' without a 'back' (even if we can only see one or the other). If we see a cat walk past a gap in a fence we would be thought more than a little mad if we said that the head of the cat caused the tail to appear. Yet when it comes to 'cause' and 'effect' we frequently make exactly this mistake; and it is those who question this error that are thought more than a little mad.

One source of this error is western languages. These impose causality as if it is inherent in perception. More accurately, the structure of these languages requires that we divide any one event into what is done and what is doing it and/or it is done to – the underlying grammar of subject/verb/predicate. In contrast, Chinese and several 'minor' languages do not distinguish clearly between verbs and nouns. The Chinese word for 'cup' does not simply denote a physical object but also the process of 'cupping'. Likewise words that we think of as verbs – such as 'to know' – are used in a more noun-like way, not least because Chinese does not require constructions such as 'I know', 'we knew' – the word 'know' alone suffices without needing a 'knower'.

Likewise evolutionary theories discuss how the species or organism adapts to the environment or ecosystem. But this way of looking at things, natural as it may be to speakers of western languages, is only one half of the actual system of experience. Step outside the subjective experience of time (what might be thought of as the 'replay' of actual events to enable us to create an illusion of cause-and-effect) and what 'adapts' is the overall experience. Evolutionary adaptations take place in both the organism and the environment – they are mutually causative.

## coincidence – the illusion of causal connections

But there are cracks in this belief system. Although events which we associate together frequently are regarded as causally connected, events that we associate together only occasionally are deemed 'coincidence'. The Enlightenment worldview, and all the philosophers and scientists who subscribe to it, has nothing useful to say about coincidence. The concept of coincidence is arguably the least rational 'explanation' bandied about on a daily basis. Indeed, 'coincidence' is a gaping chasm in the claims for material causality to explain the universe.

We are happy to live our lives with the irrational and undefined notion of coincidence 'explaining' a great deal of what happens to us. Furthermore most western people believe in something even more irrational and undefined – 'free will'. Whatever free will is – and indeed is not – has puzzled philosophers for centuries and I have no intention of summarising these unresolvable 'how many angels dance on a head of a pin' debates. Suffice to say that if there were such a thing as 'free will' it is essentially contradictory to the belief in material causality. Notwithstanding, 'free will' remains a greatly cherished illusion!

'Coincidence' is one symptom of peoples' need to seek causal connections even where they do not exist. Our minds are seemingly designed to impose order, even if the order is only imaginary. As an evolutionary strategy for hunter-gathering primates it clearly worked, and held up pretty well for the invention of agriculture. The downside is that it left the door wide open for all sorts of ideologies – religious and otherwise – to offer 'explanations'. Mystical beliefs are excellent at offering apparent order where non-believers see little or no such causality. Few people are comfortable with the idea that their lives are largely ruled by blind chance; even Einstein reputedly said that 'God does not play dice'.

Humans are fascinated by simultaneous events and attempt to make these meaningful, often in quite elaborate ways. Largely this is a continuation of the same instincts which helped us 'make sense' of the world when we were young children – accepting that many of the rationales that children develop are deeply flawed. One of the more notable example of 'rationales' for coincidence is Carl Jung's mystical discourse on what he calls 'synchronicity'. Characteristically, he serves only to further muddy what were already muddled ideas. Jung however was correct in recognising a major challenge to the Enlightenment model of causality.

## everything is always now

> If we take eternity to mean not infinite temporal duration but timelessness, then eternal life belongs to those who live in the present.
> Ludwig Wittgenstein

Modern physics has built on Heisenberg's preliminary insights into the indeterminate and probabilistic world of atoms and sub-atomic particles. In the final analysis physicists are only to be able to measure effects and make predictions. Physicists do not have an overall sense of how anything causes anything else. The so-called laws of physics are only catalogues of the habits of physics, the basis for expectations, but lacking a 'law maker', any fundamental understanding of how and why.

But the problem with the myth of causality is not that people have an out of date knowledge of physics; indeed 'old school' physics is fairly good at describing the everyday world. The problem lies elsewhere. As ever, it is inside our heads. The nature of human thinking creates a sense of time, a sense of the past and the future. This aspect of thinking is so deep that it is more part of our cognitive processes than part of our belief systems (although *how* we think about the past and future is certainly culturally acquired). Simply put, everything we experience is experienced now. There is only the present moment. The future does not 'exist' except as anticipations, whether reasonable expectations or wishful (or even harmful) fantasies. In a similar way we create a sense of the past by selectively re-experiencing memories – the past only exists so much as we continually recreate it. We tend to regard the 'past' as somehow more 'real' than the future, yet only *some* aspects of the past are 'real' and most are 're-creations'.

If you find that hard to accept then consider the following three examples. Firstly, court proceedings today may determine whether a person is guilty – or not – of transgressions in their past. However at some point in the future a legal appeal may reverse the 'truth' about the past. This is of course less a flaw in material causality (although the legal system places implicit trust in that worldview) than possible flaws in forensic and legal procedures. However such legal proceedings are at most only one step removed from two people having a major argument – for instance a married couple encountering unresolvable difficulties. Most probably, what they each say about the situation to their respective friends will bear little resemblance to the other's accounts.

The third example arises frequently, as when a major archaeological 'discovery' alters our views of the past, or a new historical monograph presents a new way of thinking about previously well-established events. This is directly analogous to the intelligence services seeing clearly *in retrospect* the build up of terrorist activities prior to an attack, although before the attack the relevant information was only a small part of the vast flow of intelligence, not sufficient to be regarded as significant.

## the past is continually reconstructed

We continually reinvent the past. More accurately, we continually recreate our explanations – the causality – of the past. Histories are written according to the ideologies of the historian. Marxist historians in the 1970s and 80s wrote very different accounts of the industrialisation of Britain in the nineteenth century compared to the established views promulgated by an earlier generation of Conservative, upper middle-class authors. Black and feminist 'reclamations' of history and archaeology followed, which led in turn to 'queer' (not necessarily in a sexual sense) readings created from the viewpoint of a wide range of people who considered themselves to be 'other' to the established perspectives. The result has been a wonderfully pluralistic variety of accounts of the past. There is no 'truth' out there for the historian to painstakingly discover, just a web of interpretations, each offering quite different connections and giving different meaning and significance.

Or, as Peter Carroll put it:

> ... our common sense strives to create an illusory certainty about the causes of events by imputing reverse causal connections. History is bullshit; it is as indeterminate as the future.

There is nothing really new about that viewpoint. The words of Samuel Butler (1835–1902) may have quite a different idiom, but the underlying insight is not dissimilar:

> It has been said that though God cannot alter the past; historians can; it is perhaps because they can be useful to Him in this respect that He tolerates their existence.

George Orwell put it more bluntly: 'Who controls the past controls the future.' No prizes for realising that considerable effort is expended on 'controlling the past' through the mass media.

## controlling causality controls the past

While we are accustomed to thinking of the past as something 'fixed', a moment's reflection will reveal that how we attribute causes and effects is not inherent in what actually happens. Certainly some things are 'fixed' – houses are built, people move in, children are born, people die, and all the physical minutiae that goes with this. But the cause and effects are complex. We tend to construct 'explanations' in simplistic ways, with the result that many different explanations can be constructed according to how the emphasis is placed. The nature of human and social identity is such that we tend to 'fossilise' key events in concise narratives. For example I often tell new friends how I 'accidentally' found the house I live in, although a more honest and complex version of the story would have to weave in a large number of 'arbitrary' events and 'mini-decisions' that would greatly reduce the sense of 'accidentally' discovering the house, albeit at the expense of making the narrative impossibly long-winded.

While there is a physical aspect to the past – houses are built, people are born – what has actually happened is only a small part of the past. The vast complexities of what has *not* happened are every bit as important. So, you and I have not died from illness or accident, for example, neither have military forces invaded my town and demolished my house, nor have a whole host of trivial things prevented me from writing this book or you from reading it.

If the notion that what has *not* happened is at least as important as what has happened sounds daft this is largely because the ideology of causality (which is incapable of considering everything that has not happened) requires that we think it is daft. The idea is much less daft if we drop the illusion of causality.

## chaos theory

If causality does not determine events in the universe, what does? Well, based on modern physicists' current models of the universe, it is perhaps something much closer to random behaviour, described by probability theories. Some of these theories fall under the umbrella of 'chaos theory'. Chaos theory recognises that all events are associated with a vast number of causative factors, many of which relate to what *does not* happen, and few of those relating to any specific event can be understood in detail. In a chaotic system there are no dominant 'primary forces'; rather everything is equally related in an extremely complex interweaving of entities, events, interdependencies and possibilities.

The best example of a 'chaotic system' is the weather, where a minor change in atmospheric conditions may (but not necessarily will) have a major change in the subsequent weather. This means that, even with the assistance of powerful super computers, predicting the weather is still unreliable. The metaphor of a butterfly flapping its wings in Brazil potentially causing a tornado in Texas is widely known; also implicit in this metaphor is that many millions of butterflies flap their wings *without* causing a tornado i.e. even though something could happen, most times it does not.

There is a technical definition of chaotic systems which relates to their lack of stability to 'internal' or 'external' changes. A more practical way of thinking of chaos theory is that it describes situations which are so complex that we cannot hope to have sufficient understanding so they might as well be chaotic. Chaos theory also teeters into the weird territory of quantum physics, where (a) events are probabilistic, and (b) the act of observation affects the outcome, such that any alteration of the present also alters the past.

Science resorts to chaos theory only when all attempts to derive more rationalistic theories are deemed impossible. Intriguingly, many of the 'big problems' of physics are among those where the light of Enlightenment causality fails to shine. As these underlie most other aspects of science, the apparent causality of science is built on much less causal chaos theories. The nature of the universe as a whole is chaotic, spontaneous, and more magical than rational.

Reason's obsessive quest for rational order requires there to be disorder which can be disciplined into order. Reason has created the concept of 'chaos' as the antithesis of its ideal. The activities of the proponents of reason have, however, not resulted in the conquest of chaos. Instead we have a deepening awareness that chaotic disorder is intrinsic and that the apparent establishment of reason over disorder is simply 'spin' based on skirmishes incidental to the overall conflict.

## evolving in a chaotic world

There is one aspect of the everyday world which most certainly is an example of chaos theory – our social world of interactions with other people. The large brains of early humans strongly suggest that they lived in larger social groups than any other species of primates. Even making and using stone tools requires numerous cause-and-effect connections that are apparently entirely lacking in other higher primates. This requires the ability to create 'mini-stories' with implicit cause-and-effect scenarios. Creating plausible cause-and-effect scenarios is seemingly what distinguishes early humans from other tool-using primates and was part of what has been dubbed the 'cognitive arms race' of early human evolution. The cause-and-effect connections required for tool making and early hominid social behaviour are almost certainly linked to the development of language. Although whether language is the cause or effect of causal thinking is an unanswered (and deeply ironic) question.

Studies of child development in the 1950s and 80s revealed that core concepts of causality are developed at an early age, even though the reasons children offer may be flawed. Anyone who has watched a child playing knows that children are spontaneous story tellers; it takes little effort to imagine an ancient ancestor muttering away to himself 'If

I do this and this to this piece of flint then that big bison I saw an hour ago will be as sure as dead. And then I can offer the tastiest parts to that gorgeous blonde back at the camp... ' OK, seriously sexist or not, 'play' involving narrative fantasies are a key part of human life. Substitute 'If I clinch that big sales deal then I'm off to buy the sports car of my dreams, and that blonde who goes down the pub every Friday night is sure to want to test out the passenger seat... ' and the boundaries between the Mesolithic and modern culture seem much less certain.

Such core narrative skills are possibly 'hard wired' into our genes, although the ability of children to acquire complex thinking – such as language – suggests that the seemingly innate appreciation of causality is acquired from other people, and most certainly refined and adapted according to the culture of our upbringing.

## divination

People are usually uncomfortable when someone challenges the belief that their lives are governed by complex processes of cause-and-effect. The idea that 'Blind Chance' (or at least her manifestation in modern physics, chaotic systems) runs counter to the human brain's innate tendencies to seek reasons, 'logical' connections, and causality, even when none exist. We impose order on the many arbitrary aspects of our experience according to patterns and ideologies that are culturally constructed, the 'norms' of our society. From an evolutionary perspective, this probably makes sense as it is better to have a belief in an inaccurate cause than to be overwhelmed by uncertainty.

People with damaged brains or severe memory problems will 'confabulate' a narrative that attempts to consistently explain (at least to themselves) their circumstances, even though their reasons are often nonsensical or comical to anyone with more normal brain functions. Indeed, every night our brains confabulate for several hours, although not everyone considers that our dreams 'make sense' or have any deeper significance.

There is a further large anomaly in the supposedly rationalistic modern world. Despite much pooh-poohing, belief in divination – from the simplistic horoscopes in every tabloid newspaper, through to individual tarot readings and the like – is widespread. The recent growth of interest in Chinese *feng shui* among the educated western middle classes shows clearly how easily modern marketing can graft 'exotic' (albeit substantially trimmed down to little more than the 'Art of Tidy Rooms') belief systems onto the less rationalistic deeper beliefs of western culture.

As the famous Rorschach ink blot tests confirm, we are willing to see significance in the most unlikely of stimuli. We also have a great ability to fit our lives according to prior expectations. So if someone practising some kind of divination or 'fortune telling' suggests that the client will meet a tall, dark, handsome stranger next week, then clearly that client is going to have different expectations of encounters with certain men than with short, blond ones. In hindsight the fortune teller will have been 'accurate', even though the encounter may have been 'inevitable' or merely the result of many arbitrary 'coincidences'.

My experience of psychics and diviners reveals that they all have belief systems of their own which, to a greater or lesser extent, provide some sort of rationale for how their mental experiences are linked to peoples' futures. Whether or not these rationales are accurate or not is irrelevant – what matters is the *belief* that their 'extrasensory perception' is in some way meaningful. I am reminded of recent studies of blindsight, a phenomena associated with certain forms of blindness where a person has no conscious sense of sight but, when prompted to guess what is in front of them, are able to make surprisingly accurate descriptions; this ability can be improved with practice. This seems rather akin to my own experiences of learning to dowse for water and buried archaeological remains, and also akin to how friends who clearly have some form of 'psychic' abilities seem to access information (I make no claims to be psychic myself). It also accords with ethnologists' descriptions of divination in traditional cultures. Perhaps blindsight, dowsing, clairvoyance and divining all make use of some so-far unknown mental processes that bypass the usually-recognised sensory perceptions and instead pop imagery directly into the areas of the brain where we create meaning and significance.

When we use divination, oracles and omens we are creating a symbolic relationship to the 'real' problem. Such symbolism is often based around metonymy, i.e. an object or image is understood to be an attribute of a more complex event. In a manner akin to play, divination allows both diviners and their client to create images, imitate and act out different aspects. Complex connections can be woven between the meaning, significance and 'reality' of the problem, projecting the subjective contents of our minds into the symbolism of the divination method. This is far more than 'telling the future'. It augments our normal 'rational' intelligence with more fluid symbolic associations. Indeed, traditional cultures often think of divination as providing access to a 'world soul' or divine mind, or the weaver of fate, or the sense of fertile chaos that empowers the world. Whatever the metaphor, there is a sense of accessing something greater than everyday human consciousness.

One key absence from human consciousness is direct knowledge of any moment in time other than the present. Combine this with our inadequate and often irrelevant notions of causality – the result is that divination readily appears as something greater than our everyday thinking, in a real sense 'divine' knowledge (both 'divine' and 'divining' derive from the Latin *divinus*, meaning 'god-like').

Knowledge acquired through divination, like all forms of knowledge, empowers both diviners and their clients. One of these aspects of empowerment is the extent to which we believe we are able to enhance the odds of a better outcome from uncertain situations.

Inherent in human survival is awareness that life does not favour risky decisions. We need to feel we are making 'calculated' decisions, even when the basis for the 'calculation' is recognised to be too complex and uncertain. Divination allows an alternative form of decision making so that we believe we are no longer simply 'taking a risk'. Divination is a way of defining reality, a means of knowledge and empowerment.

From my perspective, someone who believes that 'divination doesn't work' or 'astrology is nonsense' is fundamentally no different from the person who 'believes in' the *I Ching*, tarot readings, or whatever. Both are expounding their personal ideological myths about the nature of reality. Whether or not we believe that some or all divination techniques do or do not work is underlain by an 'implicit' belief in causality and the nature of past-present-future. Such implicit beliefs are so deeply ingrained into a culture that usually only philosophers and modern physicists question them.

If the underlying causality of the universe is essentially a chaotic system, then divination based on random outcomes – such as the tossing of coins in *I Ching* – is probably no worse (although no better) than attempting to make decisions by imagined chains of cause-and-effect. Western thinking requires decisions to be made on rational decisions based on all the relevant information. However, how do we know what information is really relevant and, especially in advance of the outcome, if we have anything like all the relevant information. Unforeseen events and 'accidents' could easily upset the most carefully researched decisions. Indeed almost any attempt to alter a

114

complex system will almost certainly have unexpected outcomes – as politicians involved in welfare, the economy and foreign affairs consistently find out. Trying to collect all the information that might be needed to understand all possible outcomes would take so long that the data would be out of date before the decision could be made – a terminal state of indecision (also demonstrated by some government departments, politicians and even business leaders, especially at the level of local government and medium-sized businesses).

The reality of decision making in politics, business and our private affairs is that we go through the motions of collecting and analysing information. Then we either get a 'hunch' or run out of time or mental energy and make a decision. In many cases an equally good decision would have been reached by chance-based divination. In other words, most of the key decisions made in the 'rational' western world are not made on a strictly rational basis. The chaotic systems which underlie the supposed causality of the modern world are best modelled by random probabilities. Little wonder then that divination 'works' so well – it is more closely related to the underlying random causality than seemingly rational decision making, which invokes largely illusory processes of cause-and-effect.

The tradition of divination which surrounds the *I Ching* requires no causal connections. The manipulation of yarrow stalks or coins and the hexagrams thereby selected have only meaningful 'correspondences'. In other words, just as people waiting on the platform do not cause a train to appear, so the hexagrams have only a correlation with the topic of divination. However these mental correlations satisfactorily side-step our unwillingness to accept that reality is the result of complex networks of events interwoven with each other and with 'chance'.

The predictions of diviners are created in the mind. But, as this book has already demonstrated, this does not distinguish such prophecies from a great deal else we regard as reality.

## causality and disease

Shared myths of causality are basic aspects of any culture. Modern western societies have relatively few cause-and-effect myths compared to traditional cultures, which incorporate a greater variety underlying assumptions about telepathy, clairvoyance, ghosts, spirits and other concepts that fit poorly with scientific ideologies. As a specific example of cause-and-effect myths, the western model of illness (with its emphasis on cells and infections) is entirely alien to most non-western and pre-modern societies where illness is not 'accidental' infection but directly caused by other people, evil eye, bad blood, guilt, witchcraft, or as a result of offending supernatural forces. Illness is retribution for violating social norms or for thoughts of envy, greed or malice. Attributing the causes of illnesses to witchcraft or divine intervention displays one key characteristic of humans' abilities to 'confabulate' causal connections: *the less one knows the more one can explain.*

Such traditional beliefs about the causes of illness are surprisingly similar throughout the world. Mythologists tentatively attribute this to the 'diffusion' of myths that originated at an early phase of human evolution. Others might attempt to attribute this to 'hard wiring' in our genes. But these are just different ways of attempting to impose causality, a sense of order, a specific ideology.

In recent decades western therapies have engaged in the creation of their own cause-and-effect myths. The history of the supposed causes of mental disease follows the evolution of western medicine. First of we blamed the gods, then the humours, then social misfortune, followed by three psychoanalytic spirits (id, ego and superego), then parenting, and – most recently – our genes. The wild goose chase for causality in physical medicine and psychotherapy looks set to run for some time. Only when we recognise that causality is essentially a socially constructed illusion will be able to recognise the underlying reality of diseases. In the meantime homeopathy and alternative therapies, while probably having wildly inaccurate models of causality, do at least give greater emphasis to the psycho-social nature of disease rather than adopt a reductionist form of materialistic 'rationalism'.

## divine as causal

Instead of recognising that reality is essentially irrational, western culture has devised a scheme whereby the human world is deemed to operate by apparent cause and effect, even though this causality is largely retrospectively created by a process of selective omission of 'irrelevant' events. Indeed, causality may be just a product of the processes of our consciousnesses and not inherent in the underlying nature of the universe.

To avert the fear that something closely akin to blind chance is running our lives we create causal connections where there are none. The human brain is naturally configured to impose 'meaningful' order according to imagined patterns. Belief systems – religious, political, economic, and all the rest – embody such patterns and thereby reinforce the sense of causality. Many of these belief systems, not just the ones that readily fall into the category of 'mystical', work on the basis that the less one understands, the more one can explain. They all pander to the universal human need to believe we live in a 'rational' world.

When our attempts to impose cause and effect break down then causality is transferred to deities, angelic beings, spirit helpers or otherworldly demonic entities. The divine and otherworldly beings are collectively distinct from the mundane world of humanity. By creating this concept of the divine we have effectively created a 'back up system' for causality for when so-called rational cause and effect fails.

If divination helps define reality (especially in areas where 'definition' is lacking) then such divine 'divination' defines divinely.

## contriving causality

All human cultures seem unwilling to accept that social interactions are sufficiently complex that attempts to make 'informed' decisions have little chance of being reliable. Nevertheless a wide range of cause-and-effect myths are contrived. Of all the ideas discussed so far in this book, the various beliefs in causality are among the most deeply-embedded myths constructed by different human cultures. I have already noted that this causality is inherent in languages. No surprise then that the next chapter looks at the deeply-embedded myths, mythic fragments and implicit metaphors that underlie all others – the myths of language.

### sources

Blackmore 2003: 263–70; Carroll 1987; 1992: 23; 1995; Dunn 1988 Ch.7; Fauconnier and Turner 2002: Ch.5; Hall 1982a; Jung 1972; Karcher 2001; Loewe and Blacker 1981; Peek 1991; Pinker 1997; Trubshaw 2003 Ch.8; Wittgenstein 1961: 6.4311.

# Chapter 10

# Myths of language

Linguistics is arguably the most hotly contested property in the academic realm. It is soaked with the blood of poets, theologians, philosophers, philologists, psychologists, biologists, and neurologists, along with whatever blood can be got out of grammarians.

Russ Rymer

Once, many years ago, I tried an ancient Cabalistic exercise – abolishing the pronoun 'I' from my speech for a week. I found the results of this exercise shocking, painful and extremely illuminating...

Robert Anton Wilson

The bait is the means to get the fish where you want it, catch the fish and you forget the bait. The snare is the means to get the rabbit where you want it, catch the rabbit and forget the snare. Words are the means to get the idea where you want it, catch on to the idea and you forget about the words. Where shall I find a man who forgets about words, and have a word with him?

Chuang Tzu


I have long been advocating the teaching of Chinese in secondary schools, not only because we must inevitably learn how to communicate with the Chinese themselves, but because, of all the high cultures, theirs is most different from ours in its ways of thinking. Every culture is based on assumptions so taken for granted that they are barely conscious, and it is only when we study highly different cultures and languages that we become aware of them. Standard average European languages, for example, have sentences so structured that the verb (event) must be set in motion by the noun (thing) - thereby posing a metaphysical problem as tricky, and probably as meaningless, as that of the relation of mind to body. We cannot talk of 'knowing' without assuming that there is some 'one' or 'what' that knows, not realizing that this is nothing more than grammatical convention. The supposition that knowing requires a knower is based on a linguistic and not an existential rule, as becomes obvious when we consider that raining needs no rainer and clouding no clouder. Thus when a Chinese receives a formal invitation, he may reply simply with the word 'Know', indicating that he is aware of the event and may or may not come.

Alan Watts

This passage by Alan Watts was written shortly before his death in 1973. His specific example of Chinese was popularising more universal ideas that had developed in the 1950s. These recognised that the structure of language influences the structure of thought. This means that a person speaking one language group subdivides the conceptual world differently from a person speaking another language group. For example all reds, oranges and browns are regarded as the 'same' colour in some African languages. Within the British Isles, blue, green and all shades of grey shared the same word in some Celtic languages.

The problem is much deeper than seeing shades of colours. For example, sentences such as 'It is raining' and 'It is snowing' are linguistic lies - there is no 'it' that is raining, there is only the rain. Sentences based on 'I know', 'I think', 'I believe', 'I desire', 'I hate' all share same lie. There is no 'I', only the knowing, thinking, believing, desiring, etc. Or, as William James put it concisely back in 1890, there is no 'I' in 'I am thinking' as 'thought itself is the thinker'.

This can be taken further as the thoughts, and their narratives and underlying ideologies, are not so much created by us as we are created by the thoughts.

'Our tales are spun, but for the most part we don't spin them, they spin us.' (Dennett 1991: 418) This can be taken a step further because, as the philosopher Julia Kristeva recognised, there is no self-awareness of self without language. Being an individual is to be part of a linguistic process. However discussions of self-identity will be deferred until Chapter 12.

Such illusions of language go deeper. All forms of the verb 'to be' (am, are, is, was, were, be, been) are also linguistic lies. No wonder one famous philosopher got bogged down with an inordinately complex discussion of 'being' – he was trying to describe a linguistic illusion that would be all-but untranslatable into some non-western languages. There is no 'being', there is only 'doing'. Which also means we are not 'human beings' but 'human do-ers'.

In the meantime we need to explore in more detail how language simultaneously helps us to understand and to represent reality.

## can language step outside the illusions of language?

'Is it possible to use language to undo the hallucinations created by language?' asked Robert Anton Wilson. He responded to his own conundrum thus: 'The task seems impossible, but Zen riddles, Sufi jokes, the works of Aleister Crowley, and a few heroic efforts by philosophers… seem able to jolt readers awake.'

And heroic the efforts indeed need to be. Individuals and societies construct and reinforce their identities through language – language is the medium through which most mythic fragments are communicated (and by which most visual symbols first gain their significance) and is intimately linked with folkloric transmission.

While language structures our thinking according to cultural norms, this does not mean that these cultural preferences are arbitrary. On the contrary, the relatively new discipline of 'cognitive linguistics' has revealed that the underlying basis of language is indeed systematic.

## the metaphors we live by

In Chapter 7 I gave some examples of way we only think about time through closely-related metaphors of time as a 'container' or as a 'flow'. Since the mid-1980s linguistics have begun to recognise that all languages describe abstract ideas through narrative metaphors that derive directly from the experience of the physical world. This approach to the underlying metaphors of human language and thinking became known as 'cognitive linguistics'. Mark Turner has provided an accessible introduction to cognitive linguistics, written from the perspective of literary criticism (Turner 1996).

The key to understanding cognitive linguistics is to recognise that meaningful sentences are built up from fairly universal metaphorical 'building blocks'. Cognitive linguists refer to these as 'schemas'. These metaphorical schemas are very varied but not arbitrary. Indeed most of the types of metaphors tend to be shared across widely different languages; the plausible reasons for this will be explored later in this chapter. These cognitive schemas might be thought of as linguistic 'building blocks' used by people who speak many different languages and cultures. They come in many shapes and colours, but there is a finite limit to the types and a very large but still finite limit to the ways they fit together.

Turner lists a great variety of schemas together with typical examples in English. I have simplified some of his finer distinctions to create the following list of key examples:

> Action is motion by a person under their own power
>> e.g. 'She is a *mover* in the entertainment industry.'
>> e.g. 'The president must make a decision, but he seems *paralysed*.'

e.g. 'He *went ahead* and gave his opinion.'

Mental states are spatial locations

e.g. 'She sees financial security as being *far off in the distance.*'

e.g. 'We cannot *return* to former conditions.'

e.g. 'He is *in* retirement.'

e.g. 'He *left* research to *go into* sales when he was thirty and *stayed there* for the next twenty years.'

Goals are spatial locations and means to goals are expressed as movement to a destination

e.g. 'I finally *reached* a solution.'

e.g. 'Why did they *stop short* of their goal?'

e.g. 'She decided that her ambitions would be met by going in a *different direction.*'

e.g. 'He found the right *avenue* to fulfil his aims.'

e.g. 'There have been a few *hold ups* but I'm *getting there* now.'

People manipulate ideas as if they are grasping objects

e.g. 'She *took* the opportunity.'

e.g. '*Hands off* my business!'

e.g. 'They had the game *in their grasp* but let it *get away.*'

e.g. 'He had a *firm grip* on delivery dates.'

e.g. 'I'm going to *hold down* this job and no one is going to *take it away from me.*'

e.g. 'She's looking to *snatch* that contract from the rival bidders.'

e.g. 'He was *juggling* too many projects and finally had to *release* some of them.'

More complex ideas are expressed by combining such schemas. So events can be construed as actors moving under their own power and the occurrence of the events as motion. e.g. 'The recession *crept up* on Britain' or 'Time *marches* on.' Alternatively events can be seen as manipulators, and the occurrence of events as manipulation e.g. 'The economy is *spinning* our business *around*' or 'The bad weather is *strangling* our profits.' One of the most prevalent schemas is the image of life as a journey, with death as departure.

What is especially interesting about these schemas is that quite abstract social and mental scenarios are constructed from simple spatial and bodily experiences. However this borrowing of metaphors only goes one way, from the more physical to the more abstract. We do not normally borrow abstract schemas to describe bodily or spatial scenarios. So, 'He's *cracking up*' and 'I *let go* of that idea ages ago' are perfectly normal metaphorical associations. However, although we would readily understand someone who says that flaking paint is 'losing its nerve' to the challenges of the weather, or that floorboards are 'conspiring' to break free from the joists, these metaphors come across as contrived and overly literary rather than typical of more spontaneous language such as speech.

Detailed research by cognitive linguists has shown that these schemas are not arbitrary but all relate more-or-less directly to bodily and spatial experiences. Despite clear evidence for some culturally-specific metaphors, these are outnumbered by cross-cultural consistency for schemas used to describe different abstract ideas. So the general schema of 'wind forcing trees over' means that we find it hard to understand a sentence such as 'The transparency of the wind wore the treetops down for spite'. Such puzzling and defamiliarising metaphors come from the realms of literature (this one is based on Robert Browning's poem *Porphyria's Lover*). In everyday use of language we prefer to use image schemas which do not contradict well-established (and seemingly culturally-independent) associations. However much remains to be understood about how we create 'easily recognised' metaphorical associations; this is one area of human thinking that remains mysterious.

The insights offered by cognitive linguistics strongly suggest that all the mythic fragments and ideologies which structure our ways of thinking – no matter how abstract – are, ultimately, derived from our physical experiences and activities. As will be discussed in the next chapter, this effectively implodes the long-standing mind-body distinction.

## representing reality

How we understand the world through linguistic constructions is only one half of language. The other half is how we use language to 'represent' reality in conversations and writing. This is an area of academic research (sometimes known as 'discourse analysis'; see Potter 1996 for an academic overview) which has grown up in recent decades fairly independently from cognitive linguistics, although both are interested in the way metaphors and categories are fundamental to the use of language.

This two-way process by which underlying concepts are shared to both 'understand' and to 'represent' reality is key to seeing language as a fundamental aspect of the social construction of reality. The same two-way process is also how more elaborate uses of language enable the sharing of mythic fragments and other narratives. The social construction of reality uses all the different 'levels' of language, with all the different embedded metaphorical schemas and categories, to simultaneously understand and represent reality.

## the stories we live by

Metaphorical schemas mostly share one characteristic that fits in well with ideas already developed in this book. These schemas are story-like, 'narrative fragments' if you like. This characteristic is inherited from the way we construct meaning from everyday spatial and bodily experiences. The wind *blows* clouds through the sky. A child *throws* a stone. Its mother *pours* a glass of water. A fish *swims* through water. Our entire everyday experience is constructed from 'pouring', 'carrying', 'throwing' and – above all – 'watching'. Our language, like most others, is based around such 'doing words' – 'Every sentence must have a verb', as has been drummed into generations of schoolchildren. So ubiquitous are these mini-stories that we take them for granted, consider them 'natural', the way things are. We simply do not recognise them for what they really are: the foundation stones and building blocks of culture.

Our cognitive processes are predisposed to create mini-stories or narrative fragments. Unsurprisingly the grammar of language has a similar narrative structure. Our language then reinforces this tendency to structure reality according to narrative, mostly according to culturally-established narrative metaphors and schemas. Myth-making is among the more fully-developed ways of imposing narrative onto ideas – you may recall that in Chapter 2 I put forward the notion that one way of thinking of myths is as ideology plus narrative.

From the perspective of cognitive science this deceptively easy capacity to recognise and construct narrative is a huge puzzle. Hearing and speaking languages both call upon hugely complex neural processes, which span many different areas of the brain. Yet all human beings recognise and act out more-or-less the same range of such mini-stories. And only humans have this ability – comparable narrative-creating skills in other highly developed mammals such as primates and dolphins seem to be far more rudimentary.

These mini-narratives are what stand between human thinking and chaotic experience. They are our way of *inventing* rational causality. And we just do it 'naturally', without consciously thinking about what we are doing. Indeed, it seems that the brain creates these mini-stories *before* it creates more rational concepts. Just as our brains process identification of shapes in a different part of the cortex from distinguishing colour, so too motion is recognised in yet another part. Somehow (and neuroscience has yet to work out how, still less if there is a specific 'somewhere' in the brain) our cognitive processes integrate shape, colour and motion to create the concept of, say, 'sparrow' or 'swallow'. Moderately experienced naturalists will be aware of this tripartite process of recognition – how different species move is often as distinctive as bodily shape and coloration. A fleeting glimpse in the undergrowth leads to the almost instantaneous conclusion 'That must have been a wren' based as much on flight characteristics as size or shade of brown.

The blending of form, colour and motion is at the level of our most basic perceptual processes. Our conception of physical objects is deeply linked to what they are *doing*. A horse is *standing* (rather than lying or cantering). That woman is *getting into* a car. Indeed our perception tends to filter out the vast number of things in our visual range which are not doing anything (or what they are doing is deemed by our cognitive processes to be uninteresting) – they are just 'background'. Only by a semi-conscious act do we step back to take in the whole of our visual surroundings, and only by an even more conscious step do we usually fully appreciate all the aural sources in our surroundings.

What this means is that our primary perception processes give significance to things which are considered to be 'doing' something. It is as if verbs are hard-wired into one part of our brains. From the standpoint of conventional scientific models of consciousness, this puts the proverbial cart completely before the horse. Conventional models argue that apparently sophisticated and 'exotic' mental activities, such as blending form, colour and motion, are based on other more basic (less 'sophisticated' or 'exotic') operations. Scientists' preferences for simplistic and stable mental concepts have been projected onto our mental processes, seeking simplistic and stable mental concepts at the core of our brains' activities. However the evidence of recent research in childhood development now suggests that blending form, colour and motion (and comparable complex cognitive processes for the non-visual senses) are *primary*. This means our simplistic 'rational' concepts are learnt, whereas these 'sophisticated' and 'exotic' forms of understanding are more innate.

This means that something as apparently simple as noticing that 'the grass is green' is not a primary perception but already contains the mini-story contracted to the verb 'is' (which, as previously noted, is more a figure of speech than something the grass is 'doing'; if it was a painting then it would be equally logical to say, referring to a particular patch of paint, 'the green is grass'). Furthermore, our cognition also uses narrative fragments to create the concepts of 'grass' and 'green'. So 'the grass is green' is nothing like a primary perception but already a concept made up of several cognitive schemas, each of which has implicit narratives.

Cognitive linguistics may have been born in the 1980s as a theory of language but by the mid-1990s it had outgrown its parents' expectations and was beginning to look more like a theory of mind, albeit a rather gawky adolescent interloper among some hoary old savants. However, two of the key players in the discipline, George Lakoff and Mark Johnson, showed there was more than just a theory of mind lurking in cognitive linguistics and developed a full-blown theory of philosophy in a book called *Philosophy in the Flesh* (Lakoff and Johnson 1999).

## a deep insight into myths as deep structures

I am deeply fascinated by the insight that 'doing' is apparently innate to our cognitive processes. If this is the case, then 'mini-stories' based on bodily and spatial experience are innate to our perception. Our more abstract thoughts are created from these 'primary' narrative fragments. Earlier in this book I have introduced the ideas that myths can be thought of as narrative plus ideology and how in the modern world myths are transmitted principally as mythic fragments. This term 'mythic fragments' (where 'mini-stories' and catch phrases allude to more encompassing narratives) matches almost exactly the cognitive linguistics concept of narrative fragments. 'Mythic fragments' can be thought of as slightly more complex or abstract cognitive narrative fragments (akin to the way molecules are made up of various atoms to provide the small 'building blocks' of the larger world).

Even more interestingly all myths are, ultimately, metaphors as well as narratives. So, if cognitive metaphors and narrative fragments are *primary* to our cognitive processes, this helps to explain why mythic fragments – also comprising of metaphors and narrative – come 'in under the radar' of our more conscious thinking. Indeed our primary cognitive processes are more 'mythic' than 'rational'. This means that the belief systems and ideologies communicated by myths are readily incorporated into our more primary thinking, before 'rational thinking' has a chance to step in. This in turn suggests that religions, politics and other mythic belief systems are *not* derived from more fundamental rational thinking but, on the contrary, such mythic systems are more fundamental than 'rational' thinking.

Furthermore, the fundamental 'narrative fragments' identified by cognitive linguistics are not merely part of our spoken and written language. They are part of our visual and aural perceptions too – we see things *doing* something, or at least as unmoving 'actors' in a mini-story. Sound, by its very nature, is always the result of something *doing* something – whether it is an owl hooting or a motorbike being revved up.

The most primary cognitive 'narrative fragment' is the act of making a distinction (see Chapter 8). Even thought the word 'distinction' is a noun, distinctions are not 'objects' floating around waiting to be picked, neither do they exist independently of human consciousness and individuals – distinctions only come about when *someone* actively *makes* them.

## culture as cognitive linguistics schema

The narrative fragments inherent in our processes of perception are shared by all means of communication and 'built in' to all aspects of our culture. They are as present in everyday speech – such as the 'folkloric' fragments which bond a group of people together, and are transmitted by folkloric processes such as word of mouth or the Internet (see Chapter 3) – as they are in the activities of the mass media.

Indeed, arguably the most focussed of mass media activities is TV advertising. I lere we see people and things 'doing something', never as static objects. What they are doing is part of the promotional message. This sense of doing can be fully developed into a mini-drama with sexy, affluent 'role model' adults promoting the product (as with the long-running Nescafé commercials) or it can be as mundane as a bottle of toilet cleaner happily bouncing around as part of a computer-generated animation. The instant coffee advert fairly transparently associates its product with sex and affluence, the other more subtly aims to impart a 'happy bouncing' feel to the decidedly mundane activity of cleaning bathrooms.

Moving from advertising to journalism, we can see the same obsession with creating narratives and mini-stories. Even the most banal of pop songs is made up of simple narrative fragments. In the promotional video, how the group members move is as important as what they wear (although the Pet Shop Boys took this to the logical limit by minimising all on-stage movement).

However before tying in the insights of cognitive linguistics with the mythic fragments of culture we need to explore the myths of how we think we think, and how we think of ourselves as individuals. Time not just for a new heading but a new chapter...

## sources

Bey 1996; Blackmore 2003: 162; Carrol 1956; 1995; Dennett 1991: 418; Eynon 2002; James 1890: Vol.1 p401; Lakoff 1987; McAfee p29; Potter 1996; Rymer 1992; Searle 1995: 59–78; Turner 1996; Taverniers 2002; Watts 1975, Wilson 1994: 89.

# Chapter 11

# Myths of consciousness

'Say! What you been doing?'
　　　　*'I've been thinking.'*
'Oh yeah? About what?'
　　　　*'I don't think that way.'*
Paul Haines

Consciousness is the perception of what passes in a man's own mind. Can another man perceive that I am conscious of any thing, when I perceive it not myself? No man's knowledge here can go beyond his experience.
John Locke (1632–1704)

... I regard consciousness as fundamental. I regard matter as derivative from consciousness. We cannot get behind consciousness. Everything that we talk about, everything that we regard as existing, postulates consciousness.
Max Planck (1858–1947)

Consciousness cannot be related to experience except
through the interposition of a particular language which
organizes the understanding of experience...

Gareth Stedman Jones

Mind is consciousness which has put on limitations.

Sri Ramana Maharshi

Human consciousness is just about the last surviving
mystery.

Daniel Dennett

It is really the most astonishing hubris to suppose that the
highest wisdom is constituted by the standpoint of
conscious reason, for we hardly begin to understand the
neural processes without which the very simplest act of
reasoning is impossible. The entire possibility of logical
and scientific thought rests upon a structure which was
formed unconsciously, which we do not understand, and
cannot manufacture. Should the finger accuse the hand
of clumsiness?

Alan Watts

Although fifty years has passed since Alan Watts wrote those
perceptive comments, we still have only the most tenuous
understanding of human consciousness. Indeed only within the last
fifteen years has there been any systematic attempt to fathom out how
we think. This comes as a profound shock to most people. Many
decades have passed since we developed the technology to put men
on the moon; and modern computer technology draws upon vast
technological expertise to enable powerful software to be in every
home. Yet, despite the best efforts of some of the best brains, we have

only a clumsy grasp of the underlying human thinking that created all this.

This is not simply because we have yet to define clearly which parts of the brain are most associated with specific tasks or emotions (although some progress has been made). It is that there is no agreement about what it is to be conscious. From the perspective of the more philosophically-inclined thinkers, we cannot even be certain that consciousness is something 'created' by our brains, rather than our brains 'filtering' a more omnipresent consciousness. There is no part of the brain where 'consciousness' is to be found – it is somehow a function of most parts of the brain acting together in some way. Yet clearly there is something about human brain functions which is more conscious than the brains of other animals, even higher primates.

One reason why we know so little about consciousness is that the scientific materialism which prevailed for much of the twentieth century dismissed consciousness. It was as if brain scientists thought that by taking the brain apart into pieces somehow there would be a part – or a set of parts working together – which correlated with the processes associated with higher consciousness. Only in the last fifteen years has there been a recognition that such materialistic approaches to the brain simply do not get us very far – most parts of the brain are involved, to some extent, in most activities. And thinking of consciousness as akin to an extra layer that has evolved on the top of a wedding cake simply does not fit the evidence, as some aspects of consciousness are created in the lower layers.

Human consciousness is far more developed than in any other species. This means that it must have evolved in the last few hundred thousand years. With hindsight we can see that this gave humans huge evolutionary advantages. But why did this change come about? Consciousness may have started out as just one among many of the narratives and rationales that our cognitive processes create to 'make sense' of our perceptions. In the course of time the 'consciousness narrative' became an increasingly dominant way for humans to 'make sense', as it were taking on a life of its own. Or maybe consciousness's close relative, self-consciousness, was the main evolutionary advantage and the rest of what we think of as consciousness was a secondary development. And it is reasonable to suppose that consciousness developed in close partnership with early humans' linguistic skills, in a 'chicken and egg' partnership. These three scenarios are not mutually exclusive although presumably we will never establish in any detail how humans became so conscious.

A key obstacle is the extent to which understanding consciousness is self-referential – the mental equivalent of lifting yourself up by the bootstraps. This means we can only use the metaphors and categorisations we already have about consciousness to understand consciousness. If the comparisons and categories are inappropriate then we will simply be barking up the wrong metaphors.

An example of such hindrance to understanding is the way philosophers and physiologists in recent decades have been seduced by the metaphor of the brain being like a computer and that 'thinking' is a subset of computational theory. Much as we may wish we could understand and adapt the brain in the same way we understand and design computers, the apparent similarities are outweighed by vastly greater dissimilarities. Frankly the 'brain is like a computer' myth is misleading and distracting. It is probably about as helpful as saying our 'brain is like a school of herrings'.

A more helpful metaphor is to think of consciousness is a *process*, a way of thinking, rather than some sort of 'thing' that can be separated from what is being thought about. Just stop for a moment and ask yourself what you are conscious of right now. Perhaps you can, but immediately your consciousness shifts to something else. We can all make a list of what we are conscious *of* at any one moment, but these change from moment to moment. Can you describe your 'stream of consciousness' apart from the sequence of perceptions and thoughts which you are thinking *of*? Can you get past this stream of ideas to reach a sense of what consciousness 'is'? Difficult isn't it? We think we are conscious but we cannot identify or describe an 'entity' which corresponds to this thought.

Is consciousness a process that originally came about as just another 'narrative' that our cognitive processes created to 'make sense' of our perceptions? Did it develop from a self-awareness narrative into what we now think of as consciousness hand-in-hand with our languages and linguistic schema? Should we think of consciousness as 'nothing but' an illusion, a trick of the brain, the neuronal counterpart to smoke and mirrors? Three tricky questions which the rest of this chapter will explore – although not necessarily answer!

## consciousness and language

Our consciousnesses are deeply intermeshed with our language in that the 'building blocks' for both are concepts and mini-narratives. This may be because consciousness developed in humans at the same time as language – the two seemingly unique aspects of humans having evolved in parallel. Language is undoubtedly a great benefit to people living in large social groups and, quite literally, languages are socially constructed.

In certain key ways our consciousnesses and linguistic concepts evolved the way they did because of social benefits and the ability for the way we think to adapt to social conditions. While I would not go so far as to suggest that consciousness is a 'side effect' of the evolution of language, the two are intimately linked.

Furthermore, consciousness is not functionally distinct from language. For example, the word 'yellow' correlates with light of a wavelength of 580nm. So my consciousness of 'yellow' is triggered by looking at a buttercup so that light of this wavelength stimulates on my retina. But my consciousness of 'yellow' is also triggered when I dream of a buttercup and my eyes are closed...

Whether our eyes are open or closed, 'yellow' only exists in our minds. Colour is not the 'property' of some external object (or, more correctly, some space-time event). Whatever the space-time event that stimulates our retina, it is our optic nerves and cognitive processes that create the concept of colour.

## consciousness as process

Because they are neither simply words, nor merely patterns of neurons, our cognitive processes vex empiricist and nominalist philosophers. However old school non-empiricists such as Plato and Aristotle, together with their neglected twentieth century counterpart George Santayana (1863–1952), regarded such concepts as 'essences'. And 'essences' are also the way we conceptualise 'abstract' mathematical structures and methods.

The neglected Greek philosopher Heraclitus (c.544–483 BCE) also understood that 'essences' are more important than specific events or objects when he famously noted that 'We cannot step twice into the same river.' While we readily recognise that a river flows on and is not exactly the same from moment to moment, we may need to be prompted before realising that that the person who steps into the river has also 'flowed on'. Yet, crucially, we have little hesitation realising that both the river and the person continue to exist from moment to moment – in other words, the 'essence' of the river, the person, and indeed all other space-time events are more fundamental than their physical existence. This has been dubbed by some the 'process' approach to philosophy, and resurfaces at the turn of the twentieth century with the book by Henri Louis Bergson (1859–1941) on

133

*Creative Evolution* (published in French in 1907 with an English translation following in 1911) and the later work of Alfred North Whitehead (1861–1947) such as *Process and Reality* (published in 1929). More recently, in his 1982 book *The Uncertain Phoenix*, David L. Hall has looked specifically at 'process philosophy', and explicitly states that such approaches have been masked by the predominate western philosophical tradition that looks not at processes but at 'objects' and 'events', thereby helping 'to ensure that the metaphysical traditions of Western philosophy would be biased toward substance over process... (Hall 1982a:174). However finding a philosophically acceptable way of understanding consciousness is beyond the scope of this chapter.

For the moment, think of consciousness as spanning many different brain functions through some exceptionally active and complex associative links. Metaphorically at least consciousness is the process by which the brain circulates sensory and conceptual information. In other words, consciousness is not something extra to the process of creating conscious phenomenal representations, it is that process. Linguistically this makes consciousness more of a verb than a noun.

## a brief history of consciousness studies

All I can do in this chapter is draw attention to issues of consciousness and theory of mind which seem to be most relevant to the broader scope of this book, i.e. how consciousness constructs a sense of reality.

The first point to make is that our understanding of how we think we think only began to take off in the late 1980s when various psychologists, philosophers, neuroscientists and others from a wide variety of backgrounds – including those with extensive experience of so-called 'altered states of consciousness' induced by eastern religious practices or by psychoactive drugs – came together to take an inter-disciplinary approach to what was termed 'consciousness studies'. Apart from the need to clear out a considerable amount of very 'dead wood' from centuries of philosophical speculation and materialist ideologies of science, there was a greater need to define what the key problems really were, and how to shed more light on these issues.

This has led to a number of wide-ranging and often heated debates. As is so often the case, these are either deeply philosophical and 'fundamental', or deal with unusual 'anomalies'. This is to be expected, as 'anomalies' which cannot easily be explained away reveal weaknesses in our explanations. So, borrowing examples from astronomy, the retrograde motion of the planet Mercury led to the realisation that the planets orbited around the sun and not around the Earth; then, about a hundred years ago, much more minor anomalies in the observed motion of Mercury led to experiments which confirmed that Einstein was right when he postulated that light passing close to the Sun was bent by gravity. In a similar manner, consciousness studies is interested in such anomalies as hallucinations, lucid dreams, amnesia, the effects of anaesthesia, synesthesia (e.g. 'seeing' sounds as colours or 'tasting' colours), and people who have difficulty maintaining a unitary sense of self, or who hear 'imaginary' voices.

Alongside these anomalies consciousness researchers are especially interested in the sense of free will and intuitive (i.e. non-algorithmic) mental activities such as creativity, especially how problems sometimes 'solve themselves' after a period of incubation during which we are not consciously concerned with the problem.

Above all, our brains continually work by unconsciously perceiving – and filtering out – a vast range of stimuli. Our conscious perceptions are only a minuscule part of our sensory experience, seemingly the tip of an iceberg mostly comprised of subliminally acquired knowledge. However they are less a 'tip' than fragmentary parts spread throughout the whole. Our conscious perceptions are *not* simply the equivalent of a computer monitor, whose display relates to a small part of the computations being performed on the motherboard. What we are conscious of is not in any sense an overview, nor is it easy to delimit which parts of our perceptions remain unconscious, as these are quite fluid as our attention changes. If we think about it for a moment, all animals experience the world through various senses, but none of them (with the possible exception of dolphins) have a developed sense of consciousness. How are our conscious perceptions different from these more prevalent and 'normal' subliminal processes? The difficulties of answering such a simple-seeming question betray the limited knowledge which consciousness research has so far achieved.

People involved in consciousness research rapidly develop a very different sense of how we think we think. Indeed, it is not only how we think we think that is thrown up in the air, but how we think about reality more generally. This may perplex those rooted only in western material rationalism, but the kind of questions raised – and even, perhaps, the tentative answers to these questions – are akin to those of Buddhism. The 'illusions' recognised by consciousness researchers are surprisingly close to Buddhism's declaration that all of ordinary experience is illusory. The Buddhist view is that everything is interdependent, so there cannot be consciousness without sensations, perceptions and actions. Buddhism takes this further and develops the doctrine of *anatta* or 'no self' but this is a topic I'll save for the next chapter.

In the last fifteen years consciousness studies has evolved from effectively nowhere to a subject of great complexity. Frustratingly, much of this literature suggests that consciousness researchers have an exceedingly narrow view of what it is to be conscious. Rather than seeking out the rich diversity of our relationships with other people and the world generally – in other words, consciousness as the *process* by which we construct reality – their emphasis is too often on an abstracted sense of consciousness as some elusive *thing* existing at the level of the neurons. If I wanted to add about 500 pages to this chapter I could attempt some sort of overview of the good and bad in this highly technical literature. Thankfully John R. Searle has saved me from this challenge with his book *The Mysteries of Consciousness* (Searle 1997) and Susan Blackmore has provided a more recent survey in her book *Consciousness: An introduction* (Blackmore 2003).

## the mind:body myth

One of the biggest illusions we have created is the sense that the 'mind' is somehow distinct from our bodies, and that the 'mind' is somehow superior to our bodies, so that human mentality is seemingly not constrained by material limitations. Clearly at a biological level this is pure bunkum – our brains are as much part of our bodies as our bowels. This mind:body dualism is a secular carryover from religious beliefs in the soul. This secularised offshoot of Christian belief comes to the fore in the sixteenth century with the writings of René Descartes (1596–1650). The superiority of mind was effectively debunked by the bleak philosophy of Friedrich Nietzsche (1844–1900), although a more sophisticated sense of mind and body as a non-distinct ongoing process was proposed by John Dewey (1859–1952). However, it was not until the work of Maurice Merleau-Ponty (1908–61) that the concept of the 'embodied mind' came to the fore. In essence, this means that everything we think about is derived from our sensory perceptions and the experience of our bodies moving through space. In the English-speaking world this idea was not well-known until after Merleau-Ponty's death, when a translation of his book *Phenomenology of Perception* was published.

In the last ten years cognitive linguistics, especially the work of George Lakoff and Mark Johnson already mentioned in the previous chapter, has added further strength to the sense of the mind being embodied, in that all abstract thought is constructed from metaphors and narrative fragments that describe more basic bodily experiences. In their book *Philosophy in the Flesh* (Lakoff and Johnson 1999) they argue for a complete system of philosophy based on the premise of the embodied mind.

Recent applications of the embodied mind approach to clinical psychiatry suggest that children regarded as dyspraxic are not simply 'clumsy' but have a poor sense of balance, literally *and conceptually*. Cognitively they seem to have no sense of 'centre' (or, more technically, a 'mid-line'). Such an inner sense of 'centre' is clearly needed for physical balance. It is also needed to develop a sense of direction and handedness – both skills which dyspraxic children struggle to develop. Likewise a sense of a mid-line is also needed for mathematics (e.g. 'What you do to one side of an equation you must do to the other') – and dyspraxic children may also find maths difficult. In a similar way the inability of autistic children to recognise other peoples' faces (at least in early childhood) and make eye contact is matched by cognitive difficulties recognising a sense of 'self' in other people.

## the Freudian myth

Another huge obstacle to understanding consciousness is the widespread popular awareness of, usually greatly misunderstood, versions of Freudian and Jungian models of how we think we think. Indeed terms such as 'the unconscious', 'ego', 'archetypes' and the like are part of everyday English, although few people using them are necessarily aware of the origins, still less the specific meanings given to them by Sigmund Freud (1865–1939) or Carl Jung (1875–1961).

Despite the everyday use of words invented by these pioneer psychotherapists, their ideas are rarely mentioned by consciousness researchers and then usually only in a derogatory manner. If this seems surprising, then an analysis of all 556 postings to the *Journal of Consciousness Studies* e-mail list made between 22 September 2001 and 9 May 2002 revealed that Freud was cited 13 times and Jung 12 times. 'Apart from one highly qualified comment about Freud recognising the "preconscious" activities of the brain, none of these 25 comments suggest that Freud and Jung are helpful to the approaches to consciousness being considered by the 600-plus list members.' (Trubshaw 2003e)

Although Freud's stratigraphy of superego, ego and unconscious id does not 'map' onto how modern consciousness researchers think about thinking, some aspects of Freud's work still have validity. He was the first to recognise that most of the brain activity that 'produces' consciousness is effectively hidden from consciousness. Also he anticipated what we now term synapses. (Credit also goes to Freud for recognising that desire is a major motivation, although not until the 1970s did this idea move forward, when René Girard recognised that we mostly desire what we think other people desire; see Chapter 5).

Rather than 'explain' human thinking, Freud mostly created a model that is as complex and inconsistent as what he was purporting to explain. It is akin to a Gothic castle, with dungeons and garrets, hidden staircases, drawbridges and moats. Freud's concepts have boundaries which can then be transgressed. Never mind that a more plausible model of consciousness would have none of these boundaries and a far more fluid sense of 'normal' behaviour with far less emphasis on transgression and aberration.

Above all Freud's model of how we think we think is mostly a reflection of his own character and social situation. It is a generalised theory of 'normality' based on observations of 'abnormal', somewhat neurotic people. For example, Freud's notion of the libido as being unconscious, unstructured lust has little validity outside western cultures where repression of sex has led to its obsessive over-valuation. Even modern day western cultural expectations have changed, making Freud's views about women seem more than a little sexist, as he regarded them as having inferior rationalism to men and did not recognise that many of his female clients' symptoms correlated with the socially-constructed passivity expected of women in early twentieth century Viennese society.

Freud's biographers refer to his obsessive sense of self-importance. To further these aims he falsified case histories of psychiatric 'cures' that we now know were anything but cures. Like all such people with a predilection for self-delusion, he successfully misled himself. This made it much easier to convince others. First of all he misled his closest followers. Although many, such as Jung and Alfred Adler (1870–1937) would subsequently disagree with at least some aspects of Freud's ideas, others would continue to promote Freud's misleading ideas long after his death. Intriguingly it was Freud himself who wrote 'No one who shares a delusion ever recongises it as such.'

In all but name Freudian psychoanalysis is a religious myth (with its cultic figure, origin myths, sacred texts, creed, initiation rituals, even procedures for excommunication) to set alongside Christianity, Islam and the rest. Referring to it as 'Freudianity' would be highly appropriate, although is unlikely to catch on, if only because most people hearing the word for the first time would think he speaker had said 'fraud-ianity' (an interesting 'Freudian slip'!).

The fraud at the heart of Freudian psychoanalysis is that terms such as id, ego and superego arc used in the same way that astrologers and Tarot card readers use a 'mumbo jumbo' of correspondences. Where psychoanalysts differ is by charging much more and making claims to alleviate mental problems, which no self-respecting astrologer or Tarot reader would consider doing. Or we can take the approach of Alan Watts, who wrote:

> ... [psycho]analysis is not really a system. It is an intimate personal relationship, and when, as usual, it is paid for, it is actually – like marriage – a most delicate and refined form of prostitution.

What wheat there is among the chaff of Freud's ideas would have probably been sorted soon after his death in 1939 if his youngest daughter, Anna (1895–1982), had not repeatedly crushed any debates about her father's ideas. Thanks to persistent *ad hominem* attacks led by Anna against critics the whole Freudian edifice survived almost intact until well into the 1970s.

The critiques of Freud's fantasies commenced in 1956 with Herbert Marcuse's *Eros and Civilisation* and Erich Fromm's *Sigmund Freud's Mission* in 1959. Various investigations of specific aspects followed over the years (e.g. Ellenberger 1970; Roazen 1975). Thomas Szasz provided the first hard-hitting attack on the Freudian edifice in 1978 with *The Myth of Psychotherapy*. E. Fuller Torrey joined the fray in 1992 with *Freudian Fraud*. One of the more recent and thorough demolitions of the Freudian myth is Richard Webster's 1995 book, *Why Freud was Wrong*. Among the vast number of other books about Freud see also Fisher and Greenberg 1985; Grunbaum 1984 and Robinson 1993.

Freud's writings tell us a great deal about the 'social construction' of Jewish society in Vienna in the early twentieth century. They are also 'cautionary tales' in that they reveal the weaknesses of his intellectual argument and understanding – bear in mind that Freud intentionally distanced himself from universities and academics of his time, and therefore from any potential critics, preferring to indoctrinate his 'disciples' in his own training institutes.

Beyond their historic interest as one of the most sustained 'cons' in the last hundred or so years, Freud's ideas are largely worthless. Worthless, but vastly influential. Despite the Freudian model of psychology being fundamentally flawed, ever since Alfred Hitchcock's pioneering films of the 1950s (such as *Psycho*) Hollywood scriptwriters have based their model of 'how we think we think' – the causality of human actions – on badly distorted versions of the Freudian model. As a result, for the last 40 or more years, western culture's ideas about 'how we think we think' have been largely been based on these errors.

Rather than cinema in some way reflecting reality, cinema provides us with the deep mythic structures that create our notions of reality. Little wonder then that, despite the number of devastating critiques, the cult of Freudian psychoanalysis is only slowly waning. The 'talking cure' is still a billion-dollar business in America. So the sitcom *Frasier* gently made self-conscious fun of father-son relationships, but fell well short of full frontal anti-Freudian stances.

## Jung

The ideas of Freud's one-time protégé, Carl Jung, have fuelled even wilder fantasies about how we think we think. Jung went several stages further than Freud in creating a mythic system that was even more mythic and mystical. Archetypes and the collective unconsciousness may be seriously seductive but require whole new ontological categories. Carl Jung's belief that 'Nothing to which the psyche belongs or which is part of the psyche is ever lost. To live fully, we have to reach down and bring back to life the deepest levels of the psyche from which our present consciousness has evolved.' (Jung 1960) requires a model of reality that is 'out there' along with the least logical of New Age sentiments.

For all that Jung asserted the frequent and universal occurrence of key symbolism, no convincing evidence has ever been presented. His ideas have to be accepted as an act of faith. According to Jung, the 'collective unconscious' is instinctive and pre-cultural. From it come archetypes, which manifest in dreams and myths. In a mystical manner, these archetypes operate independently of man's conscious mind. Since the archetypes exist *a priori*, man does not invent them but simply inherit or receives them. As the folklorist Alan Dundes notes:

> ... several of Jung's archetypes are so general – the great mother, the child, the wise old man, etc. – that they probably are very widespread and maybe even universal. It is hard to imagine a culture which has no image of a mother figure. But

even if a general mother image were universal, there would be no need to postulate that such an image was part of one's genetic inheritance. That image might be acquired through the mediation of culture....

There is unquestionably a mystical, anti-intellectual aspect of Jung's thought. Since the archetypes are part of the collective unconscious, they cannot, Jung maintains, ever be made fully conscious. They are therefore not completely susceptible to rational definition or analysis.
(Dundes 1984: 244–5)

Jung uses the universal themes of myths as evidence for his notions of the collective unconscious. He is interested in a 'static' ideal that can be discerned in the symbolism of myths and not the 'dynamic' life of mythic motifs and narratives. As William Doty coyly states, 'To be fair to Jung, we must note that he wrote before the development of modern structuralism or semiotics.'

In my opinion all of Jung's perceived parallels and correlations can be explained far more elegantly by the 'mythic fragments' suggestions made earlier in this book, and without entering the realms of mysticism and innovative ontology. In all fairness, Jung's contemporaries in psychology were less than impressed with his ideas with the result that his vast output of writing is better known *outside* of psychology and psychotherapy.

Even wonkier versions of the Jungian myth of psychology were picked up by Hollywood scriptwriters, with the result that versions of a very specific hero myth prevail, from the overt racism of cowboy films, through the imperialism of *Star Wars*, Neo of *The Matrix*, and legions of other manifestations. And reality really does imitate this fiction, as was explored in Chapter 5 in the examples of American presidents who have re-enacted events from action films.

## consciousness as a socially-constructed process

I hope this brief overview of an exceptionally complex subject has indicated that our models of consciousness – how we think we think – are socially constructed. How we think we think (which may have little to do with how we actually think) is most certainly socially constructed as, since the 1950s, popular awareness of psychology has been disseminated by the mass media, especially cinema and TV.

Unfortunately these models of our mental actions and rationales are mostly pure bunkum. How we think we think is now an invention that is not merely socially constructed but, intentionally or otherwise, deeply implicated into the hegemony of the mass media.

Current academic thinking about consciousness suggests we should think of consciousness as a process. This means that consciousness is as much about performance – how each of our brains 'perform' at being each of us. Seemingly consciousness is about sustaining a personal 'narrative', an overall sense of a life story which makes me the main actor, and sustains the sense of me being me rather than a series of different entities. Intriguingly, psychopathology shows that some people do have difficulties sustaining such personal narratives. Time to look at the myths of individuality...

## sources

Baron-Cohen, Tager-Flugsberg and Cohen 1993; Blackmore 2003; Chalmers 1996; Cioffi 1998; Crews 1998; Dennett 1991: 21; Doty 2000:159; 203; Dufresne 2003; Dundes 1984: 244–5; 1999: 179–80; Ellenberger 1970; Eynon 2002; Fauconnier and Turner 2002; Fisher and Greenberg 1985; Freud 1930 (quotation cited appears in *Standard Works* Vol.21 p81); Fromm 1959; Golsan 2002; Graham and Stephens 1994; Grunbaum 1984; Guattari 1996: 155–6; Haines 1976; Hall 1982a; Lawrence and Jewett 2002; McMahon 2003; Marcuse 1956; Planck 1931; Ripley, Daines and Barrett 1997; Roazen 1975; Robinson 1993; Searle 1997; Stedman Jones 1983: 101; Stephens and Graham 2000; Szasz 1978 ; Torrey 1992; Trubshaw 2003a; 2003e; Watts 1954, 1972: 341; Webster 1995.

# Chapter 12

# Myths of self identity

... the very act of making sense of ourselves and others is only possible in and through the fabric of narrative itself.

Mark Freeman

One shouldn't write one autobiography but ten of them, or a hundred because, while we have only one life we have innumerable ways of recounting that life to ourselves.

J.B. Pontalis

The feeling of 'I' and 'mine' is the result of ignorance.

Sri Ramakrishna

The world is seen not as it is, but in its various relationships to the 'me' of memory.

Krishnamurti

Most people are fairly receptive to the idea that politics and religions are based on ideologies, and take little persuading that these ideologies are mostly transmitted by mythic fragments. A good number of other people (especially those not so deep in the belief system as to be unable to see the proverbial wood for the trees) can be persuaded that commerce and science are also based on ideologies which are also sustained by mythic fragments. And, if science is ultimately a belief system, then by logical extension, any scientific understanding of how we think must also be constructed in similar ways.

But most people have great difficult in accepting that the sense of self, their own individuality, is similarly constructed. This cuts away every sense we have of being who we are. So this chapter may be the hardest for most people to understand, still less accept. And if you do understand and accept, you may find the resulting uncertainties difficult to cope with. This is the 'red pill' or the 'blue pill' moment. Don't say you weren't warned…

## 'I' and 'me', 'person' and 'self'

In conversation we often say 'I did so-and-so' or 'I will do such-and-such'. We refer to 'me' and 'myself', which seems in some way distinct from 'my self'. When I refer to me as a 'self', what is the difference from me as a 'person', or me as an 'individual'?

Ah, if only there were an easy answer. The more philosophically inclined have debated such questions long and hard. Their answers often suggest that we are looking at little more than different shaped shadows cast by the same illusion.

Chapter 10 included a discussion of the suggestion that, just as there is no 'it' in 'it is snowing', so too there is no 'I' in 'I know', only the knowing. So too there seems to be no 'I' in 'I am thinking', as 'thought itself is the thinker'. More basic acts of perception, as when we say 'I see the flower' do not require an 'I', as there is only the seeing (although our consciousness – our sense of self and 'I' – quickly steps in with feelings and reactions to what we see). Sentences such as 'I believe this', 'I think that', 'I hate whatever' are more persuasive than simply stating this, that or whatever. The downside is such sentences create the illusion of an 'I' who has beliefs, thoughts and desires who is separate to the believing, thinking and desiring.

And yet, and yet… Somehow there is a strong sense of an entity which is behind the perceptions, thoughts, remembered knowledge, an 'entity' which is more than a linguistic lie, a trick of language. And yet… we still seem to be looking into a kaleidoscope of multiple reflections, such that this sense of the self exists only because this sense of self asserts that there is a sense of self.

For the purposes of this chapter I will use the term 'person' to refer to the material body which has mental images of itself that interact with the external world and which has physical, intellectual and spiritual achievements and aspirations. Such a person is also an individual. When referring to myself as such a person it is convenient to use the terms 'me' and 'my'.

However the sense of being a person and individual is not without its problems. Are we referring to the 'embodied individual' (the one who eats, walks, makes love, sleeps)? Or to the 'thinking individual', made up of a seemingly sequential stream of thoughts? Or to the 'social individual' who takes part in ever-varying relationships with a variety of other people? Some of these social relationships are close, as with family. Some are transient, such as perfunctory exchanges with shop assistants in a strange town. Some are more abstract, as each social interaction is part of a wider 'politics of power' – who has power over who, and how this power is traded. Furthermore, in the modern western world at least, there is the sense of individual*ism* – that individuals have independence of thought and action.

In contrast the word 'self' is used in a narrower sense which allows for any one person to have a number of 'selves' depending on the different social situations he or she encounters. Each of our selves can act as an agent to manipulate other people and things. Our sense of self also allows that our various selves are volitional, i.e. they have the capacity for voluntary and intentional activities.

This sense of 'selfness' (or subjectivity) persists through a variety of changing activities and situations – it is the 'essence' of an on-going process, not an 'object' that exists independently of the activities, situations and on-going process. The last chapter raised the suggestion that consciousness is more of a verb than a noun. So little surprise then that the sense of self – a product of consciousness – is also more of a process than a thing; this is a topic I will return to later in this chapter. For the moment just one comment – whatever this process may or may not be, it is a long way from literary concepts of the 'stream of consciousness' as perpetrated in the writings of Virginia Woolf, James Joyce and other twentieth century authors.

## self as a boundary

Thinking of 'self' as a process raises several important issues. The first is: how does self relate to consciousness? This begs a closely-related question: where is this sense of self 'situated'? To answer these questions requires thinking in terms of a three-level distinction. We have little difficulty making a distinction between, on the one hand, the external world of objects and other people and, on the other hand, our internal mental world of thoughts (even though many of these thoughts relate to 'external' objects and people). However there is a two-way interface between the external and the internal. Incoming sensations, perceptions and feelings are matched by the various ways in which we interact with and manipulate the external world. 'Self' is that interface, that semi-permeable boundary. If this sounds odd, think of what happens when the sense of self is disrupted by hallucinogenic plants or drugs, where the experiences render that boundary very fluid or seemingly non-existent.

## self as singular

The biggest of the issues about the sense of self is: why do I think I am *one* person living in *one* world, who (usually) has a strong sense of being an individual over an extended period of time?

This in turn raises two subsidiary issues. Firstly, why do I think I am a unified self at any one moment? Secondly, why do I seem to be the same self as I was a few minutes/hours/months/years ago?

These seemingly similar questions do not necessarily have the same answer. Cheating for a moment and giving you the 'answers' before the reasons, the sense of being a unified self at any one time is perhaps a direct consequence of our consciousness. The sense of self over a period of time is far more fluid. Some people have a well-developed sense of such personal continuity whereas others do not, others are consistent only in their inconsistency, perhaps to the extent of pathological behaviour. Just as a minority of people have well-developed narratives of their past, so too some are able to construct long-term plans into the future. The majority of 'normal' people fall into a much more muddled middle ground, even if social norms require us to mask the muddle as much as possible.

The muddle is inevitable. 'Social norms' allow each of us to change and adapt, sometimes quite dramatically, over time. Social norms require a certain amount of psychological continuity – for example, most people are, initially at least, a little perturbed if friends or acquaintances reveal trans-gender 'discontinuities', whether transient cross-dressing or enduring surgery.

## me, I'm multiplex

Our sense of being a unified person, of being 'me', normally copes with different parts of our personas to come to the fore in different social environments. My day job self is distinct from my sport-playing self. Both are distinct from my religious self, and also from my roles within the family. Indeed most of these personae have evolved over time, quite markedly when there is a clear discontinuity, as with starting a new job or taking up a new sport or religion. While it is not part of my personal experience, some family roles – such as becoming a parent or being required to act as full-time carer for an ailing parent – are also transformative.

Society does not usually regard such changes in roles and personae as abnormal. Only if some of the roles transgress social mores do we begin to worry about cross-contamination (i.e. don't admit to have 'kinky' leisure interests if you plan on being promoted to senior management by a conventionalist managing director). We also distinguish the normal range of multiplex personae from clinically-recognised multiple personality 'disorders'. By and large we accept multiplex selves as normal, even though this means our sense of being a person is an extremely complex construction. The most perplexing aspect is adjusting this awareness of multiplex selves to the idea of a singular self. In other words: which sense of self is aware of the other selves?

However in practice, the main problem with such multiplexing of roles and identities is simply how many different roles (and rapidly changing roles) are required by modern western society. As one modern day sage, Peter Carroll, has observed, 'If you consider yourself as a single being capable of playing various roles, then you have yet to play them *in extremis.*'

Most of us deal with this dilemma pragmatically by constructing a 'hierarchy' of our personae, with one of the personae being dominant in specific contexts, although the others are never far away and can be called upon if necessary.

## self as narrative

To a greater extent than we realise, all of us are the authors of our selves. We continually re-narrate our own origin and identity myths. We create narratives which paper over vast discontinuities and create a sense of unity. We also project these narratives of the past into the future as desires, aspirations and plans. Even if only some of our plans are achieved, or we only plan for as little change as possible – as with an archetypal retired person – what happens in our futures is in large part determined by rehearsing and reiterating narratives about our past. At some later date we will create retrospective cause-and-effect narratives outlining how either our plans reached fulfilment or 'fate' intervened.

Or, in the case of people suffering from multiple personality disorders, there is a failure to integrate – to the extent that sufferers report that their different selves sometimes display different allergic reactions, or have differing visual defects. In contrast, severe amnesia prevents even one sense of self from being constructed.

Some self narratives are more fictional than others, as when we construct lies, adopt a pseudonym, or seek to live under a different identity (for nefarious or other reasons). Converts to eastern religions are often given new names, with the explicit intention of helping to create a new persona (within Christianity this rite has lost its sense of re-naming because most denominations baptise soon after birth, and those who baptise as adults – such as the eponymous Baptists – do not rename). However in western culture it is conventional for women to change their surname when they get married, although this is mostly regarded as a symbolic change rather than a psychological 'tool' to assist the bride adjusting to her new roles (and, indeed, the custom originated when marriage denoted legally-binding ownership of the wife by the husband).

Our sense of personal identity is constructed by narratives. In this we are no different from groups of people who, as already mentioned in Chapter 5, also construct their identity from narratives shared among group members, whether the group is as small as a handful of people who share the same office, or as large as a nation. And, in the same way social groups define themselves by who they exclude (e.g. excluding people who cannot share current in jokes) so too our sense of self is as much a process of *exclusion* and quickly feels perturbed by any boundary violations.

People who hear 'alien' voices inside their heads are understandably troubled by this boundary violation. Whether the voices are auditory hallucinations or mis-attributed *sotto voce* self-produced thoughts still remains for the specialists to determine. Within traditional societies such voices were presumably the basis for notions of possession. Robert Louis Stephenson famously dramatised such possession in his 1886 novel *Dr Jekyll and Mr Hyde*. His demonisation of Mr Hyde epitomises a characteristic of human nature – we define ourselves (either as individuals or as social groups) mostly by defining the 'other', what we think we are not. This process of categorisation frequently demonises the 'other'. Stephenson perpetrated the social norms of his day by defining the respectable Dr Jekyll in contrast to the demonic Mr Hyde. This is little different to modern tabloid newspapers who define acceptable social behaviour by demonising 'hooligans', 'muggers', 'travellers', and other such invented mythic notions.

## losing the plot

Our sense of self largely dissolves in dreams and trance states. The collective term 'altered states of consciousness' includes a variety of categories (and causative reasons) for what might equally validly be deemed 'altered states of self' – or, perhaps more accurately, 'altered states of selves'. Some of these altered states include out of body experiences, where the sense of self seems to have been physically removed from our bodies.

Furthermore our tendency to think in terms of a stream of self-narratives is diminished when we are engrossed in some demanding physical or mental activity, or are triggered into some artistic or numinous sense of unity or ecstasy. Similar 'blissed out' states can be triggered by orgasm. But not too long afterwards our sense of narrative returns, and our recent 'timeless' state becomes incorporated into our narrative making.

Our personal narratives are habits of thought. The next few times you meet someone new and recount significant events in your life, keep a mental note of how you tend to use almost the same words, and rarely add different details or emphasis when telling new friends about key events in your life. Indeed we do exactly the same when informing established friends about a recent significant event.

At one level self identity is a collage of self-quotations. The sense of self is the centre of a narrative gravity, a useful fiction. But, while we are capable of massive self-deception, there are limits to how much autobiographies can differ from the facts and remain plausible, especially to others who share the relevant 'facts'. However human memory is deeply flawed. Not only do we forget, but suitable 'prompts' can cause us to invent details that were not part of the original experience. Eye witnesses to criminal events have been proved to be seriously unreliable, even though juries follow their common sense in attributing a high degree of confidence to such witness accounts.

The extent to which we rely on memory to construct – and maintain – our sense of identity was wonderfully explored in Philip K. Dick's novel of 1968 *Do Androids Dream of Electric Sheep?* which was adapted to the 1982 film *Blade Runner.* The plot revolves around the ability for memory – and thereby identity – to be fabricated, and the inability to distinguish between the 'manufactured' memories of the cyborgs and 'real' memories and identities. Dick and the screenwriters intentionally posit a large question mark over the nature of 'real' memories and identities.

In recent decades a handful of psychotherapists have created a monstrous phenomenon known as 'false memory syndrome'. These therapists use hypnosis and various more-or-less subtle cues during therapy sessions to 'manufacture' memories of childhood abuse, even though the patient has no prior memories of such abuse. When the patient confronts the abuser (usually a parent or guardian) with these false accusations considerable psychological damage may arise to all concerned.

## self is always in the past

Although we plan for and anticipate the future, our sense of self becomes much more hazy as we look into the future. Indeed, for most of us we find it hard to relate the only inevitable event in our futures – our death – with any sense of self we currently hold. Various metaphors for after life and reincarnation, sustaining some sense of self into some sense of forever, abound in a variety of belief systems.

To a very large extent there is no sense of self in the present moment, only the present moment of consciousness from which we need to 'step back' and put into some sort of historic context, some sort of mini or meta narrative, before we can impute a sense of self. We respond to the present according to the personality traits of the self who is currently dominant, but we can only with difficulty ask that self to 'step aside' and allow different personality traits to come to the fore. Counsellors helping clients with, say, aggressive behaviour, or religious gurus imparting a sense of peace and contemplation, or sports coaches encouraging more assertive performances, or military training experts teaching recruits how to kill have all developed tricks of their trades to switch mental states at appropriate times. Indeed numerous self-help books will impart these tricks. Nevertheless, without training we do not usually have control over our selves *in the present moment* in the same way we construct our self narratives about past events.

While I have a continuous physical existence, whatever makes up 'me', the combination of 'selves', exists principally in the past and only projects tentatively into the future. What Freud referred to as our 'ego' would be better referred to as our mental habits, habits which entrap our awareness of the present within the narratives which construct our sense of self in terms of our past. We drive into the future looking almost entirely at the rear view mirror. The world is seen not as it is, but in its various relationships to the narratives that my various selves create to invent and sustain the sense of being me.

Looking at this from a slightly different perspective, the events in our lives 'make sense' only when they are part of a suitably-constructed narrative. Such 'autobiographical' accounts are not produced as a *consequence* of life – such accounts are in themselves the process by which we create and determine our lives.

## the tales tell us

We are the authors of our personal narratives. But the more we rehearse, repeat and revise these stories as part of our social interactions, the more other people use them as the basis for their social interactions with us. Within specific social situations these self-narratives reflect back on us and play a large part in defining who we are. As Henry Floyd Allport wrote back in 1924:

> … our consciousness of ourselves is largely a reflection of the consciousness which others have of us… My idea of myself is rather my own idea of my neighbor's view of me.

When people meet for the first time there is a mutual process of finding out what work they do, whether they have children, what TV programmes they watch, what films they enjoy, their preferences for music, what books they read, where they go on holiday, whether they support a football team, play golf, squash. All these answers – which are all, to a greater or lesser extent, narratives – locate us and them socially and culturally (as do our accent, use of language, manners, not to mention our clothes, car, and the general consumption of 'material culture'). Between people who know each other already then the social interactions, the processes of maintaining social and cultural identities, become a little more subtle but nevertheless equally effective, and invariably comprise of narrative fragments.

I started this chapter by suggesting that sense of the self is akin to looking into a kaleidoscope of multiple reflections (that this, our sense of the self exists only because this sense of self asserts that there is a sense of self). So too the narratives by which we create and sustain this sense of self in our social interactions also seems in the nature of a vast ever-shifting kaleidoscope. Not for nothing is there a mirror fetish in *The Matrix* (see Danser 2004 for further details).

At some point we created our personal narratives. But by the combined processes of 'internal' mental rehearsal and 'external' repetition in social interactions these narratives take on the semblance of reality. And subsequent social interactions reflect these narratives back to us and so really do seem to be 'real'. For most of our lives our thoughts are not such much created by us as we are created by the established narratives of our thoughts, our mental habits. 'Our tales are spun, but for the most part we don't spin them, they spin us' is the metaphor used by Daniel Dennett in *Consciousness Explained.* Or think of the 'power of positive thinking' schools of self-development that have been with us for about a hundred years – if you think you can do something then there is a good chance you will be able to do it; if you think you can't do something then you certainly never will.

## self as socially constructed

Individuals and society are two sides of the same dualism. Self identity is always in the context of a social group, even if the group is absent or imaginary. Only when other people are aware of us does our self identity really come into existence. This puts another twist on the take that we define ourselves by defining (or at least developing an implicit awareness of) the 'other', that which we are not.

Society is, as the starting point for many other possible definitions, an aggregate of individuals. The potential social interactions between individuals are unconscionably complex. An individual is not simply the sum total of possible social variables such as age, ethnicity, sex, gender, class, social status, religion, education, aspirations, and so on and so on. An individual is capable of *all possible permutations* of these seemingly limitless variables, few of which are constant even within quite short spans of time as different 'selves' and personae come to the fore in different social contexts.

As the previous chapters of this book have attempted to illustrate, all the concepts that make up what we think of as reality are constructed through the complexities of these social interactions. Even our fantasies are intimately linked with cultural expectations, as we desire what we think other people desire.

Western society is founded on a deep-seated illusion that we can establish meaningful cause-and-effect rationales out of this intense complexity, and still have a well-defined sense of individual*ism* – i.e. that all individuals have independence of thought and action. Traditional societies have a wide range of ways of thinking about individuality but do not suffer from this illusion that individualism is more significant than group interests and actions.

Furthermore, in traditional societies causality is 'devolved' into cosmologies where divinities and malign spirits have as much influence as human agency. The western sense of evolutionary superiority makes us dismiss such cosmologies as 'superstitious', yet we fail to recognise our own rationales are at least as fanciful.

If, at least for the moment, we consider the complexities of human social interactions as so complex and inter-determinate that they are best considered as 'chaotic systems' (and note that this terminology, borrowed from mathematics, does not mean that they are simply 'chaotic') then conventional cause-and-effect models simply do not provide accurate predictions, even if in retrospect we construct the illusion of plausible cause-and-effect rationales. It is not simply that a 'chance' meeting with a friend can lead to learning about a job opportunity which results in a whole new career with much better pay, which in turn means we can afford a better house, expensive holidays, and the fulfilment of other aspirations. Rather, the consequences of 'chance' social interactions are leading to a whole range of less conspicuous outcomes *all the time.*

## self as performance

Human existence relies on the sense of self. Social interactions require the production, indeed the performance, of our self narratives. And we consume the self identities produced and performed by others. Even something as 'real' as gender has been shown to be to be neither natural nor optional, but instead is socially constructed – although in this instance the biases of western languages provide constraints that make the 'normal' binary options seem 'inevitable'. Only in recent years has the possibility of a plurality of genders surfaced, and we are still a long way from such non-dualist attitudes being considered normal (although we should not forget that 'normal' dualist heterosexual attitudes were constructed only in recent centuries). Any awareness of popular culture in recent decades reveals the extent to which a variety of 'transgressive' gender options – including a variety of expressions of homosexuality, transvestism, and the like – have been 'constructed' and performed privately and publicly in night clubs and 'Gay Lib' parades.

The construction and performance of different aspects of our personae is, in the modern world, not simply reflected back as part of face-to face interactions with other people but also constructed by commercial interests. The desire for self-expression offers rich pickings for both the media and manufacturers to offer a cornucopia of 'life style marketing', whether we are teenagers creating – indeed performing – self-identity through cultish enthusiasm for a pop group, or their parents expressing their status with BMWs, Barbours and a cottage in the country.

While we think of ourselves as the authors of our self identities, social interactions have a major part in the construction of our selves and of all the social factors at work the efforts of the marketing executives are by far the most pervasive. Who we think we are is, to a far larger extent than most people will readily admit, constructed by magazine articles, TV adverts, pop music moguls, and Hollywood films.

As I already noted in Chapter 2, all too often individuals create a 'reality' which is a defective version of an illusory ideal; and their sense of self constrained by these illusions. This is one reason why 'socially agreed reality is akin to a bleak Monday morning', as Alan Watts put it nearly fifty years ago. If people were soap operas then most of them should sack their scriptwriters and recruit someone with considerably more imagination and a 'can do' attitude. The script also needs to allow for a greater diversity of ideals, such as ones empowering for people who are labelled 'disabled' according to current concepts, and ones that make 'normality' seem less akin to a disabled state of existence.

Not that many decades ago, western cultures created a sense of identity which was fairly limited and any changes were restrained. Identity was felt to be 'singular' rather than 'multiple' (even if this feeling did not quite match how identities were multiplex to a certain extent). This allowed for a sense of completeness to our identity, indeed one that appeared timeless and universal. However in recent decades identity has become much more fluid, essentially multiplex, and part of the continual processes of change. This in turn leads to a sense of incompleteness and an implicit recognition that they are culturally- and historically-specific.

Whereas at one time dissatisfaction with one's identity was expressed as an urge to *discover* your self, now it is seen as need to *reinvent* your self. In practice, this usually means 'reinventing' our cultural consumption, which can also be thought of as differentiating our self (in some suitably conspicuous way) from our previous self. Self identity is only partly belonging; in much greater part it is about exclusion from what we do *not* want to belong to.

## the consequences of the illusion of self

'Our sense of being a conscious agent who does things comes at the cost of being technically wrong all the time' observed Daniel Wegner. It is perhaps an honest error. The idea of an 'inner self' is an illusion created by projecting our physical bodies onto our sense of self. Arguably we cannot exist without such an illusion. However the consequence is that this illusion seriously constrains our thinking. Even the most innocuous habits of thought, word and deed act as anchors which constrain us to previously established patterns of thinking and acting. Our social interactions reflect these constraints back at us, such that our sense of identity is contained within our concepts of social reality. We identify with ideas of what we are expected to be much more than what we wish to be. Reality becomes something that happens to us; this illusion totally obscures the ability to recognise that reality is something we construct.

Our various selves are the processes by which we look at external reality. While I prefer to think of self as a process rather than a thing, if there were such a thing as the self then it is more in the nature of the lenses of spectacles – something we normally look through rather than look at. (Although trying to look objectively at our sense of self has something of the paradox of trying to look at the inside of our own eyeballs.)

The more attentive of you will realise that I used exactly the same metaphor of lenses back in Chapter 2, as one way of thinking about myths. Quite intentionally I have closed the loop with the same metaphor. If, as I have been consistently illustrating throughout this book, the concepts which largely make up what we conventionally think of as 'reality' are all socially constructed then the same underlying rationale should be present whether we are considering the fairly explicit mythology associated with, say religious, political or economic ideology, or the better disguised 'myths' of how we construct knowledge, consciousness and the sense of self.

This is akin to the Buddhist doctrine of *anatta* or 'no self', which runs counter to most other major religions (indeed it is not accepted by all Buddhists) as it is diametrically opposed to belief in a soul. However the realisation that the 'self' is an illusion unites Buddhist mystics with the latest generation of western philosophers and consciousness researchers.

## sources

Blackmore 2003: 162, 243, 249, 412–3; Brook 1999; Butler 1990; Carroll 1995: 12; Cavallaro 2001: 121–3, 129–30; Crews 1995; Danser 2004; Danzinger 1997; Dennett 1991: 418; Edelmann 2000; Flanagan 1994: 135–44; Freeman 1993: 21; Gray 2002: 71–2; Krishnamurti 1971: 9; Leary 1997: 28; Meskell 1999: Ch.1; Morris 1991; Olson 1999: 49; Pickering 1997, 1999; Rahula 1959; Rosenwald and Ochberg 1992; Scott 1986; Strawson 1999; Stephens and Graham 2000; Storey 1999; Wegner 2002: 342; Williams, Loftus and Deffenbacher 1992.

# Chapter 13

# Recapitulation and application

… nature is a structure of evolving process. The reality is the process.
Alfred North Whitehead

Identification with a nation or a belief is a favourite trick to cheat loneliness.
Krihsnamurti

… in contemporary societies, cynical distance, laughter, irony are, so to speak, part of the game. The ruling ideology is not meant to be taken seriously or literally.
Slavoj Zizek

The whole aim of practical politics is to keep the populace in a continual state of alarm (and hence clamorous to be led to safety) by menacing them with an endless series of hobgoblins, all of them imaginary.
Henry Louis Mencken

In some respects this book has so far been rather like steadily peeling away the layers of an onion, starting with political and religious myths, moving on to myths of commerce and economics, then to the myths of science, knowledge and causality which underlie western culture, then moving on to the even more concealed 'myths' which are embedded in language and our understanding of consciousness and self identity.

With all these topics I have attempted to illustrate that these myths are created and sustained by social interactions, such that all the concepts which make up what we think of as 'reality' are socially constructed. This process of construction takes place partly through the mass media and – to a greater extent than is often recognised – through 'unmediated' face-to-face conversations and their counterparts on the Internet. The 'building blocks' of this construction (and the ongoing adaptation and reconstruction) are best described as narrative fragments or mythic fragments which allude to larger narratives, although these are rarely expressed in their entirety. Handy labels, metonymic allusions (whereby a part stands for the whole), quotations, slogans and even non-verbal icons or rituals substitute for the complexities of the overall idea or ideology. Frequently used metonyms include 'according to the Oval Office... ', 'a White House spokesperson said...', 'the Pentagon reports that... ', 'Number Ten alleges... ', 'the police' (when referring to a few specific officers not the entire force), 'Hollywood' (unless pertaining only to the geographical area) and a whole variety of expressions used in popular speech such as 'men in suits', 'Liverpool lost to Madrid', 'lend me your ears', and many more.

These narratives not only give 'shape' and 'substance' to underlying ideological ideas but also disguise them. We do not normally see the ideologies by which we structure reality. The mythic narratives act as a sugar coating for the ideological pill and enable it to be swallowed unknowingly. Or, to reiterate a metaphor used previously, myths are like the lenses in spectacles – we ordinarily look through them, not at them.

Similar concepts of narrative fragments are also encountered in cognitive linguistics and consciousness studies. Indeed, our sense of self is created and maintained by narrative fragments, such that our sense of self is also akin to a lens we look through rather than at. Although we are in part the authors of identities – as individuals and as members of numerous groups – in large part the narrative tales we create to express our identities are reflected back and 'the tales tell us'.

Furthermore, the sense of *process* and narrative sequence is deeply embedded in our cognitive processes. It is not so much that we create narratives about 'things' but more than we differentiate and create 'things' (and a great many other concepts) out of the underlying narrative processes. Attempting to understand such concepts as 'consciousness' and 'self' requires us to think of them more as processes than things. There is no 'thing' that is a whirlpool (you can't take a whirlpool home in a big bucket…), there is only water that is whirlpooling. There is no 'thing' that is a candle flame, only a constantly renewing stream of incandescent particles. Likewise there is no thing that is consciousness or self, only a delightfully complex renewing of the processes of consciousness and self-awareness.

Seemingly, our minds are disposed to think more in terms of verbs than nouns, which means that mini-narratives are implicated in the lowest levels of our minds, well before conscious rationality begins to intervene. No wonder then that the ideologies embedded in the mythic fragments transmitted via the mass media or conversations with friends also slip in 'under the radar' of rational scrutiny. Do we really stop to analyse such Humpty Dumpty words as 'democracy', 'the free world', 'terrorism' and 'insurgents' to assess whether they are being used in a paradoxical or hypocritical context?

## evolution of human consciousness

If these suggestions are correct then, by implication, they are tied in with the evolution of human consciousness. While we can only guess about the processes of mental development in early hominids, clearly a defining characteristic is the ability to think in terms of concepts, ideas and narratives.

Ideas are very different to things, even if the idea is about some thing. If I have an apple and you have a banana and we swap over then we still have only one item of fruit each. Whereas if I have idea 'A' and you have idea 'B' and we exchange them, then we both have two ideas. This makes ideas very valuable assets. Unlike physical assets, giving away ideas does not limit our ability to use them. We can indeed have our cake and eat it too. OK, there may be tactical or strategic reasons why *some* ideas – like knowing where the best bananas are growing – are best kept to ourselves rather than shared. Combine this with a skill which humans share with the higher primates – the ability to tell lies, to spread misinformation – and the cognitive race is on. Now you need to outsmart other members of the social group who are getting better at thinking about what you are thinking about what they are thinking.

Social behaviour is key to understanding hominid evolution. There is a direct correlation between the brain size of primates and the size of the social group they live in (the only notable exception is the almost solitary orang-utan). As the primates with the largest brains by far, early hominids almost certainly lived in larger social groups than other primates, probably in the order of several hundred individuals. Such social groups bring with them competition for food, water, mates and nest sites. It brings the risk of treachery such as theft, extortion and adultery, and maybe also infanticide or cannibalism. As Jean-Paul Sartre famously remarked, 'Hell is other people'. Forming coalitions, exchanging favours, enforcing repayment of debts and collectively punishing cheaters are all good social strategies. Being 'smart', even shrewd, would score very well in such social groups and help to cope with all the arguments and stresses inevitable in such large social groups. Being 'smart' enabled us to evolve into domesticated primates.

Even though modern social life has subverted the original reasons, our brains still work along the same old lines. Whereas once seeing attractive members of the opposite sex unclothed could only be done in physical proximity where mating was a possibility, after the successive invention of representational drawings, photographs, films and videos the physical proximity became the exception rather than the norm. Before there were plays, films and TV dramas, we only witnessed the emotional struggles of people you had to out-psych every day. Before reliable contraception, status and wealth were converted into children; the wealthier you were the healthier your children should be. Now children can be postponed, temporarily or permanently, and wealth can be accumulated in other ways. When lean years are never far away – and for most of the world that is now, not the past – there are good reasons to eat sweet and fatty foods. Nowadays watching soap operas is less stressful than dealing with real families, watching porn less challenging than seeking sexual partners, climbing the corporate ladder more wealth-creating than childbearing, and excessive eating is interrupted not by famine but obesity-related illnesses.

## meanings not things

The inherent ability of our brains to think in terms of mini-narratives means things and people are in a sense secondary to the potential ways in which things and people interact, and the meaning and significance we give to those interactions. Reality is more about the totality of meaningful and significant interactions than it is about the things and objects.

This is hardly a new idea. Western philosophers and academics have been drawing the same conclusions, from a wide variety of starting points, for over a hundred years. Indeed, apart from some of the work on consciousness, many of the underlying ideas in this book were known twenty or more years ago. And they are even better known in non-western cultures – as already noted at the start of Chapter 1, Hindus and Buddhists have long taught that the world is maya, an illusion. More specifically, this illusion comes from our concepts not our senses.

> Since they have no essence, phenomena do not exist as true or false, as delusion or non-delusion, but because the mind has identified the objects, saying, this is a faculty, these are senses, and this is a house; and it discriminates and clings to them as subject and object.

So wrote Tulku Thondup Rinpoche, commenting on Nagarjuna's *Mulamadhyamakakarika XIV*. Something akin to this was in Jeremy Narby's mind when he wrote:

> We see what we believe, and not just the contrary; and to change what we see, it is sometimes necessary to change what we believe.

It does not help that most 'educated' western people cannot distinguish between a symbol and the thing the symbol stands for. Christopher S. Hyatt adopted a more provocative stance regarding how we learn to structure reality:

> Almost everything people believe in as grown ups consists of lies they were told as children. Culture is nothing more than agreed upon lies.

Most people are so absorbed within the 'structure' of reality that they acquired as children that they have no awareness that entirely different world views are possible. It is as if they live inside bubbles with perfect internal reflection. Others may be able to see into their bubbles but they cannot see out. Indeed, too many people have an 'inlook' on life not an outlook.

Our concept of reality is artificial and culture-bound. Reality is a projection of our self identities, which have been formed by the social world (with all its commercial, political and religious ideologies) which controls economies and families alike. The western notion of 'reality' is the world of jobs and 'leisure', money and progress, success (in which conspicuous consumption of status-enhancing goods and services is more important than fame or respect), and a whole pyre of cultural baggage.

Our so-called 'education' systems are processes which lead to the undiscriminating acceptance of middle class myths and values. They lead away from any kind of inner awareness. Is this why so many adolescents want to 'get out of their heads'? Is it because they feel that their heads are not their own? Is it any wonder that children from non-middle-class social backgrounds rebel against these educational processes, even if modern society fails to offer a more empowering alternative than crime.

Our concepts of 'reality' are habits we adopt, like good manners and wearing particular kinds of clothes. One of the concepts of the western habits of reality is the false assumption that there is a definite and definitive 'real world' out there.

This is a fallacy born out of the Renaissance. According to it, knowledge is simply a process of correctly categorising and comprehending a finite reality which adheres to the laws of physics. Our so-called common sense blinds us to the 'cognitive templates' that shape reality. These cognitive templates can also be thought of as societies' deeply-rooted myths, ideologies and metaphors.

Such cognitive templates are not adopted by any conscious learning process. Rather they are internalised by cumulative exposure, exposure to fragments of the overall myths. Such truncated references to complex beliefs and assumptions are rarely challenged. This may be one reason why people hold on to prior assumptions when presented with contrary evidence or arguments. The mind that holds an idea becomes held by it. Indeed, as Laurens van der Post noted:

> Human beings are perhaps never more frightening than when they are convinced beyond doubt that they are right.

## prevalent illusions

We live our lives seeking such illusions as progress, happiness, love, security and freedom. We attempt to distinguish between such illusions as sanity and insanity, right and wrong, equality and inequality. We fear change, not understanding that everything is always changing, because change is inherent in how we think about time. We then attempt to impose cause-and-effect scenarios that project into the future from our self-created narratives about our past. We identify with groups and belief systems to trick ourselves into thinking we belong, although in so doing we divide society into numerous mutually exclusive entities, each of which has the potential to act aggressively against any other.

We cannot live without such illusions. These shared illusions are what separates us from the unfathomable and unbearable chaotic complexities that underlie the concepts we regard as 'reality'. In other words, such illusions are our 'reality'.

Those who say 'I don't have an ideology' are still seeing the world through an ideology, a deeply-rooted Christian preconception that the world is ruled and controlled by God, whose intentions are inscrutable and beyond human comprehension, so there is little point into looking too far into the underlying causes of events.

This is entirely contrary to the views of this book, that all meaning is created – and continually recreated – by human thinking. When we look for 'God' and higher causes we are not looking for something inscrutable but, rather, a reflection of our prior assumptions, a mirror created by our own culture. Those with the most ardent religious beliefs are those least able to cope with uncertainty and, through their faith, find an illusory certainty. They then need to defend their illusion from any criticism to retain the sense of certainty they have attained. This leads to the attitude that 'If only everyone else thought like me then the world would be a much better place' and related varieties of bigotry.

## irrationality

One of the key assumptions of western culture is that reality is essentially logical and rational. This illusion is clearly sustained against frequent everyday experiences which suggest otherwise. It is also a deeply-rooted illusion. Indeed it goes back to the Classical and Hellenistic Greek cultures. As is revealed from the literature of that era, the Greeks did not understand irrationality and intuition. So they simply ignored them. And western cultures ever since have laboured under the delusion that irrationality and intuition can be ignored or, if they are not ignored, are somehow far less important than so-called 'rational' thinking.

In recent decades neuroscience has suggested that our right brain hemispheres operate more 'intuitively' and 'irrationally' than the left hemisphere. It is as if for over two millennia western culture has worked hard to sustain the delusion that half our brains do not exist to sustain the illusion that the world is essentially rational. Yet, despite these deep-seated beliefs, there is no scientific evidence that the universe works in the rational way envisaged by the Enlightenment. Indeed, what evidence that has been produced by modern physics suggests that at the level of sub-atomic particles the universe is very 'irrational' indeed. Would we have done better if for two millennia we had ignored our *left* ('rational') brain hemispheres?

## we create gods according to our desires

As discussed in Chapter 9, when our attempts to impose cause and effect break down then causality is transferred to deities, angelic beings, spirit helpers or otherworldly demonic entities. By creating this concept of the divine we effectively created a 'back up system' for causality for when so-called rational cause and effect fails. Gods and the like are very useful for plugging this major error in our attempts to understand reality.

Gods are useful in other ways too, of course. They overcome the problem that we can only see reality from a single, embodied point of view – we need gods (or the concept of gods) to provide omnipotent, all-seeing overviews. As Mark Turner put it:

> A person has a single life, by which I mean not that we live only once, true as that is, but that as human being – a mind in a brain in a body – leads a singular rather than a general existence. A God's-eye view is a general view – it can belong only to a being whose existence is without limit or locale. Since God's eye is everywhere, eternal, and all-seeing, it is undifferentiated. To the eye of God, there would not be alternative ways of seeing, but only seeing pure and absolute and permanent. A human being does not have a God's-eye view. A human being always has only a single view, which is always local. This is so unacceptable as to have been sufficient reason for the invention of God.

And humans have invented a great many gods. Those who need an ever-loving, all-forgiving father figure can turn to Jesus. But if you want compassion without being lorded over then perhaps the Buddhist goddess Kuan Yin, the Iron Goddess of Mercy, is more your type, or her Tibetan precursor Avalorkitesvara. If you have problems with women's sexuality and just want an idealised mother who will take an interest in your most juvenile anxieties, then the Virgin Mary will cater to your problem. If you want female role model who is not one-dimensionally idealised, then Isis or Kali might take your fancy. Those with a preference for autocratic and revengeful deities may find the Old Testament Yahweh fits the bill, although he has plenty of competition from his protégé Allah, not to mention the wrathful deities of Buddhism, Hinduism and various African cults. Those who are concerned that mankind [sic] is about to turn the all world's ecosystems into something akin to Biblical deserts usually think that women are not part of the problem, so to them it is logical that the biosphere is sentient and to all intents and purposes an all-enveloping nurturing goddess. So in recent decades we have invented Gaia in accordance with this sexual-stereotype fantasy, and modern pagans have come up with number of Earth Mother goddesses, the likes of which were never part of historical paganism. And those who have moved towards recognising their selves are multiplex tend to be more in tune with pantheism, as monotheism is an expression of a unitary concept of self identity.

Just as all social groups define themselves largely by what they exclude, so we define our sense of being human by what we are *not*. One aspect of being human is that we are not deities or otherwise supernatural. Therefore the concepts of deities and the supernatural are a necessary part of our understanding of being human. But having invented these concepts of our 'excluded other' we have a tendency to believe that they really exist.

Little imagination is required to realise that we create gods in our own image, according to our own desires, and even according to our own perversions. By 'offloading' responsibility to the deities, the followers of a belief system can advance their own interests while claiming to be divinely inspired. Some of the better exponents combine this with expressions of humility to conceal, at least from themselves if not from others, their megalomania.

Having created our gods, we then become enslaved to the ensuing beliefs. Much of this is driven by personal insecurity which organised religions pander to by offering the illusion of certainty, peace of mind and a whole host of 'subsidiary illusions' such as salvation. Religions revolve around charismatic preachers and cult leaders with a thinly-disguised sense of their self-importance. Their preaching techniques are largely 'borrowed' from recognised hypnotism techniques. Dick Sutphen has provided an excellent description:

165

If you'd like to see a revivalist preacher at work, there are probably several in your city. Go to the church or tent early and sit in the rear, about three-quarters of the way back. Most likely repetitive music will be played while the people come in for the service. A repetitive beat, ideally ranging from 45 to 72 beats per minute (a rhythm close to the beat of the human heart), is very hypnotic and can generate an eyes-open altered state of consciousness in a very high percentage of people. And, once you are in an alpha state, you are at least 25 times as suggestible as you would be in full beta consciousness. The music is probably the same for every service, or incorporates the same beat, and many of the people will go into an altered state almost immediately upon entering the sanctuary. Subconsciously, they recall their state of mind from previous services and respond according to the post-hypnotic programming.

Watch the people waiting for the service to begin. Many will exhibit external signs of trance--body relaxation and slightly dilated eyes. Often, they begin swaying back and forth with their hands in the air while sitting in their chairs. Next, the assistant pastor will probably come out. He usually speaks with a pretty good 'voice roll.'

A 'voice roll' is a patterned, paced style used by hypnotists when inducing a trance. It is also used by many lawyers, several of whom are highly trained hypnotists, when they desire to entrench a point firmly in the minds of the jurors. A voice roll can sound as if the speaker were talking to the beat of a metronome or it may sound as though he were emphasizing every word in a monotonous, patterned style. The words will usually be delivered at the rate of 45 to 60 beats per minute, maximizing the hypnotic effect.

The content of the preaching is typically a parable, that is a story which purports to tell one tale but is simultaneously telling another tale at a different level. The brain is quickly confounded trying to rationally resolve the ideas at one level while being presented with a narrative at the other level. As Christian sermons are frequently based on Biblical parables, this introduces at least one further level of complexity – the 'level' of the preacher's narrative which structures the sermon.

Furthermore, sermons commonly make use of framing stories ('A funny thing happened on my way to the church. A little girl came up to me and asked me… ') creating stories within stories nested four or more deep that bamboozle attempts to rationalise the ideologies contained within the narratives.

If, in common with many people, you find it hard to envisage a world without a god then avoid creating one in the image of humans, and thereby sharing our various foibles. If you must have a god in your reality, create one worthy of respect and who has more going than the motley crew who get most of the attention. Thinking of god as an all-encompassing aspect of the universe (what Hindus would recognise as Brahman, the immeasurable being of ultimate reality) puts no limitations on god, least of all the political and partisan entanglements of established concepts of deity. Neither does the believer need to withdraw tortoise-like from the everyday world to seek the illusion of 'an inner god'. If you so desire, such an infinite sense of deity can be thought of as manifesting as a variety of lesser deities, whether anthropomorphic or zoomorphic (again, Hinduism provides abundant examples of deities such as Shiva and Ganesha which are regarded as 'aspects' of Brahman). As I said earlier, we create gods according to our own desires – so set your 'desires' to the top of the range rather than settle for a down market conception!

## why are they telling us this?

Throughout most of this book I have reiterated that what we think of as reality is constructed by a two-way process that involves each of us as individuals interacting with various social groups and cultures. While we in part *produce* our self identities, in much greater part our identities are a consequence of what we *consume*. And we consume films, TV dramas, documentaries and news programmes in great quantities. Our social identities are mostly based on our consumption of television. Thinking of TV as being an opiate of the people masks its far more powerful role as the creator and sustainer of social identities. Clearly TV moguls from time to time make some evolutionary changes, mostly small and incremental, although occasionally more abrupt.

As well as promoting a wide (but most certainly restricted) range of ideologies, television also offers the illusion of understanding. We feel that having watched a half-competent documentary that we 'understand' what the topic was about. We rarely have the ability to assess the ideological biases, the excluded objections, the biases and/or competence of 'experts' etc.

George Monbiot, with customary insight and indigence, observes:

> Picture a situation in which most of the media, despite the
> overwhelming weight of medical opinion, refused to accept
> that there was a connection between smoking and lung
> cancer. Imagine that every time new evidence emerged, they
> asked someone with no medical qualifications to write a
> piece dismissing the evidence and claiming that there was no
> consensus on the issue. Imagine that the BBC, in the interests
> of 'debate', wheeled out one of the tiny number of scientists
> who says that smoking and cancer aren't linked, or that giving
> up isn't worth the trouble, every time the issue of cancer was
> raised. Imagine that, as a result, next to nothing was done
> about the problem, to the delight of the tobacco industry and
> the detriment of millions of smokers. We would surely
> describe the newspapers and the BBC as grossly irresponsible.
>
> Now stop imagining it, and take a look at what's happening.
> The issue is not smoking, but climate change. The scientific
> consensus is just as robust, the misreporting just as
> widespread, the consequences even graver.

News coverage of major political stories – such as George W. Bush's invasions of Afghanistan and Iraq, and the overall so-called 'war on terror' – are increasingly constrained by the activities of political spin doctors and Pentagon directives. Indeed both invasions of Iraq have become 'show pieces' of how to control journalists and only feed them with information that conforms with American presidential goals. Just how dangerous 'uncontrolled' sources of information can be was dramatically revealed when photographs of American soldiers abusing Iraqi prisoners were published in the *Washington Post* followed by photographs of British troops allegedly abusing Iraqi looters.

## fear of phantom threats

The Pentagon has always been deeply devious in its use of the media. In recent years it has become clear that the short films created in the 1950s about how people should protect themselves in the event of atomic bombs were specifically intended to create widespread *fear* of a nuclear war rather than offer any useful advice. 'Duck and cover' may be a snappy catch phrase but is cynical in the extreme as a way of contending with blast waves and gamma radiation, still less a nuclear winter.

Since then the Pentagon and associated presidential advisors (together with what are little more than subagents working for the British Prime Minister) have become if anything more devious. When TV news starts telling us once more about a 'real threat' of terrorism in a major western city, we should be asking 'Why are they telling us this?'. There is nothing newsworthy about there being a more-or-less constant threat of terrorism in America and Europe. There may be some pragmatic reasons for reminding people to be alert to unattended baggage or other suspicious behaviour, but that seems hardly to be why such news reports are issued. The underlying reason we are regularly reminded of the risk of terrorism seems to be more akin to the Cold War 'propaganda' – to create and sustain a level of fear.

In an era where politicians no longer expect ever-improving prosperity for their voters, and the phrase 'You've never had it so good' applies to an ever-diminishing (although increasingly disproportionately affluent) percentage of the population, they have stopped offering dreams and instead promise to protect us from nightmares.

Only the politicians, they claim, can avert dreadful dangers that we cannot see or understand. At the heart of this darkness is a powerful and sinister network of international terrorism, that can only be countered by a sustained 'war on terror'.

But, like the Emperor's new clothes, the threat of terrorism is a fantasy which has been exaggerated and distorted by politicians. The same fantasy also benefits the grandeur of the terrorists. Undoubtedly there are guerrilla fighters throughout the world who are contesting real and perceived oppression. Some are seeking to displace secular regimes with ones based on fundamentalist religious practices. But almost all of these groups have limited aspirations, usually relating to bringing about changes in a specific country. A good example is in the UK's backyard, where Irish nationalist groups have a long tradition of terrorist activities. However connections between such terrorist groups are minimal and usually deeply distrustful.

Since the beginning of 2001 the American security services have built up a myth (originally instigated by the FBI as part of 'creative' legal proceedings to prosecute Osama bin Laden) that there is an international terrorist organisation called al-Queda. There is no evidence that al-Queda exists, outside the minds of Pentagon and CIA experts. Osama bin Laden only used the term himself after the attacks on the World Trade Centre on 11 September 2001, after George W. Bush used the term to refer to his supposed organisation. Clearly it suits bin Laden to promote the myth that he is at the hub of a web of 'sleeper cells' and not, as all the evidence shows, simply the financier (but not commander) of a very small number of the most extreme Islamists. Other than this small group Osama bin Laden has no formal organisation – apart from the phantom one the Americans have invented for him...

The 'reality' of al-Queda is a dark illusion that has spread unquestioned through governments around the world, the security services and the international media. It is an illusion promoted by American neo-conservatives (such as Paul Wolfowitz, Richard Perle, Donald Rumsfeld and Dick Cheney) to reassert the myth of America as a unique country whose destiny is to struggle against evil throughout the world. It is little different from the scriptwriters of *Star Wars* and a whole host of Hollywood action films taking charge of the White House. The reality of the 'war on terror' is a 'war on phantoms', in effect a war of lies.

In an age when all the old school political ideologies have lost credibility, the only means politicians have left for maintaining their power is to create fear of a phantom adversary.

## American presidents as archetypal alpha males

If the fear of phantom threats is not enough to empower politicians, then they adopt the tactics that any frustrated playground bully adopts – they start bullying. The first President George Bush, perceived by many as a 'wimp' simply invaded a small, Third World country (Panama was the victim of choice). An easy victory came within a week, the 'wimp' image vanished and Bush's popularity soared. Son 'Dubya' upped his credibility by trashing the Afghanistan military forces (which could muster 100 tanks, 200 artillery guns and 45,000 men against the world's most powerful military power). Any alpha male of a gorilla or chimpanzee pack would have done likewise if his status was being questioned. Legions of medieval kings did too – and Shakepeare's dramatisation of Henry V's dominance-enhancing strategies is still part of our culture.

The neo-conservative scriptwriters appointed by George W. Bush to key posts in his administration invented the supposed links between the (phantom) al-Queda and Afghanistan. Then they contrived connections between al-Queda and Saddam Hussein, while profoundly misrepresenting intelligence reports about Iraq's 'weapons of mass destruction'. The outcome hardly puts American imperialist intervention in a good light. Afghanistan has been left with a power vacuum where the intimidation of local war lords is the nearest to civil government. And the strategies of 'shock and awe' which opened the second Gulf War have crumbled to human rights abuses by US troops and an ever-growing series of suicide bombings.

In this climate of ever-growing mistrust of the 'Dubya' administration, there is ever-growing speculation that the attacks on the World Trade Centre on 11 September 2001 were instigated by America's own security services to provide a pretext for implementing the already-drafted PATRIOT Act and the attacks on Afghanistan and Iraq. Whether or not such 'conspiracy theories' are correct or not is essentially irrelevant – what is key is that in a climate of neo-conservative fantasies then contrary fantasies are as readily accepted.

The creation of 'iconic' mythic moments is clear when the Stars and Stripes were raised on the rubble of the World Trade Centre by three New York fire fighters as a clearly intentional invocation of the photograph taken by Joe Rosenthal towards the end of the Second World War when six American soldiers raised their country's flag on the Japanese island of Iwo Jima.

Deceit is clear from the 'upbeat' acronym of 'PATRIOT Act' for the seriously repressive legislation which has the full title of 'Uniting and Strengthening America by Providing Appropriate Tools Required to Intercept and Obstruct Terrorism'. The the deceit is doubled when 'Patriot Act' is misleadingly written rather than the acronym PATRIOT. Depending on who is deemed a 'terrorist' – a terminology that has proved to be used very flexibly in the past – depends on exactly how the wide-ranging powers of the PATRIOT Act will be implemented.

Intentional and wide-ranging deceit is clear from the remarks of a White House aide interviewed by Ron Suskind in October 2004:

> The aide said that guys like me were 'in what we call the reality-based community,' which he defined as people who 'believe that solutions emerge from your judicious study of discernible reality.' I nodded and murmured something about enlightenment principles and empiricism. He cut me off. 'That's not the way the world really works anymore,' he continued. 'We're an empire now, and when we act, we create our own reality. And while you're studying that reality – judiciously, as you will – we'll act again, creating other new realities, which you can study too, and that's how things will sort out. We're history's actors... and you, all of you, will be left to just study what we do.'

As these remarks were published just as the final draft of this book was being prepared, I had a real sense of the extent to which reality is continually be recreated by the hegemonic forces. If there is any evidence that the so-called 'war on terror' was planned from the outset as a war of lies, then this aide's remarks are about as explicit as we can reasonably expect.

## belief is rarely fixed

This chapter has picked up on a few of the more prominent ways in which religious, political and economic myths pervade modern society. As the previous chapters will have indicated, these myths are the more 'superficial' of those which make up reality – underneath the religious and political mythmaking are several levels of myths about the nature of knowledge, consciousness and self. The overall outcome is that what we take to be reality comprises of a variety of shared belief systems.

However there is one aspect of belief systems that I have so far ignored. That is that, in practice, everyone's beliefs on a specific issue vary according to who they are talking to, or other different contexts. While belief systems can usually be expressed in terms of strongly polarised distinctions (such as 'good' and 'evil'), in most contexts beliefs are *not* strongly polarised. We usually qualify our remarks with 'maybe', 'sort of', and such like, so that our opinions fall somewhere nearer the middle. Rather than expressions of firm belief, such as 'Oh yes, I do believe that – without question', we are more likely to say 'Not really, but… ' or 'Possibly there could be something in it'. Even outright disbelief is softened to 'It's not that I don't believe in it, but…', 'I don't really think so' or 'I usually take no notice of that sort of thing'. Indeed disbelief is even more commonly expressed as laughter rather than verbal contradiction or counter-argument.

Above all, we change the certainty of our expressions according to who were are with. Most of the time we seek to conform to other people's views by trying to find an overlapping point of view, or choose to contest quite specific aspects of otherwise shared belief systems. We avoid social confrontation by passing over in silence the views of people with seemingly quite different beliefs (although behind their backs we may make disparaging remarks about them being 'nutters'). Out and out expressions of bigotry – my belief system is the only right way and the world will be a much better place if everyone agreed with me – is, thankfully, the exception rather than the norm.

# beliefs are contradictory

In the postmodern, multi-cultural society that most western people under about forty have been brought up in, the sort of stance associated with 'my belief system is the only right way' places the exponent of such views in the intellectual kindergarten. Taking one's belief system too literally tends to be associated with contradiction, unwitting hypocrisy, and psychological problems.

In practice, most of us spontaneously adapt our belief systems according to our social situation. Quite commonly we adopt contradictory stances at different times, although maintaining the illusion of them being consistent within some broader belief system. As noted earlier in this chapter, lying and deception are traits shared by many higher primates, so perhaps we should regard all forms of this – including self-deception – as inevitable.

For example there are people who say quite emphatically that they don't believe in newspaper horoscopes but when asked why they don't read them, respond with a statement such as 'Well they might say something unpleasant may happen… ' – which betrays that they do have some degree of belief in their significance.

Such contradictory stances appear frequently among people who hold religious beliefs that require followers to adopt a specific moral code, such as avoiding marital infidelity. Moral codes, it seems, apply to everyone else – but only to me when I feel like it. Christians have long since been able to combine the Biblical injunction 'Thou shalt not kill' with widespread slaughter of religious and political opponents. This long-standing contradictory stance has been sustained by George W. Bush and Tony Blair, both practising Christians yet the instigators of a war which, by the time of writing, has led to the deaths of in excess of 50,000 Iraqis. The belief system which led to this war values control of the largest oil reserves in the world more than the lives of all those on both sides of the conflict who have died, been injured or had their lives ruined as a consequence of this Christian-led invasion.

Contradictions and hypocrisy have long been part of politics but their blatant use, hidden behind the thinnest of 'spin', has become endemic to American-led consumerism and the global capitalism which is sustained by this consumption. And anyone who has watched Matt Groening's characters in *The Simpsons* – such as Mayor Quimby, Chief Wiggum, Reverend Lovejoy and Mr Burns – will be well aware of the extended satire scripted around their hypocritical actions that seem only one step removed from the 'reality' of suburban America.

## necessary myths

All belief systems may be illusory and ultimately arbitrary. Nevertheless most people would agree that some 'myths' are necessary. My personal preferences include the right not to be assaulted or murdered and for other people to recognise that I would deeply unhappy if they removed many of the books and chattels which clutter up my home. I also prefer that friends only stay or move into my home by invitation, and that my neighbours don't disturb me unnecessarily. On the other hand I expect to have the freedom to do just about anything that does not infringe other people's rights – I want the right to wave my arms around wildly, but recognise that this right extends no further than the tip of your nose.

By a process of extension these same rights extend to my neighbourhood and, because Britain is a relatively small island, my concept of 'neighbourhood' may at times extend as far as the country's coastline. This means that implicitly I 'believe in' the armed forces, policing and a legal system (although I certainly do not believe in the basis behind many of the laws which criminalise no-victim crime or, worse, prosecutes the *victims* of organised crime such as many drug users and prostitutes).

There is also a need for democratic political systems which enable individuals to collectively challenge corporate interests. (While both British and American political systems were founded on this premise, in recent decades the political systems in these – and most western countries – have been subverted such as they now support corporate interests, leaving individuals disenfranchised and enslaved to the corporate order of things.)

The upbringing of children, both within the family and through the education system and 'peer group' influences, is in large part the transmission of a society's ideologies. Culture-less 'anarchy' is neither desirable nor achievable – seeking some sort of social identity is fundamental to human instincts – although I would prefer to see considerably more self-awareness of ideological prejudices within families and school curricula. At the present time education can easily be confused with a process for ensuring that people grow up being unable to think for themselves, to be placidly exploited in poorly-paid service industry jobs.

Likewise, mass media, the entertainment industries and religion are all key aspects of how we create, develop and limit ideologies. Life would be more than a little boring without any of these, although a full range needs to be promoted from which people can 'pick and mix' in a flexible, indeed at times inconsistent or even self-contradictory, manner. The only belief system which has no place is the one which asserts that any specific belief system is better than any other. You can have any belief you like, except bigotry.

Thinking of beliefs as somewhat arbitrary is not simply cynicism or postmodern relativism taken to excess. In essence, it means beliefs can be thought of more like the different tools in a tool box – just as a screwdriver is of limited use for driving nails in, so too a hammer is ineffective for putting paint on. Thinking of beliefs as tools for achieving specific effects is far from being cynical, it is both enlightening and hugely empowering.

## sources

Bronksi 2003; Carroll 1987, 1995; Cavallaro 2001: 120–30; Dodds 1951; Doty 2000: 177; Gray 2002: 29; Holt 2001; Hyatt 1992; Kearney 2002:   112; Krishnamurti 1971: 41; Kristeva 1990; Monbiot 2004; Narby 1998; Pandit 2005; Pinker 1997; Suskind 2004; Thondup Rinpoche1986; Said 1978; Sutphen 1984; Trubshaw 2002; Turner 1996: 116; Warner 1994; Watts 1972: 391, 1997: 35; Weir 1996; Wilson 1990:147–8; Zizek 1989. Also *The Power of Nightmares* (three one-hour programmes directed by Adam Curtis and broadcast on BBC2 Autumn 2002).

# Chapter 14

# Empowerment and enlightenment

People are always blaming their circumstances for what they are. I don't believe in circumstance. The people who get on in this world are the people who get up and look for the circumstances they want, and if they can't find them, make them.

George Bernard Shaw (whose own life was a steady climb from a difficult background; recognition only came when he was nearly fifty)

The world of a happy man is a different one from that of the unhappy man.

Ludwig Wittgenstein

Perhaps the closest we can get to saying anything positive about enlightenment is that it is losing something – dropping the illusions.

Susan Blackmore

If we cannot exist without beliefs – and all the evidence supports that belief – then we need to replace literalism and exclusive belief systems with belief systems that tolerate pluralism. This requires us to step outside of belief systems, recognise that all belief systems are arbitrary, and adopt them only so long as they are useful. We need to continually ask 'Which belief system is the best to adopt or use?' and then choose the most effective or the most exciting. As Alan Watts wrote back in 1972:

> I do not consider it intellectually respectable to be a partisan in matters of religion. I see religion as I see such other basic fascinations as art and science, in which there is room for many different approaches, styles, techniques, and opinions.

Since then western society has become increasingly multi-cultural, such that it ceases to be respectable to be partisan in many other matters, such as politics and economics through to self-identity. Even the belief that reality is a belief system (the leitmotiv of this book) is just an option and can be 'switched on' for, say, the purposes of a money-making day job and, ideally, 'switched off' at the weekends to pursue family and leisure interests. Despite the inevitable contradictions and compromises, the underlying attitude is a 'proactive' selecting of options, rather than a reactive 'it's the way things are' response.

## become dis-illusioned and dis-enchanted

By recognising belief systems as 'options' rather than as literal, you become dis-illusioned, maybe even dis-enchanted. You can employ thoughts, ideas, concepts and words without being blind to their illusory certainty or spell bound by their magic. According to Buddhist beliefs, you have recognised reality as maya, and reached the state of mokta, the dropping away of illusions. Hooray! You are now differently sane, as sane as before but equipped with necessary *dis*beliefs. You are capable of feats of magic, but not the magic of bending spoons. Your mind has been permanently altered, but not in the way of taking a red pill. (Indeed, to pursue this allusion to *The Matrix,* just as there is no spoon, so too the red pill is also a construct.)

There are as many ways of thinking about the concepts – the constructs – of reality as there are ways of grouping stars into constellations. Although we can create convenient concepts of things, events and 'facts', these are not fixed – they are ideas that have been invented and therefore can be 'uninvented' and reinvented. There is no 'one and only' way of understanding the complexity that underlies reality; we can be aware that 'it is' without saying exactly *what* it is. It is a sense of 'cosmic consciousness' without the usual numinous or spiritual significance. Into the sea of cosmic consciousness such concepts as 'right and wrong' slip like droplets of rain into an ocean, ceasing to be significant or meaningful in the bigger context.

What once seemed comforting certainties that offer meaning and a sense of belonging become confining chains. The ability to adopt a range of different ideas and beliefs enables you to operate effectively in many more different social groups while simultaneously freeing you from the in-look of any one of them. If enough people become empowered by this 'enlightenment' it would bring about a socio-psychological revolution far more radical than any political or economic insurrection.

By seeing your own belief systems as just a range of possibilities among many others, there is less tendency to literalism. You begin to see all beliefs, including your own, as essentially metaphoric in nature. You begin to recognise how people express their social identities and sense of belonging through the ways they consume. While value judgements are of course just part of personal belief systems, you may find yourself thinking that there is something deeply pathological about people whose sense of identity seems to rely on supporting a Premiership football team, or driving a specific make of car.

If this is beginning to read rather like a rant then bear in mind that the only psychotherapeutic techniques which have proven to be reasonably efficacious are *not* those of psychoanalysis – all talk and no cure – but those known as 'cognitive therapies' where clients are taught to reframe and rethink the narratives by which they sustain their self identity and social interactions.

## adding to the tool kit

Once you get used to the idea of beliefs being akin to tools then there is much to be said for adding some fairly powerful belief systems to your personal tool kit. Allow me to show off some that I have found especially useful.

Let's start with multiplex selves. As briefly mentioned in Chapter 12, one of the more profound changes in western consciousness in recent decades has been the recognition that the sense of being a 'unitary' self is fragmenting. In its place there is increasing recognition that we all, to varying extents, lead our lives with multiplex personalities, with different personas coming to the fore in different social contexts.

There are good reasons to suppose that the illusion of monolithic self-identity is intimately linked with monotheistic religions (although whether or not our self-identity is constructed in imitation of the supreme god is very much a chicken-and-egg question). Peter Carroll made a characteristically colourful pronouncement:

> Some philiosophers and psychologists bemoan the disintegration or fragmentation of the self in the contemporary world. We celebrate this development. The belief in a single self stems from religious monotheisms having only a single god. Let us throw out the baby with the bath water.

He goes on to offer the following equally colourful and even more powerful insight:

> If you consider yourself an 'individual', in the sense of 'indivisible', you have not lived. If you merely consider yourself as a single being capable of playing various roles, then you have yet to play them *in extremis.* The selfs must allow each self a shot at its goal in life, if you wish to achieve any sense of fulfilment and remain sane.

Another 'tool' that is more like a Swiss army knife with innumerable blades are the insights of NLP. This stands for 'neuro-linguistic programming', although don't let that frighten you away. Unfortunately too many of its exponents have degraded the term 'NLP' into little more than a pyramid-selling scam. But NLP's origins were a way of closely observing people who were widely considered to be exceptional at what they did, and then attempting to model and recreate their successful techniques. Out of this came a whole raft of insights, some of which are tricky to summarise, but others fall under such rubrics as:

- Experience has structure
- A map is not the territory
- The mind and body are one system
- People work perfectly (although not necessarily appropriately)
- If something is possible for one person it is possible for everybody
- Everyone has all the resources they need
- There is no failure, only feedback

- If what you are doing is not working, do something else
- You do the best you can at the time
- Every behaviour has a positive intent
- The meaning of a communication is the response it elicits

But NLP is not really about snappy labels, it is more about awareness of how we automatically construct and use concepts, metaphors and language, then learning specific ways of using them most effectively. The only really good book about NLP I know of is *Introducing Neuro-Linguistic Programming* by John O'Connor and John Seymour; many of the more recent introductions to NLP are too heavily diluted to be worthwhile.

Two really powerful ideas which I picked up from NLP are dubbed 'reframing' and 'chunking down'. 'Reframing' is reminiscent of long-established ideas at the core of Taoism where any idea is regarded as one part of an encompassing dualism. NLP's 'reframing' is about looking at situations – especially problematical ones – from a new perspective. This is akin to cognitive psychotherapy seeking to 'change the metaphors'. The Taoist perspective on reframing tries to identify what is *excluded* by a specific concept. Sometimes this can be a simple dualism – the concept of 'light' excludes 'dark'. Other times there are multiple 'opposites' – as when the concept of 'nature' can be contrasted variously with humanity, man-made, urban environments, and such like. Sometimes a concept that embraces the distinction or dualism can be easily recognised – for instance 'hot' and 'cold' are examples of a bigger concept of 'temperature'. Other times we struggle to find a pre-existing concept for the greater entity but can begin to recognise that there is something that equates to the sum of the concept and its excluded 'other'. For example, most western people can happily distinguish 'sacred' and 'profane' but the distinction is very much either:or and struggle to think of how actions and places can be simultaneously regarded as both hallowed and mundane.

Sometimes the greater concept uniting two ideas can itself be seen to be part of an apparent distinction or dualism. Indeed, in principle at least, we should always be able to step back far enough to recognise that any specific concept is just one way of distinguishing an aspect of one overall unity – what Taoists would call 'the Tao' but perhaps the sublime sense of unity alluded to by mystics of many different backgrounds, or even more accurately a sense of undifferentiated 'everything' that lies beyond even the mystical awareness of unity.

There is another way of applying reframing, which has already been mentioned in the previous chapter. When the media – especially news programmes – present us with information, it is often helpful to ask 'Why are they telling us this?' So, the latest unspecified 'terrorism alert' on the evening news is more likely to be a part of an orchestrated long-term sequence of such alerts which ensure that every few weeks the anxiety states of the populace are pumped up.

The counterpart to reframing is 'chunking down'. This refers to taking a complex situation or task and identifying how it can be broken down into achievable steps or phases. When we identify something that is 'not right', whether at work, in our personal lives, or on the wider social stage, there is a series of three simple-sounding questions that need to be asked:

What to change?

What to change to?

How to bring about the change?

So, although the ideas in this book are ultimately about making other people think differently and thereby aiming for a significant change in the social construction of their sense of reality, this is not something I consider capable of doing directly. But I decided that I could write a book about my ideas. But to write a book I needed to do more research on various topics. I also need to re-prioritise my work schedule to make time for the writing. And so on and so on. Each of these steps is 'chunking down', creating tasks small enough that they can be achieved before moving on to the next one. This negates any doubting thoughts about how difficult it would be to write a book, I could never find the time, and all the usual procrastinations.

However the deep irony about writing this book is that it requires imposing a narrative structure on ideas, even though the book is drawing attention to the arbitrary and misleading nature of narrative structures. However, at the risk of getting impossibly self-referential, I did apply one of my own 'tools' and developed a new writing persona which brings together the more relevant aspects of my self-identity, and simultaneously assists with 'casting off' the less relevant aspects.

## the ultimate heresy

The recognition that reality is a socially-constructed illusion is an invisible act of profound liberation and empowerment. It enables you to step outside the prejudices, opinions and ideologies of cultures, societies, relationships, family and even the beliefs and ideas ossified in your own personality.

Recognising that reality is constructed is one step from recognising that it can be re-constructed. This is the ultimate heresy to the figureheads of the economic hegemony, who want us to unquestioningly believe that there is no alternative to their belief systems, reinforced by the elitist mentality that western belief systems are superior to any that have gone before.

The hegemonic system currently dominating western culture has had around three hundred years to insidiously present itself as the 'necessary' 'development' in the 'evolving' 'progress' towards an 'ideal'. In the last fifty years the projection of these values has, indeed, become dominant, to the extent where many people genuinely believe there is no alternative.

Thankfully, when fundamental presuppositions begin to lose their efficacy we are more likely to recognise them. However the hegemonic forces sustaining to the old worldview are more certain, self-righteous, and morally accusative; while those seeking new solutions appear more tentative and sometimes apologetic, and often find themselves on the moral defensive. The pluralism of innovative ideas means that the established hegemony has plenty of opportunities to divide and conquer. However the apparent order of established worldviews is simply that – apparent.

All belief systems, all hegemonies (no matter how pervasive) are ultimately constructions. All constructions can be dismantled, even if the cost is high. All constructions can be reconstructed or replaced. All hegemonies outside military dictatorships are ultimately consensual.

While mass media will inevitably help disseminate new myths, it is more likely to trivialise or demonise them. Specialist media – especially magazines, books and films – will remain key to the broad dissemination of new ideas. These ideas will be developed further within more folkloric processes, whether in good old fashioned face-to-face ways, or via Web sites, blogs, discussion lists and one-to-one emails.

If this sounds idealistically optimistic then modern paganism provides clear evidence that ideas can successfully develop from the grass roots *without* hierarchical structures. What we now think of as modern paganism has its roots in H.P. Blavatsky's Theosophy Society but was largely created in the 1940s and 50s, notably Gerald Gardner's reinvention of witchcraft, known as Gardnerian wicca. While Gardner created hierarchical covens with formal processes of initiation, in the 1970s his ideas 'escaped' to West Coast America and met up with the feminist and pioneer eco-protestor known as Starhawk. By the 1980s British paganism was changing to a non-hierarchical, pluralistic range of beliefs that encompassed various schools of wicca, hereditary witchcraft, revived druidry and Germanic paganism and modern day ('urban') shamanism. All of these were deeply influenced by the feminism and eco-protest movements, together with deeply romantic notions of history and traditional myths.

In contrast to 'top down' religions, there are as many versions of modern paganism as there are pagans – everyone has their own 'take', and that usually evolves and adapts over time. It sounds like a prescription for pandemonium. Instead, through various privately-produced 'zines and an umbrella organisation (the Pagan Federation) to facilitate contacts and regional meetings, British paganism has thrived. This growth owes everything to the processes I have previously dubbed 'folkloric transmission' and nothing to the mass media. Indeed the media has usually treated paganism as 'whacky' and as a result media attention is avoided or treated as suspect by all but a few anomalous publicity-seeking pagans. Neither do modern pagans relate to even the more constructive media versions of 'paganism' – so no one turns up at a pagan conference dressed up as *Buffy the Vampire Slayer*, *Selena*, characters from *Charmed*, still less from *Harry Potter*. Indeed, all of these dramatisations are regarded by modern pagans as entirely unrelated to their beliefs and practices.

Modern paganism is certainly not the only non-hierarchical counter culture, but is a thriving example which other contemporary 'tribes' have yet to match.

## The Many not The One

This book has tried to show that western culture is constructed from identifiable 'bricks' and 'mortar' – i.e. mythic fragments and their processes of transmission. If we do not like the style of the bricks or the overall style of the edifice, then we need to design a new one. And this is a process of *social* construction – there is no need for a Grand Architect, a Neo – we are all The One.

Contrary to Hollywood, we do not need yet more myths of super-hero saviours. The myth of salvation by The One, whether called Moses, Jesus, Buddha, Mohammed, Guru Nanak (the original prophet of Sikhism), Joseph Smith (founder of the Mormon church) or the cinematic heroes personified by the likes of John Wayne, Clint

Eastwood, Sean Connery and the many others. The myth that we need another One, a new Neo, is most in need of dropping. Our salvation will come from the Many, from each of us being empowered.

## reality's not real, it's realistic

From the way our consciousnesses create distinctions and mini-stories as part of the cognitive processes, through to the way we create and maintain our sense of self-identities and group identities, we spend our lives constructing narratives and retelling these as narrative fragments.

These tales are partly inspired by other peoples' narratives, both those encountered in face-to-face encounters (and their Internet equivalents) and through the complex interactions of the mass media. Mostly these narrative fragments come fully loaded with ideological considerations, although we rarely recognise – and only with considerable conscious effort fully recognise – this hidden payload.

The processes of production and consumption of these narratives of meaning reflect back on each other with considerable complexity but manage to create belief systems shared by specific cultures or subcultures, while still changing and evolving. It is these shared, mutually-created, belief systems that construct the many levels of meanings and significance that we take to be reality.

In our everyday lives we lose sight of how these belief systems are constructed and therefore have little or no awareness that they are constructed. This is wonderfully convenient for those who consider that their belief system is the 'one true way' and 'there is no alternative' to this system if things are to 'progress' for the 'good' of some ideal. Such bigotry, whether religious or economic or a combination of both, have left a long history of oppression, violence and intellectual impoverishment.

Ultimately all our belief systems are illusions, even if they appear to be real. My belief system is that reality is not real, it is merely realistic. Which is still an illusion...

## enlightenment, empowerment, and beyond

Understanding the social construction of reality – including our self identity – through myths, narrative fragments and folkloric processes requires understanding the ways we give meaning and significance to objects and events. More especially it means seeing 'objects and events' as aspects of processes, so you can't step twice into the same river because both the river and you have changed (although there is still something that we and others recognise as the 'same' river and the 'same' person). Objects and events are conceptualised partly by what they are and, more importantly, by what they are not, what they exclude. This is especially so with social activities and groups. However such dualistic distinctions do not have an independent existence but are continually reaffirmed, continually recreated as part of a dialectical process.

The enlightenment and empowerment that comes from understanding the 'myths of reality' also bridges is the self:not-self dualism. So on the one hand it leads to states of self-awareness known to Eastern mystics for millennia, such as the spiritual condition known to Buddhists as moksha (i.e. awareness that the world is an illusion; see Chapter 1). And on the other hand it enables awareness and deconstruction of the powerful modern day myth-making processes of the political, economic, technological and mass media hegemony.

Mystical self-awareness may seem to be many to be miles apart from, say, recognising the 'war of lies' currently being promulgated by George W. Bush and Tony Blair but they are simply two aspects of the social processes by which we construct the 'myths of reality'. If this book has begun to enlighten and empower you about these processes then it has achieved its aim – but now you need to seek further as this book is itself a construct of the myths of reality…

## sources

Blackmore 2003: 404; Carroll 1987, 1995; Flanagan 1994; Hall 1982a: 47; Kramer and Alstad 1993: 161; Krishnamurti 1971: 41; O'Connor and Seymour 1990; Pandit 2005: Ch.4; Samuels 2000; Watts 1954: 16, 1958: 35, 1972: 72

# Bibliography of works cited

**Armstrong**, Karen, 2004, 'From Buddha to Beckham', *The Guardian*, 12 June, 23.
**Ashman**, Keith and Philip **Baringer** (eds), 2001, *After the Science Wars,* Routledge.

**Badiou**, Alain, 2003, *Infinite Thought*, Continuum.
**Baron-Cohen**, S., **Tager-Flugsberg**, H., **Cohen**, D.J., 1993, *Understanding Other Minds: Perspectives from autism*, Oxford UP.
**Barthes**, Roland, 1973, *Mythologies*, Paladin.
**Barthes**, Roland, 1977, 'The death of the author', in *Image, Music, Text*, trans. S. Heath, Fontana.
**Baudrillard**, Jean, 1983, *Simulations*, Semiotext(e).
**Baudrillard**, Jean, 1990, *Revenge of the Crystal*, Pluto.
**Baudrillard**, Jean, 1994, *Simulacra and Simulation,* translated by Sheila Faria Glaser, University of Michigan Press (1st publ. Éditions Galilée 1981).
**Bennett**, W. Lance, 1980, 'Myth, ritual and political control', *Journal of Communication*, 30, 166–79.
**Berger**, P. and T. **Luckmann**, 1966, *The Social Construction of Reality*, Doubleday.
**Bernardi**, Bernardo, 1987, 'Jomo Kenyatta and the myth of origins of the Kikiya: the cosmic order as an expression of political argument' in *Mythology and Cosmic Order*, René Gothóni and Juha Pentikkäinen (eds), Studia Fennica: Review of Finnish Lingusitics and Ethnology (Suomalaisen Kirjallisuuden Seura), Helsinki.
**Bernays**, Edward, 1928, *Propaganda*, Horace Liveright.
**Bey**, Hakim, 1996, 'Aimless wandering', *Fringeware Review*, 10; online at multiple locations.
**Blackmore**, Susan, 1999, *The Meme Machine*, Oxford UP.
**Blackmore**, Susan, 2003, *Consciousness: An introduction*, Hodder and Stoughton.
**Bronski**, Michael, 2003, 'Arabian night sweats', *Boston Phoenix*, 16 July.

**Brook**, Andrew, 1999, 'Unified consciousness and the self'', in Shaun Gallagher and Jonathan Shear (eds), *Models of the Self*, Imprint Academic.

**Brooker**, Will, 1998, *Cultural Studies*, Teach Yourself.

**Brown**, G. Spencer, 1972, *Laws of Form*, Allen and Unwin.

**Butler**, Judith, 1990, *Gender Trouble*, Routledge.

**Carrol**, J.B. (ed.), 1956, *Language, Thought and Reality: Selected writings of Benjamin Lee Whorf*, MIT Press.

**Carroll**, Peter J., 1987, *Liber Null and Psychonaut*, Weiser; (*Liber Null* previously published 1978).

**Carroll**, Peter J., 1992, *Liber Kaos*, Weiser.

**Carroll**, Peter J., 1995, *Psyber magick: Advanced ideas in chaos magick*; page references to 1997 New Falcon edition.

**Cavallaro**, Dani, 2001, *Critical and Cultural Theory*, Athlone.

**Chalmers**, D., 1996, *The Conscious Mind*, Oxford UP.

**Chandler**, Daniel, no date, 'Notes on the Construction of Reality in TV News Programmes';
www.aber.ac.uk/media/Modules/TF33120/news.html

**Cioffi**, Frank, 1998, *Freud and the Question of Pseudoscience*, Open Court.

**Cocchiara**, Giuseppe, 1981, *The History of Folklore in Europe*, Institute for the Study of Human Issues; English translation by John N. McDaniel of *Storia del folklore in Europa*, Editore Boringhieri, 1st edn 1952, 2nd edn 1971.

**Cohen**, H.F., 1994, *The Scientific Revolution: A historiographical inquiry*, University of Chicago Press.

**Crews**, Frederick, 1995, *The Memory Wars: Freud's legacy in dispute*, New York Review.

**Crews**, Frederick (ed), 1998, *Unauthorized Freud: Doubters confront a legend*, Viking.

**Cutlip**, Scott, 1994, *The Unseen Power: Public relations – a history*, Erlbaum.

**Danser**, Simon, 2003, 'Beyond anti-capitalism',
www.indigogroup.co.uk/foamycustard/fc011.htm

**Danser**, Simon, 2004, '*The Matrix* as metamyth',
www.indigogroup.co.uk/foamycustard/fc045.htm

**Danzinger**, Kurt, 1997, *Naming the Mind: How psychology found its language*, Sage.

**Dawkins**, Richard, 1976, *The Selfish Gene*, Oxford UP (revised edition 1989).

**Dawson**, Kim A., 2004, 'Temporal organization of the brain: Neurocognitive mechanisms and clinical implications' *Brain and Cognition* 54(1),75–94;
www.kdlwebdesigns.com/dawson/assets/pdffiles/article.pdf

**Dean**, Tim, 2003, 'Lacan and queer theory', in Jean-Michel Rabeté (ed), *The Cambridge Companion to Lacan,,* Cambridge UP.

**Dégh**, Linda, 1994, *American Folklore and the Mass Media*, Indiana UP.

**Delacampagne**, Christian, 1996, *A History of Philosophy in the Twentieth Century*, John Hopkins UP; trans M.B. DeBevoise; originally published in French 1995.

**Dennett**. Daniel C., 1991, *Consciousness Explained*, Little, Brown and Co.

**Dodds**, Eric R., 1951, *The Greeks and the Irrational,* reprinted 1973 University of California Press.

**Doniger**, Wendy, 1998, *The Implied Spider: Politics and theology in Myth*, Columbia UP.

**Doniger**, Wendy, 2005, 'Tsunami myths', *Times Literary Supplement*, 5311 (14 Jan), 11–12.

**Doty**, William G., 2000, *Mythography: The study of myths and rituals*, University of Alabama Press; 2$^{nd}$ edn (1$^{st}$ edn 1986).

**Dufresne**, Todd, 2003, *Killing Freud: Twentieth century culture and the death of psychoanalysis*, Continuum.

**Dundes**, Alan, 1980, *Interpreting Folklore,* Indiana UP.

**Dundes**, Alan (ed), 1984, *Sacred Narrative: Readings in the theory of myth*, University of California Press.

**Dundes**, Alan, 1999, Introduction to Freud's 'Interpretation of dreams', in A. Dundes (ed), *International Folklorists*, Rowman and Littlefield.

**Dunn**, Judy, 1988, *The Beginnings of Social Understanding*, Harvard UP.

**Easton**, Tom, 2003, 'Perfidious Albion: an end to deceit?', *Lobster*, 46, 9–11.

**Eco**, Umberto, 1987, *Travels in Hyper-reality*, Picador.

**Edelmann**, Gerald M., 2000, *A Universe of Consciousness: How matter becomes imagination*, Basic Books.

**Eliade**, Mircea, 1958, *Patterns in Comparative Religion*, Sheed and Ward.

**Ellenberger**, Henri, 1970, *The Discovery of the Unconscious*, Basic Books.

**Ewen**, Stuart, 1996, *PR! A social history of spin*, Basic Books.
**Eynon**, Terri, 2002, 'Cognitive linguistics', *Advances in Psychiatric Treatment*, 8, 399–407.

**Fauconnier**, Gilles and Mark **Turner**, 2002, *The Way We Think: Conceptual blending and the mind's hidden complexities*, Basic Books .
**Feyerabend**, Paul, 1975, *Against Method*, New Left Books.
**Feyerabend**, Paul, 1987, *Farewell to Reason*, Verso.
**Fisher**, S. and R.P. **Greenberg**, *The Scientific Credibility of Freud's Theories and Therapy*, Columbia UP.
**Fiske**, John, 1987, *Television Culture*, Routledge.
**Flanagan**, Owen, 1994, 'Multiple identity, character transformation, and self-reclamation', in George Graham and G. Lynn Stephens (eds), *Philosophical Psychopathology*, MIT Press.
**Flood**, Christopher G., 1996, *Political myth: A theoretical introduction*, Garland.
**Flowers**, Betty S., 2000, 'Practising politics in the economic myth' in T. Singer, *The Vision Thing: Myth, politics ands psyche in the world*, Routledge.
**Ford**, James L., 2003, 'Buddhism, mythology and *The Matrix*', in Glenn Yeffeth (ed), *Taking the Red Pill: Science, philosophy and religion in* The Matrix , Summersdale.
**Foucault**, Michel, 1977, 'The political function of the intellectual', in *Radical Philosophy*, 17, 12–14.
**Freeman**, Mark, 1993, *Rewriting the Self: History, memory, narrative*, Routledge.
**Freud**, Sigmund, 1930, *Civilisation and Its Discontents*; reprinted in *Standard Edition of the Complete Psychological Works of Sigmund Freud*, Vol 21, ed. James Strachey, Hogarth Press (series publ. 1953-74).
**Fromm**, Erich, 1959, *Sigmund Freud's Mission: An analysis of his personality and influence*, Grove Press.

**Gallagher**, Shaun and Jonathan **Shear** (eds), 1999, *Models of the Self*, Imprint Academic.
**Girardot**, N.J., 1983, *Myth and Meaning in Early Taoism*, University of California Press.
**Goldhill**, Simon, 2004, *Love, Sex and Tragedy: How the ancient world shapes our lives*, John Murray.
**Golsan**, Richard, 2002, *René Girard and Myth*, Routledge.

**Goodwin**, Barbara, 1992, *Using Political Ideas,* 3rd edn, John Wiley.

**Govinda**, Lama Anagarika, 1960, *Foundations of Tibetan Mysticism,* Rider (page references to 1969 paperback edition).

**Graham**, George and G. Lynn **Stephens** (eds), 1994, *Philosophical Psychopathology,* MIT Press.

**Gray**, John, 2002, *Straw Dogs: Thoughts on humans and other animals,* Granta.

**Grey**, William, 2000, 'Metaphor and Meaning, *Minerva,* 4; www.ul.ie/~philos/vol4/metaphor.html

**Grunbaum**, Adolf, 1984, *The Foundations of Psychoanalysis: A philosophical critique,* University of California Press.

**Guattari**, Felix, 1996, *Soft Subversions,* Semiotext(e); essay cited first published in French as 'Le divan du pauvre', *Communications* 23 (1975).

**Gutting**, Gary (ed), 1980, *Paradigms and Revolutions: Applications and appraisals of Thomas Kuhn's philosophy of science,* Notre Dame UP.


**Habermas**, Jurgen, 1972, *Knowledge and Human Interests,* trans J.J. Shapiro, Heinemann.

**Hacking**, Ian, 1999, *The Social Construction of What?,* Harvard UP.

**Haines**, Paul, 1976, sleeve notes to Evan Parker's *Saxophone Solos* LP (Incus 19).

**Hall,** David, 1982a, *Uncertain Phoenix: Adventures toward a post-cultural sensibility,* Fordham UP.

**Hall,** David, 1982b, *Eros and Irony,* State University of New York Press.

**Hamilton**, Carol V., 2004, 'Being nothing: George W. Bush as presidential simulacrum', *CTheory,* 27, article 144; www.ctheory.net/text_file.asp?pick=427

**Heath**, Joseph and Andrew **Potter**, 2002, 'The rebel sell'; www.thismagazine.ca/36_3/f_4.html

**Hebdige**, Dick, 1979, *Subculture: The meaning of style,* Methuen.

**Hertz**, Noreena, 2001, *The Silent Takeover: Global capitalism and the death of democracy,* Heinemann.

**Hine**, Phil, 1989, *Two worlds and Inbetween.*

**Hobsbawm**, Eric, 2000, *The New Century,* Abacus.

**Hobsbawm**, Eric, and Terence **Ranger** (eds), 1983, *The Invention of Tradition,* Cambridge UP.

**Holt**, Jason, 2001, 'Springfield hypocrisy', in W. Irwin, M.T. Conard and A.J. Skoble, *The Simpsons and Philosophy: The D'oh! of Homer,* Open Court.

**Hyatt**, Christopher S., 1992, *The Tree of Lies*, New Falcon Publications.

**Illich**, Ivan, 1976, *Medical Nemesis: The expropriation of health*, Pantheon.
**Illich**, Ivan, 1983, *Gender*, Pantheon.
**Irwin**, W. and J.R. **Lombardo**, 2001, '*The Simpsons* and allusion: "Worst essay ever"', in W. Irwin, M.T. Conard and A.J. Skoble (eds), *The Simpsons and Philosophy*, Open Court.

**James**, Simon, 1999, *The Atlantic Celts: Ancient people or modern invention?*, British Museum.
**James**, William, 1890, *The Principles of Psychology*.
**Joll**, J., 1997, *Gramsci*, Fontana.
**Jung**, Carl G., 1960, *Collected Works Vol.8: The structure and dynamics of the psyche*, RKP.
**Jung**, Carl G., 1972, *Synchronicity: An acausal connecting principle*, RKP.

**Kapell**, M. and W.G. **Doty**, 2004, *Jacking in to the Matrix Franchise: Cultural reception and interpretation*, Continuum.
**Karcher**, Stephen, 2001, *The Kuan Yin Oracle: The voice of the goddess of compassion*, Little Brown.
**Kearney**, Richard, 2002, *On Stories*, Routledge.
**Kelly**, George A., 1955, *The Psychology of Personal Constructs*. Vol. 1: *A theory of personality*; Vol. 2: *Clinical diagnosis and psychotherapy*, Norton.
**Kick**, Russ (ed), 2001, *Everything You Know is Wrong*, Disinformation.
**Kick**, Russ (ed), 2002, *You are Being Lied to*, Disinformation.
**Kilbourne**, Jean, 1999, *Deadly Persuasion: Why women and girls must fight the addictive power of advertising*, Free Press.
**King**, Lucien, 2002, *Game On: The history and culture of videogames*, Laurence King.
**Klein**, Naomi, 2000, *No Logo: Taking aim at the brand bullies*, Picador.
**Koven**, Mikel J., 2003, 'Folklore studies and popular film and television: a necessary critical survey', *Journal of American Folklore*, 116 (460), 176–95.
**Kramer**, Joel and Diana **Alstad**, 1993, *The Guru Papers: Masks of authoritarian power*, Frog.
**Krishnamurti**, J., 1971, *The Urgency of Change*, Victor Gollancz.

**Kristeva**, Julia, 1990, *Strangers to Ourselves*, trans. L. Roudiez, Columbia UP.

**Kuhn**, Thomas, 1970, *The Structure of Scientific Revolutions*, University of Chicago Press.

**Kuper**, Adam, 1988, *The Invention of Primitive Society*, Routledge.

**Lacan**. Jacques, 2001, *Ecrits*, Routledge.

**Lakoff**, George, 1987, *Women, Fire and Dangerous Things: What categories reveal about the mind*, University of Chicago Press.

**Lakoff**, George, 1991, 'Metaphor and War: The Metaphor System Used to Justify War in the Gulf'; online at multiple locations.

**Lakoff**, George and Mark **Johnson**, 1999, *Philosophy in the Flesh: The embodied mind and its challenge to Western thought*, Basic Books.

**Lawrence**, John Shelton and Robert **Jewett**, 2002, *The Myth of the American Superhero*, William B. Eerdmans Publishing.

**Lewis**, Justin, 1991, *The Ideological Octopus: An exploration of television and its audience*, Routledge.

**Loewe**, Michael and Carmen **Blacker** (eds), 1981, *Divination and Oracles*, George Allen and Unwin.

**Lutus**, Paul, 2001, 'How we confuse symbols and things', www.arachnoid.com/lutusp/symbols.html

**Lyotard**, Jean-François, 1984, *The Postmodern Condition: A report on knowledge*, trans. G. Bennington and B. Massumi, Manchester UP.

**McAfee**, Noëlle, 2004, *Julia Kristeva*, Routledge.

**McMahon**, Brendan, 2003, 'Psychotherapy, myth and meaning', *The South Trent Training E-journal* No.1; www.indigogroup.co.uk\foamycustard\fc046.htm

**Mailer**, Norman, 1964, *The Presidential Papers*, Andre Deustch.

**Mandeville**, Bernard, 1970, *The Fable of the Bees,* Penguin.

**Marcuse**, Herbert, 1956, *Eros and Civilisation: A philosophical inquiry into Freud,* RKP.

**Merleau-Ponty**, M., 1962, *Phenomenology of Perception*, trans. C. Smith, RKP.

**Meskell**, Lynn, 1995, 'Goddesses, Gimbutas and "New Age" archaeology', *Antiquity*, 69, 74–86.

**Meskell**, Lynn, 1999, *Archaeologies of Social Life*, Blackwell.

**Miller**, Daniel, 1987, *Material Culture and Mass Consumption*, Blackwell.

**Molyneaux**, Brian Leigh and Piers **Vitebsky**, 2001, *Sacred Earth, Sacred Stones*, Duncan Baird.

**Monbiot**, George, 2004, 'The Fossil Fools', *Guardian,* 27th April.

**Morris**, B, 1991, *Western Conceptions of the Individual*, Berg.

**Morris**, R.J. 1977, in *Bulletin of the Society for the Study of Labour History*, Autumn 1977 pp62–3; cited in Thompson 1993 p85 fn1.


**Narby**, Jeremy, 1998, *The Cosmic Serpent: DNA and the origins of knowledge*, Phoenix.

**Nathan**, Paco Xander, 2004, 'Corporate metabolism', *Tripzine* 6; online at www.tripzine.com

**Nelkin**, Dorothy, 1996, 'Perspectives on the evolution of Science Studies', in S. Aronowitz, B. Martinsons and M. Menser (eds), *Technoscience and Cybercultre*, Routledge.


**O'Connor**, J. and J. **Seymour**, 1990, *Introducing Neuro-Linguistic Programming*, Crucible.

**Olson**, Eric T., 1999, 'There is no problem of the self', in Shaun Gallagher and Jonathan Shear (eds), *Models of the Self*, Imprint Academic.

**Ortony**, Andrew, 1993, 'Metaphor: A multidimensional problem', in A. Ortony (ed), *Metaphor and Thought*, Cambridge UP (2nd edn; 1st edn 1979).


**Pandit**, Bansi, 2005, *Explore Hinduism*, Explore Books.

**Peek**, Philip M. (ed), 1991, *African Divination Systems: Ways of seeing,* Indiana UP.

**Pickering**, Andrew, 1995, *A Mangle of Practice: Time, agency and science*, University of Chicago Press.

**Pickering**, John, 1997, 'Selfhood is a process', in J. Pickering (ed), *The Authority of Experience*, Curzon.

**Pickering**, John, 1999, 'The self is a semiotic process', in Shaun Gallagher and Jonathan Shear (eds), *Models of the Self,* Imprint Academic.

**Pinker**, Steven, 1997, *How the Mind Works*, Norton; reprinted Penguin 1999.

**Planck**, Max, 1931, *The Observer*, 25 January.

**Potter**, Jonathan, 1996, *Representing Reality: Discourse, rhetoric and social construction,* Sage.

**Puhvel**, Jaan, 1987, *Comparative Mythology*, John Hopkins UP.

**Rahula**, Walpola, 1959, *What the Buddha Taught*, Gordon Fraser.

**Rampton**, Sheldon and John **Stauber**, 2003, *Weapons of Mass Deception: The uses of propaganda in Bush's war on Iraq*, Robinson.

**Rather,** Dan, 2004, *60 Minutes*, CBS TV, 6th June.

**Ripley** K., B. **Daines** and J. **Barrett**, 1997 *Dyspraxia: A guide for teachers and parents*, David Fulton.

**Roazen**, Paul, 1975, *Freud and His Followers*, Meridian.

**Robinson**, Paul, 1993, *Freud and His Critics*, University of California Press.

**Rorty**, Richard, 1980, *Philosophy and the Mirror of Nature*, Blackwell.

**Rose**, Nikolas, 1999, *Governing the Soul: The shaping of the private self* (2nd edn), Free Association Books.

**Rosenwald**, G.C. and R.L. **Ochberg**, 1992, 'Introduction', in G.C. Rosenwald and R.L. Ochberg (eds), *Storied Lives: The cultural politics of self-understanding*, Yale UP.

**Rowling**, J.K., 1997, *Harry Potter and the Philosopher's Stone*, Bloomsbury.

**Rudhart**, Jean, 1980, 'Mythe, langue, et experience religieuse', *NUMEN* 27, 83–104.

**Russo**, Peggy A., 1992, 'Uncle Walt's Uncle Remus: Disney's distortions of Harris's hero', *Southern Literary Journal*, 25 91), 19–32.

**Rymer**, Russ, 1992, *New Yorker*, 13 April, p48; cited in Turner 1996: 140.

**Said**, Edward, 1978, *Orientalism*, Routledge and Kegan Paul.

**Samuel**, Raphael and Paul **Thompson** (eds), 1990, *The Myths We Live By*, Routledge.

**Schalit**, Joel (ed), 2002, *The Anti-Capitalism Reader: Imagining a geography of opposition*, Akashic Books.

**Samuels**, Andrew, 2000, 'The politics of transformation: the transformation of politics', in T. Singer (ed), *The Vision Thing: Myth, politics and psyche in the world*, Routledge.

**Scott**, Joan, 1986, 'Gender: A useful category of historical analysis', *American Historical Review*, 91, 1053–75.

**Searle**, John R., 1995, *The Social Construction of Reality*, Simon and Schuster (references to Penguin 1996 edition).

**Searle**, John R., 1997, *The Mysteries of Consciousness*, New York Review of Books; reprinted Granta 1998.

**Schön**, Donald A., 1993, 'Generative metaphor: A perspective on problem-setting in social policy, in A. Ortony (ed), *Metaphor and Thought*, Cambridge UP (2nd edn; 1st edn 1979).

**Shapin**, Seven, 1994, *A Social History of Truth: Civility and science in seventeenth century England*, University of Chicago Press.

**Simmons**, Ian, 2004, 'Big Bang is not so steady', *Fortean Times*, 187 (Sept), 55.

**Sivier**, David, 2004, 'Mindscapes', *Magonia*, 84, 3–11.

**Slessor**, Tim, 2004, *Lying in State: How Whitehall denies, dissembles and deceives* (2nd edn), Aurum.

**Smail**, David, 1984, *Illusion and Reality: The meaning of anxiety*, Constable.

**Solomon**, Norman and Reese **Erlich**, 2003, *Target Iraq: What the news media didn't tell you*, Context.

**Sorel**, Georges, 1961, *Reflections on Violence* (trans. T. Hulme and J. Roth), Collier.

**Stedman Jones**, Gareth, 1983, *Languages of Class*, Cambridge UP.

**Stephens**, G. Lynn and George **Graham**, 2000, *When Self-consciousness Breaks: Alien voices and inserted thoughts*, MIT Press.

**Storey**, John, 1999, *Cultural Consumption and Everyday Life,* Arnold.

**Storey**, John, 2003, *Inventing Popular Culture*, Blackwell.

**Stauber**, John and Sheldon **Rampton**, 1995, *Toxic Sludge is Good for You: Lies, damn lies and the public relations industry*, Common Courage.

**Strawson**, Galen, 1999, 'The self', in Shaun Gallagher and Jonathan Shear (eds), *Models of the Self*, Imprint Academic.

**Suskind**, Ron, 2004, *New York Times Magazine*, 17 October.

**Sutphen**, Dick , 1984, 'The battle for your mind: persuasion and brainwashing techniques being used on the public today'; www.dicksutphen.com/html/battlemind.html

**Szasz**, Thomas, 1978, *The Myth of Psychotherapy*, Syracuse UP; citations are to 2nd edn 1988).


**Tavernlers**, Miriam, 2002, Metaphor and Metaphorology: A selective genealogy of philosophical and linguistic conceptions of metaphor from Aristotle to the 1990s, Academia Press.

**Taylor**, Charles, 1989, *Sources of the Self: The makings of modern identity,* Harvard UP.

**Taylor**, Charles, 1999, 'Conditions for an unforced consensus on human rights', in Joanne Bauer and Daniel Bell (eds), *The East Asian Challenge for Human Rights,* Cambridge UP.

**Thompson**, Edward P., 1980, *The Making of the English Working Class,* Gollancz; first edition 1963, revised edition 1980.

**Thompson**, Edward P., 1993, *Custom and Culture,* New Press.

**Thompson**, Richard L., 2003, *Maya: The world as virtual reality* Govardhan Hill.

**Thondup Rinpoche**, Tulku, 1986, *Hidden Teachings of Tibet,* Wisdom Books.

**Torrey**, E. Fuller, 1992, *Freudian Fraud: The malignant effect of Freud's theory on American thought and culture,* HarperCollins.

**Trubshaw**, Bob, 1997, 'Making time', www.indigogroup.co.uk/foamycustard/fc008.htm

**Trubshaw**, Bob, 2002, *Explore Folklore,* Explore Books.

**Trubshaw**, Bob, 2003a, *Explore Mythology,* Explore Books.

**Trubshaw**, Bob, 2003b, 'Hegemony', www.indigogroup.co.uk/foamycustard/fc027.htm

**Trubshaw**, Bob, 2003c, 'The politics of culture', www.indigogroup.co.uk/foamycustard/fc006.htm

**Trubshaw**, Bob, 2003d, 'The English and the "Other"', www.indigogroup.co.uk/foamycustard/fc012.htm

**Trubshaw**, Bob, 2003e, 'From psychoanalysis to cognitive linguistics: psychology and the study of folklore and mythology', www.indigogroup.co.uk/foamycustard/fc044.htm

**Trubshaw**, Bob, 2005, *Sacred Places: Prehistory and popular imagination,* Alternative Albion.

**Turner**, Mark, 1996, *The Literary Mind: The origins of thought and language,* Oxford UP.

**Turner**, Mark, 2000, *Death is the Mother of Beauty: Mind, metaphor, criticism,* Cybereditions.

**Tye**, Larry, 1998, *The Father of Spin: Edward L. Bernays and the birth of public relations,* Crown.

**Warner**, Marina, 1994, *Managing Monsters: Six myths of our time,* Vintage.

**Warner**, Marina, 2004, *Fantastic Metamorphoses, Other Worlds: Ways of telling the self,* Oxford UP.

**Watts**, Alan, 1954, *Myth and Ritual in Christianity,* Thames and Hudson.

**Watts**, Alan, 1957, *The Way of Zen,* Pantheon (page references to 1962 Pelican edition).

**Watts**, Alan, 1958, *This is It and other essays on Zen and spiritual experience,* Rider.

**Watts**, Alan, 1972, *In my own way*, Pantheon (page references to 1973 Vintage Books edition).

**Webster**, Richard, 1995, *Why Freud was Wrong: Sin, science and psychoanalysis*, HarperCollins.

**Weir**, Anthony, 1996, 'Time and place: the TV of our minds', *At the Edge* 1; www.indigogroup.co.uk/edge/Timeplac.htm

**Wegner**, Daniel M. , 2002, *The Illusion of Conscious Will*, MIT Press.

**Whitworth**, Michael H., 2003, 'Physics: "A strange footprint"', in D. Bradshaw (ed), *A Concise Companion to Modernism*, Blackwell.

**Wiener**, Martin J., 1981, *English Culture and the Decline of the Industrial Spirit 1850–1980*, Cambridge UP.

**Williams**, K.D., E.F. **Loftus** and K.A. **Deffenbacher**, 1992, 'Eyewitness evidence and testimony', in D.K. Kagehiro and W.S. Laufer (eds), *Handbook of Psychology and Law*, Springer-Verlag.

**Wilson**, Robert Anton, 1990, *Quantum Psychology*, New Falcon.

**Wilson**, Robert Anton, 1994, *Chaos and Beyond* , Permanent Press.

**Wittgenstein**, Ludwig, 1961, *Tractatus Logico-Philosophicus*, trans. D.F. Pears and B.F. McGuiness, RKP; first German edition 1921.

**Woolf**, D.R., 1997, 'The writing of early modern European intellectual history, 1945–1995', in *Companion to Historiography,* Michael Bentley (ed), Routledge.

**Woolley**, Mark, 1996, 'Beyond simulation: production and the nostalgia industry' www.geocities.com/Athens/Sparta/4883/html/baudrillard.html

**Worthington**, Andy, 2004, *Stonehenge: Celebration and subversion,* Alternative Albion.

**Zizek**, Slavoj, 1989, *The Sublime Object of Ideology*, Verso.

# Index

*Also from Heart of Albion Press*

# Explore Folklore

## Bob Trubshaw

**'A howling success, which plugs
a big and obvious gap'**

Professor Ronald Hutton

There have been fascinating developments in the study of folklore in the last twenty-or-so years, but few books about British folklore and folk customs reflect these exciting new approaches. As a result there is a huge gap between scholarly approaches to folklore studies and 'popular beliefs' about the character and history of British folklore. *Explore Folklore* is the first book to bridge that gap, and to show how much 'folklore' there is in modern day Britain.

*Explore Folklore* shows there is much more to folklore than morris dancing and fifty-something folksingers! The rituals of 'what we do on our holidays', funerals, stag nights and 'lingerie parties' are all full of 'unselfconscious' folk customs. Indeed, folklore is something that is integral to all our lives – it is so intrinsic we do not think of it as being 'folklore'.

The implicit ideas underlying folk lore and customs are also explored. There might appear to be little in common between people who touch wood for luck (a 'tradition' invented in the last 200 years) and legends about people who believe they have been abducted and subjected to intimate body examinations by aliens. Yet, in their varying ways, these and other 'folk beliefs' reflect the wide spectrum of belief and disbelief in what is easily dismissed as 'superstition'.

*Explore Folklore* provides a lively introduction to the study of most genres of British folklore, presenting the more contentious and profound ideas in a readily accessible manner.

ISBN 1 872883 60 5. Published 2002. Perfect bound, demi 8vo (215x138 mm), 200 pages, **£9.95**

# Explore Mythology

## Bob Trubshaw

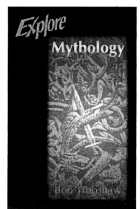

Myths are usually thought of as something to do with 'traditional cultures'. The study of such 'traditional' myths emphasises their importance in religion, national identity, hero-figures, understanding the origin of the universe, and predictions of an apocalyptic demise. The academic study of myths has done much to fit these ideas into the preconceived ideas of the relevant academics.

Only in recent years have such long-standing assumptions about myths begun to be questioned, opening up whole new ways of thinking about the way such myths define and structure how a society thinks about itself and the 'real world'.

These new approaches to the study of myth reveal that, to an astonishing extent, modern day thinking is every bit as 'mythological' as the world-views of, say, the Classical Greeks or obscure Polynesian tribes. Politics, religions, science, advertising and the mass media are all deeply implicated in the creation and use of myths.

*Explore Mythology* provides a lively introduction to the way myths have been studied, together with discussion of some of the most important 'mythic motifs' – such as heroes, national identity, and 'central places' – followed by a discussion of how these ideas permeate modern society. These sometimes contentious and profound ideas are presented in an easily readable style of writing.

ISBN 1 872883 62 1. Published 2003. Perfect bound. Demi 8vo (215 x 138 mm), 220 + xx pages, 17 line drawings. **£9.95**

# Flying Saucerers

## A social history of UFOlogy

## David Clarke and Andy Roberts

Since August 1945 the Western world has been fascinated with the notion of 'flying saucers', subsequently termed 'Unidentified Flying Objects' or 'UFOs'. Numerous 'experts' have offered explanations, often involving extraterrestrial entities. These early experts promoted their beliefs enthusiastically. Some were undoubtedly sincere – although somewhat maverick – while a few might have been intentional 'psychological con men'.

The various opinions of these 'experts' generated extensive tabloid and media attention in the 1950s and 60s with the result that reported sightings became wrapped up in any number of beliefs and legends. David Clarke and Andy Roberts carefully unpick the origin of these beliefs, looking carefully at the key individuals involved. This reveals how the paranoia of the Cold War era generated its own myths and also shows that many aspects of the subsequent 'New Age' ideology had their origins in the UFO cults.

*Flying Saucerers* is not written for people who believe in UFOs. Readers are not expected to believe in their 'nuts and bolts' existence, still less the prospects of a Close Encounter of the Third Kind. Instead it is both a social history and a history of ideas, revealing how the notions of a few inspired 'experts' evolved into one of its most pervasive modern day myths.

ISBN 978-1-905646-00-5. Published 2007. 245 x 175 mm, 231 + xii pages, 99 b&w photos, 11 line drawings, paperback. **£14.95**

*Also from Heart of Albion Press*

# Stonehenge:
## Celebration and Subversion

### Andy Worthington

This innovative social history looks in detail
at how the summer solstice celebrations at
Stonehenge have brought together different
aspects of British counter-culture to make
the monument a 'living temple' and an icon
of alternative Britain. The history of the celebrants and counter-
cultural leaders is interwoven with the viewpoints of the land-owners,
custodians and archaeologists who have generally attempted to
impose order on the shifting patterns of these modern-day
mythologies.

The story of the Stonehenge summer solstice celebrations begins with
the Druid revival of the 18th century and the earliest public gatherings
of the 19th and early 20th centuries. In the social upheavals of the
1960s and early 70s, these trailblazers were superseded by the
Stonehenge Free Festival. This evolved from a small gathering to an
anarchic free state the size of a small city, before its brutal
suppression at the Battle of the Beanfield in 1985.

In the aftermath of the Beanfield, the author examines how the
political and spiritual aspirations of the free festivals evolved into both
the rave scene and the road protest movement, and how the
prevailing trends in the counter-culture provided a fertile breeding
ground for the development of new Druid groups, the growth of
paganism in general, and the adoption of other sacred sites, in
particular Stonehenge's gargantuan neighbour at Avebury.

The account is brought up to date with the reopening of Stonehenge
on the summer solstice in 2000, the unprecedented crowds drawn by
the new access arrangements, and the latest source of conflict,
centred on a bitterly-contested road improvement scheme.

ISBN 1 872883 76 1. Published 2004. Perfect bound, 245 x 175 mm,
281 + xviii pages, 147 b&w photos, **£14.95**

# Heart of Albion

Publishing folklore, mythology and
local history since 1989


Further details of all Heart of Albion titles online at
**www.hoap.co.uk**

All titles available direct from Heart of Albion Press.

Please add £1.30 p&p (UK only; email **albion@indigogroup.co.uk**
for overseas postage).


To order books or request our current catalogue please contact

**Heart of Albion Press**

113 High Street, Avebury
Marlborough, SN8 1RF


Phone: 01672 539077


email: albion@indigogroup.co.uk
Web site: www.hoap.co.uk